QUEER GEAR

HOW TO BUY & COOK EXOTIC FRUITS & VEGETABLES

Carolyn Heal and Michael Allsop

Illustrated by Brian Dear

CENTURY
LONDON

ABOUT THE AUTHORS

Carolyn Heal has been interested in international food for most of her life. With an English-Swiss-French upbringing Carolyn has an excellent background knowledge of her subject. Carolyn Heal's first book, *Cooking with Spices*, co-authored with Michael Allsop, was published in 1983. The idea of *Queer Gear* came to her during the writing of the spice book as a logical sequence, since many of the spices are associated with the other exotics now widely available in this country.

Michael Allsop, a scientist by training, has worked and travelled widely in Africa and, more recently, in the Caribbean and Far East. His interest in exotic food stems from his early life spent on a plantation in Kenya where many of the subjects of *Queer Gear* were grown.

This book is dedicated to
Elizabeth Anne Law Allsop
and
Michael Heal

Copyright © Carolyn Heal and Michael Allsop 1986

All rights reserved
First published in Great Britain in 1986
by Century Hutchinson Ltd,
Brookmount House, 62–65 Chandos Place,
Covent Garden, London WC2N 4NW

British Library Cataloguing in Publication Data

Heal, Carolyn
    Queer gear: how to buy and cook exotic fruits
    and vegetables
    1. Cookery (Fruit)   2. Cookery (Vegetables)
    I. Title   II. Allsop, Michael
    641.6'4   TX811

ISBN 0 7126 0963 6
        0 7126 0770 6 (pbk)

Designed by Robson Lamb Design Associates
Typeset by Deltatype, Ellesmere Port
Printed and bound in Great Britain by
Butler & Tanner Ltd, Frome, Somerset

CONTENTS

ACKNOWLEDGEMENTS

To Mick Clark, who has been our collaborator on this book, we record our thanks and appreciation for all he has done and especially for his very own special brand of wit and humour that has sustained us all through the time it took to write.

We have had help of all kinds from all over the world and would like to mention particularly the following:

Trinidad and Tobago: Finlo and Maggie Paish, Judith Procope, Jean Deoki, Yasmin Baksh (National Herbarium), Dr D. R. Kumar (UWI), Lesley and Selwyn Carrington (UWI), Dr Maura Imbert (UWI). Florida, USA: Rafael Cuellar, Pablo Lara (Tropical Experimental Station, Homestead). The Far East: Brenda Jackson, the Tan family, Soo Kee, Nancy and Wee Khiang (Singapore), Karl and Linda Close (Hong Kong), Raviwan Suksawangnong, Dolf Riks (for his superior knowledge of international foods) (Thailand), Christian and Michaela Gumayao, Mercedes Peña (Philippines). West

Africa: Ted Button (Ghana, Sierra Leone), Jean H. Diawara (Senegal). Australia: David and Jan Snowball. Egypt: Marie Kalfayan. Italy: D. H. van Sloten (FAO).

At home we are indebted for information to Laura Ponsonby (Royal Botanic Gardens, Kew), Barrie Collingridge (Covent Garden) and Jenny Macarthur. For their interest and assistance we thank Charles and Eileen Pocklington, Janet Phillips, Anna Cox, Ann Collingridge, Richard Seal, Julia Boost and Sarah Hibbs.

We also extend our thanks to the following Embassies and High Commissions in the UK: Bangladesh, Brazil, Chile, Indonesia, New Zealand, Thailand and Uruguay, for information and assistance.

Finally, we wish to thank our two families who have assisted and supported us throughout, in particular Louisa Heal for cooking many of the recipes and Carole Allsop for her research in Paris.

INTRODUCTION

'Queer Gear' is the Covent Garden term for unusual produce. This book introduces the new-found wealth of curious and intriguing fresh produce daily arrayed before us in street markets, shops and supermarkets. Britain's multiracial communities have brought the flavours of the world into our high streets. Make the most of them—you need not go to India, Singapore or the West Indies—stay at home and relish them here.

To begin with, the fruit and vegetables we have chosen are described, in alphabetical order, under the following sections:

Names   The main name is that in most common use. Non-English names have been adopted in several cases, for example, MONGRI (rat-tailed radish). It would be pointless to ask for rat-tailed radish in an Indian shop. The botanical names and synonyms (old names now replaced) are included for the scientifically minded. As with most plant products, fruit and vegetables often have alternative names and these too are given. Some of these may refer to the plant itself. Parts of names in brackets may be omitted. To facilitate identification of the exotics we also give extensive lists of names in Asian and West Indian usage. These will be of immense help in UK markets and shops and invaluable, if not essential, for the traveller in Asia and the Caribbean. The

spelling of foreign names is always a problem, therefore we often list several common variations. With some practice, and more luck, you will probably manage to make the shopkeeper understand what you require!

You will often see Indonesian names containing 'oo'. This is the Dutch equivalent of the English 'u'. The West Indian names come from all over the Caribbean and include Spanish and French words.

Description   The description, used in conjunction with the illustration, should enable any unfamiliar fruit or vegetable to be recognised. Some descriptions may sound highly technical or over-detailed, since we aim to give as useful and as complete a guide as possible to the accurate identification of these often maddeningly evasive specimens. The flavour of both the raw and cooked fruit or vegetable is described to assist choice in recipes and menus.

Selecting the Best   Brief notes are given on the best ways to select fruit and vegetables and when they are likely to be available. The UK is now a market for many items and as such is subject to the usual vicissitudes of market and product developments. Eventually, we trust most items will be available in most places at most of the time, and familiar enough not to need buying advice. Until then, these notes, together with a wary eye and some common sense, will have to suffice.

Storage and Preparation   Fresh fruit and vegetables, especially the exotics, always pose a problem of storage, if indeed they will store at all! Most specimens that will keep can be frozen, or stored in the refrigerator or in a suitable open place. Full storage instructions are given where appropriate. As for preparation, this is very often the key to the enjoyment of Queer Gear. Without correct information, recipes may prove disastrous, but armed with the right knowledge the enterprising cook will coax the subtle secrets out of the most reluctant exotic. With the instructions we give, the most forbidding fruit can become a successful addition to an exciting new dish.

Culinary Uses   Here, as many culinary uses of Queer Gear as we have been able to assemble are succinctly described. They are more of a guide to ideas and adaptations than a list of instructions. They cover traditional methods from their regions of origin, adaptations to English cuisine and special creations of our own and from world-wide contributors. Unfamiliar terms are explained in the Glossary of Culinary Terms on page 213.

Herbal Properties   Most exotics have a vast repertoire of uses in traditional folk medicine. In many cases we have given only a few of these and the interested reader is recommended to consult more specialist sources. *A word of warning! On no account try any remedy without full medical supervision.*

Facts and Features   This section 'tidies up', giving any useful or interesting information not covered by the other sections. We recommend it to readers as a final rounding off of the features of these fascinating fruit and vegetables.

Recipes
Recipes have been drawn from all over the world and almost each item of Queer Gear has been included in one or more. Many recipes for fruit can be interchanged with others.

Further Reading
Within the text there are several references to and quotations from historical and modern writers on food, plants, herbalism etc. Of special interest is the Renaissance botanist Gerard, whose magnificent *Herbal*, available in facsimile, is still a source of reference, admiration and amusement today.

Queer Gear Today and Tomorrow
Yesterday we would have only been able to list places where you could obtain at most a few of the items included in this book; today many of them can be found in supermarkets, greengrocers and street markets; but tomorrow they will be so common that there will be no need to offer market advice. Finally, we beg you to keep asking in your high street shops for what you know is available elsewhere. After all, 400 years ago British explorers discovered most of the fruits and vegetables we have described. Is it too soon to enjoy them?

PART ONE

QUEER GEAR
FRUITS & VEGETABLES

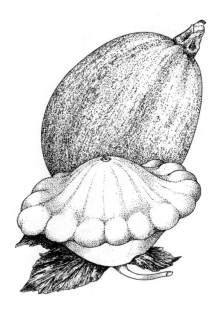

General Note: Nutritional Values Standard composition values are given for each fruit and vegetable where these are available. For convenience, the table headings have been abbreviated and as the quantity units are the same throughout, their symbols have been omitted. All values are for 100g (3.53oz) samples.

cal = calories
pro= protein g
fat = fat g
car = carbohydrate g
fib = fibre g
Ca = calcium mg
P   = phosphorus mg
Fe = iron mg
Na = sodium mg
K   = potassium mg
A   = vitamin A in international
       units (iu)
B_1 = vitamin B_1 (thiamine) mg
B_2 = vitamin B_2 (riboflavin) mg
B_5 = vitamin B_5 (niacin) mg
C   = vitamin C (ascorbic acid) mg

Note that a blank = no data; − = insufficient data; 0 = nil value; ( ) = imputed value.

Our fruit and vegetables are imported from a large number of different countries and it is an established fact that composition values vary between environments; thus the figures given for each fruit or vegetable must be taken as a guide only. Several are the averages from more than one source.

Many exotics are highly nutritious and excellent sources of vitamins and minerals, far more so than conventional fruit and vegetables in many cases. Therefore most can be highly recommended in all types of diets.

ARROWHEAD
China

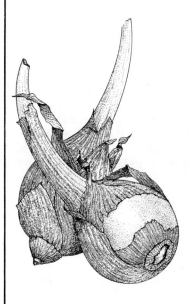

Sagittaria sagittifolia
syn *S. chinensis, S. sinensis*

Fam Aponogetonaceae

Arrow-head, Arrowleaf, Common Arrowleaf, Duck Potato, Marsh Potato, Old World Arrowleaf, Swamp Potato, Swan Potato, Wapato, Water Archer

China: chee koo, is ze kn, ma tai koo, sha koo, tsee goo, tsz koo, tzu ku; India: chotakut, muya muya; Indonesia: bea bea, etjeng; Japan: kuwai; Malaysia: beea beea, etjeng; Philippines: gauai-gauai

Nutritional Values
Arrowhead has approximately 10 per cent more energy value than the ordinary potato. The carbohydrate is mostly starch with about 2 per cent sugar.

cal	91	Ca	7–16	A	0
pro	5.5	P	155–260	B_1	0.23
fat	0.2	Fe	1.1	B_2	0.04
car	21	Na		B_5	1.4
fib	0.7	K		C	5

Don't look for a vegetable like an arrowhead as the name describes only the leaves. At first sight arrowheads might be mistaken for tulip bulbs, which they closely resemble in size and shape. They vary from 4–8cm (1½–3in) in length and 2.5–4cm (1–1½in) in diameter. The smooth skin is beige coloured, with darker papery surface tissues leaving dull rings where they have been removed or rubbed away. According to the age of the tuber, the head may be developing a sprout. The firm white flesh turns creamy textured on cooking. It is fairly bland but vaguely nutty in flavour.

Selecting the Best
Available from December to February from Chinese food stores. Select arrowheads that are round and firm with little or no sprout.

Storage and Preparation
Can be kept in the salad drawer for up to a month. Remove any sprouts and peel off the skin. Arrowheads may be left whole, sliced or halved, and are best slightly bruised with the flat of a cleaver before stir-frying. This latter method helps other flavours to be absorbed.

Culinary Uses
It seems that arrowheads are little known outside China, where they appear most often in recipes from the provinces of Tunnan and Sichuan in braised and stir-fried dishes. They are also popular in Cantonese dishes, especially for New Year celebrations. Otherwise arrowheads may be treated like potatoes and favour the addition of butter and a few chopped herbs.

Herbal Properties
Like other members of this family, arrowhead plants contain acrid juices which are diuretic and antiscorbutic. The Chinese believe they stimulate the female genitalia and have anti-emmenagogic properties.

Facts and Features
The plant is a small aquatic, about 1.2m (4ft) high, common in the water margins of China. European, North and South American species are closely related. The Chinese variety has spread through Asia to the tropics where it appears to be equally happy. Gerard (1597) mentions arrowhead or waterarcher occurring in ditches

Recipe:
Braised Arrowheads with Pork, page 184.

around Oxford and Chelmsford, St George's field and '. . . in the ditch neere the place of execution, called Saint Thomas Waterings not far from London'. There is no record of Europeans eating the tubers but the North American and Chinese varieties have been a popular food for centuries.

ARTICHOKE, GLOBE
Mediterranean

Cynara scolymus
Fam Compositae

Choke, French Artichoke, Garden Artichoke, Leafy Artichoke

China: chiu sin kai; France: artichaut; Germany: Artishchoke; Greece: agkinara; India: hathichak; Italy: carciofo; Levant; ardishawki; Middle East: al-kharshuf; Portugal: alcachofra; Spain: alcachofa

Nutritional Values
Globe artichokes contain 85 per cent water and about 10 per cent carbohydrate, raw or cooked. The carbohydrate portion is largely inulin, an indigestible polysaccharide.

Globe artichokes are the unopened flowers of a thistle-like plant. They consist of a dense bunch of 'leaves', 'petals' or 'scales', olive-green in colour, sometimes with a purplish tinge or a light-grey down. Artichokes vary from tiny, 5cm (2in), sometimes tapering, to large and round, 13cm (5in), in diameter. The leaves have a tough skin with a fleshy edible inner base. The leaves are bunched around the 'choke' which consists of thousands of tiny, smooth spikes clustered in the shape of an onion dome and which must be discarded from mature artichokes. The bottom or 'fond' is arguably the choicest part and is disc-shaped, cupped and creamy-white in colour.

Selecting the Best
Artichokes are available all the year. Select them quite tightly closed and green with a fresh bloom. Avoid brownish and dull-looking ones.
Artichoke hearts and bottoms are also canned and frozen.

Storage and Preparation
Eat as fresh as possible: store in a cool place. To clean: put them stalk end up in salted water for an hour to get rid of any hidden insects or earth. For eating whole: twist or cut off the stalk and rub the base with lemon juice. Boil in a non-metallic pan in salted water, with a good squeeze of lemon juice for each artichoke, for 30–45 minutes according to size and quality. Test for tenderness by trying a bottom leaf. Drain upside down. If you like them cold, eat them the same day. For artichoke cups for stuffing: remove the stalk and with a very sharp knife trim off all tough outer leaves. Now cut the top off about a third of the way down and remove the choke with a spoon, taking care to leave all the flesh on the bottom. Fleshless, papery leaves may also be removed. Plunge immediately into acidulated water. For artichoke bottoms: pare away the leaves of a cooked artichoke and remove the choke or prepare as for cups, then pare away remaining

However, during storage inulin is converted to sugars (fructose). Iron and iodine are useful elements occurring in modest amounts. Vitamins H and E also occur in small amounts.

Cooked:

cal	29	Ca	51	A	150
pro	2.8	P	69	B_1	0.07
fat	0.2	Fe	1.1	B_2	0.04
car	9.9	Na	30	B_5	0.7
fib	2.4	K	301	C	8

Recipes:
Cyprus Artichokes, page 192; Mushroom-filled Artichokes, page 195

leaves. Tinned artichokes should be drained and rinsed before use.

Culinary Uses
This distinctive vegetable, beloved in the Mediterranean, can be eaten in divers ways. The cooked, whole artichoke is consumed in two manoeuvres. First the leaves are detached, starting from the bottom outside, dipped in the appropriate sauce (see below) then the fleshy base of the leaf is scraped off between the teeth; a delicious and satisfying experience. After this, the choke is removed and the base eaten with a knife and fork. This way it may be served hot—just with melted butter—or try a Hollandaise, Maltaise or egg and lemon sauce. Cold, they are good with a lemony mayonnaise or tartare sauce. If you can get them, or better still grow them, whole baby artichokes are delicious battered and deep-fried or stewed in oil. Artichoke cups can be stuffed with meat or herbed breadcrumbs and braised, or even filled with seafood and creamy dressings. The bottoms are a prestigious garnish for rather grand roast meat dishes, often filled with peas, other vegetables or rich sauces, but they may also be cooked 'Cypriot style' with oil, red wine and coriander seeds or tossed in an oil and lemon dressing as an hors-d'oeuvre.

Herbal Properties
Artichoke is cholagogic, diuretic, contraceptive and aphrodisiac. A bitter principle, cynarine, and an enzyme occurring in the leaves, stem and root are useful to improve liver function, increase bile production and thus assist fat metabolism. Extracts are also used as a rennet substitute and in aperitifs. Jaundice, dyspepsia, arteriosclerosis, albuminuria and anaemia are all said to be mitigated by artichoke products. Henry VIII is reputed to have been fond of artichokes probably as both a liver tonic and an aphrodisiac. Gerard (1597) says 'It stayeth the involuntary course of the natural seed either in man or woman' and that root decoctions are a diuretic body deodorant.

Facts and Features
The artichoke is an ancient vegetable known to the Arabs (who called it *harshaf, al Khars(h)uf,* or *Kharchiof*), Greeks and Romans. It disappeared during the Dark Ages to be resuscitated by Catherine de Medici who brought it from Florence to the tables of France in the sixteenth

century, whence it spread to England and the rest of the world. Its delicacy of flavour, exotic shape, complex manner of being eaten and tonic properties all contribute to its reputation as an aphrodisiac. Artichoke's bitter substance is an ingredient of the aperitif *cynar* from Italy where it is almost as popular as vermouth.

ARTICHOKE, JERUSALEM
Canada

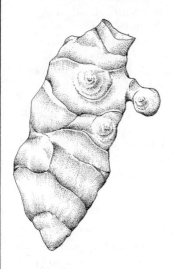

Helianthus tuberosus
Fam Compositae

Canada, Canadian Apple, Canadian Truffle, Canada Potato, Fartichoke, Girasole, Pig Nut, Root Artichoke, Sun Choke, Sunroot, Topinambur

China: chiu sin kaai, kuk oo; Cyprus: pseudokolokasia; France: topinambour; Germany: Erdartischocke, Knollensonnenblume; Holland: aardpeer; India: brahmokha, hathipick, hatichuk; Italy: carciofo di Gerusalemme, carciofo di Giudea, carciofo di terra, elianto tuberoso, pera di terra; Japan: kiku-imo, yatsugashira; Middle East: tartufa;

This vegetable resembles a small, knobbly potato, although recent cultivars are relatively smooth. The colour is usually 'white', that is buff or potato-white, but some varieties are red or purple. The tubers bear faint rings at intervals, in which dormant buds are visible. When cut, the flesh is moist, pale and crisp, very like a potato. Fresh tubers taste nutty, somewhat reminiscent of the globe artichoke, whence the name.

Selecting the Best
Available from mid-autumn to spring in the UK. '. . . it is a root fit to eat about Christmas when it is boiled' (Townsend, seedsman, 1727). To minimise waste, select the smoothest and firmest artichokes.

Storage and Preparation
Freshly harvested artichokes have the best flavour; however, they are more digestible if kept a while. Store in a polythene bag in the refrigerator salad drawer for up to 2 weeks. Smooth artichokes may be scrubbed and peeled before cooking. Keep them in acidulated water. Boil knobbly ones first, to facilitate removing the skins. Steam for 20–25 minutes or boil for 15–20 minutes. Do not overcook—this toughens them.

Culinary Uses
Popular in the US, Europe and the Middle East, this delicate tuber, although a notorious provoker of flatulence, may be enjoyed in a multiplicity of ways. Jerusalem artichoke soup (Palestine soup) is widely considered to be one of the finest. Artichokes may also be puréed, chipped, fried, steamed or concocted into a soufflé. In Nantes, the eponymous duck is often accompanied by three vegetable purées—potato, celeriac and Jerusalem artichoke, the latter enlivened with a dash of nutmeg, lemon juice and cream. In Mediterranean countries, artichokes are combined with the more robust flavours of tomato and

North America (Amerindian):
kaischue penauk; Philippines: cotufa;
Spain: aguaturma, cotufa, pataca

Nutritional Values
As in globe artichokes, the
carbohydrate is chiefly inulin. This is
indigestible so the tubers are low in
calories and safe for diabetics.
Vitamins B₁ and B₅ are in useful
amounts.

Raw:

cal	7–75★	Ca	18	A	20
pro	0.9–3.2	P	88	B₁	0.2
fat	0.1–0.4	Fe	3.4	B₂	0.06
car	8–18	Na	—	B₅	1.3
fib	0.3–3	K	—	C	4

★fresh–long storage

Recipes:
Jerusalem Artichoke Purée, page
194; Jerusalem Artichokes with
Tomatoes and Dill, page 194;
Palestine Soup, page 180

garlic. They are rewarding as a salad vegetable, grated straight into the dressing.

Herbal Properties
Jerusalem artichokes have no peculiar properties. The inulin content, however, provokes flatulence, of which John Goodyear (1621) remarks: '. . . they stirre and cause a filthie loathsome winde within the bodie, thereby causing the belly to bee pained and tormented, and are a meat more fit for swine, than man . . .'

Facts and Features
Jerusalem artichokes are neither from Jerusalem nor are they artichokes, but tubers of a sunflower native to Canada, brought to Europe by explorers in 1616. Named artichokes after their similar flavour, the epithet 'Jerusalem' is a corruption either of 'girasole' or of the hawkers' cry 'artichokes van Ter Neusen'—an area in Holland where they were originally cultivated. These tubers are a commercial source of fructose; in fact, in the 1920s it was predicted they would replace cane and beet as a sugar source. Pheasants find them irresistible. They are easy to grow: plant tubers 10–15cm (4–6in) deep, in any soil, February to April, 45cm (18in) apart; harvest in the autumn.

ARVI LEAVES
Southeast Asia

There is no special English name for the leaves of the dasheen, widely used as a vegetable, so we adopt the names common in Indian shops: arvi, also *patra* and *callaloo* (West Indies). The leaves are unmistakable: large, velvety and lush green, they are an elongated heart shape, with pronounced ribs on the underside. They are profusely and beautifully veined, in dark and light green on the upperside, and red and purple on the underside. The flavour when cooked is quite strong—comparable to kale or spring greens.

Selecting the Best
Avoid parched or discoloured leaves, and tough ones larger than 23×30cm (9×12in). You will find them all the year round in Indian and West Indian markets.

Storage and Preparation
Fresh leaves will keep for several days in the refrigerator salad drawer. Wash thoroughly.

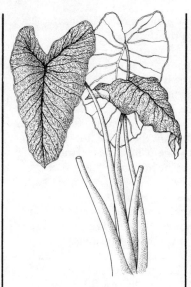

Colocasia esculenta

Fam Araceae

Callaloo, Dasheen Leaves, Patra,
West Indian Kale

India: arvi, patra; Indonesia:
loomboo; West Indies: callaloo

Nutritional Values
Arvi leaves are an excellent source of
vitamin A and a useful one of
vitamin B₂.

cal	31	Ca	98	A	18,000
pro	2.7	P		B_1	0.17
fat	0.7	Fe		B_2	0.35
car	5.95	Na	2	B_5	0.8
fib	1.45	K		C	11

Recipes:
Callaloo Soup, page 179; Patarvel,
page 205

Remove the tough central spine by folding the leaf in two, stalk end outermost, and cutting out the stalk downwards. To chop easily, stack the leaves and roll into a cylinder. It is unnecessary to blanch them before stuffing, but they do need cooking somewhat longer than kale or spinach, both of which can substitute for arvi.

Culinary Uses
Arvi leaves are predominantly used in India and the Caribbean. *Callaloo*, perhaps the most famous Trinidadian soup, is based on arvi, okra, crabmeat and coconut milk. There are many variations. An Indian snack known as *patra* or *patarvel* or, in the West Indies, *sahina*, is indeed worth trying. Robust in flavour and texture, arvi leaves adapt well to more familiar recipes such as stuffed cabbage, or can be just plain boiled or steamed and served with a knob of butter.

Herbal Properties
Arvi leaves have no special properties.

Facts and Features
Arvi or dasheen is indigenous to Southeast Asia, thriving in moist tropical conditions. It is today common throughout the tropics. It spread to the West Indies by virtue of a competition organised by the Royal Geographical Society to develop a cheap slave food. 'Dasheen' is a corruption of '*de la Chine*'. The young leaves of the related taro are also used as a vegetable, but are acrid, while those of tannia, another relative, contain bitter calcium oxalate crystals.

AUBERGINE
India

Solanum melongena

Fam Solanaceae

Apple of Love, Bringall, Brinjal, Egg Fruit, Egg-plant, Garden Egg, Guinea Squash, Jew's Apple, Mad(de) Apple, Melongene, Raging Apple, Widow's Comforter

Burma: kayan; China: jie zei, ('ng)ai gwa; East Africa: mbilingani (Swahili); France: aubergine, melongene, morelle; Germany: Aubergine, Eierfrucht, Eierpflanze; Greece: melitzana; India: baingan, bataun, begun, bengen, bhata, brinjal, katrikai, vangi; Indonesia: terung; Italy: melanzana, petonciano; Japan: nasu, nasubi; Malaysia: terung; Middle East: badinjan; Nigeria: afufa (Ibo), gauta (Hausa), igbo (Yoruba); Philippines: talong; Portugal: berinjela; Spain: berenjena; Thailand: makua-kung (yellow), makua-mooang (purple); West Indies: antrovers, b(a)igan, balangene, balanger, bo(u)langer, brown-jolly, chuber, egg fruit, egg-plant, garden egg, melongae, melongene, melonger

Nutritional Values
From the table below it can be seen that aubergine has very little

Aubergines are readily hybridised and today there is an unbelievable multiplicity of fruit shapes, sizes and colours from the tiny green 'pea' aubergine, *Solanum torvum*, to the familiar big purple ones commonly seen in Europe. Whilst the latter are as smooth as a Martian's bottom some Asian varieties bristle with thorns or spines. Ordinary purple aubergines average 340g (12oz). The shiny skin is thin, the flesh creamy-grey and spongy. When cut the seeds and some fibre ends oxidise rapidly to brown, but the flesh retains its colour for some hours. The aroma suggests banana and potato; the raw flesh tastes of the latter. The flavour of cooked aubergine is unique.

Selecting the Best
Whatever size, shape or colour you decide on for an appropriate recipe, select unblemished, tight-skinned and shiny ones.

Storage and Preparation
Fresh aubergines will keep for at least a week in the cool. Once cut they will discolour so rub or mix them with lemon juice if you want to retain their creamy lightness. To extract the rather bitter juice, cut surfaces are sprinkled with salt, left to drain for 30 minutes, rinsed and dried. Asian recipes often omit this process. For puréeing, the flesh may be scooped out of the skin after turning the aubergine over a hot flame or roasting it until tender; 2–6 minutes in a microwave oven is ideal.

Culinary Uses
Aubergines are popular in countless dishes all over the world. They are made into soups, puréed, stewed, stuffed, fried and pickled. In India, even the 2cm (1in) baby aubergines are cored, stuffed with spiced meat and fried to make a delightful addition to a meal. The Turkish *imam bayeldi* is the most familiar stuffed dish, but similar recipes appear in the Mediterranean, Caribbean, Philippines and India, each flavoured with its own regional spices. *Ratatouille* has one counterpart in India—spiced with chilli, cumin and fresh coriander—and another in Sri Lanka and Indonesia, flavoured with coconut milk and lemon grass. Aubergine fritters are enjoyed as far apart as Greece, served with *skorthalia* (see page 202), a garlic sauce; India (*pakoras*), served with chutney; and Japan in the famous *tempura* (see page 182) accompanied by radish, ginger and a dipping sauce.

nutritional value, being low in minerals and vitamins. Its function being highly absorbent, it is probably more a vehicle for other nutrients.

Cooked:

cal	19	Ca	11	A	10
pro	1	P	21	B_1	0.05
fat	0.2	Fe	0.6	B_2	0.04
car	4.1	Na	1	B_5	0.5
fib	0.9	K	150	C	3

Recipes:
Aubergine Pilaf, page 190;
Aubergine with Tahini, page 203;
Moussaka, page 186

Herbal Properties
Aubergine contains a bitter principle, irritating to the mucous membranes of the alimentary canal. It is removed before cooking by the osmotic action of salt. In India, it is used in Ayurvedic medicine, and the white variety is reckoned beneficial in diabetes. It is perhaps carminative; as Jane Grigson observes, the Sanskrit name, *vatin-ganah*, means 'anti-wind vegetable'. The *Kama Sutra* prescribes it in a concoction for 'enlarging the male organ for a period of one moon'.

Facts and Features
The aubergine belongs to the vast family Solanaceae, which includes tomato, potato, tobacco and capsicum. Indigenous to India, it has spread across the world, the Arabs taking it to Spain and the Spaniards to the New World. The name aubergine is claimed to be a derivative of *auberge*, from *alberge* (French: a peach and apricot variety). Others cite its etymological forefathers as Spanish *berenjena* via Arabic *al badinjan*, from Sanskrit *vatin-ganah*. Aubergines grow on small shrubs up to about 1.5m (5ft) high. The leafy part at the top of an aubergine is typically prickly so have a care when handling.

Avocado
Central America

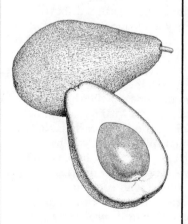

Persea americana
syn *P. gratissima*
Fam Lauraceae

These pear-shaped tropical fruits now come in a number of sizes and types, but four distinct varieties grace most greengrocers' and supermarket shelves—'Ettinger', oblong in shape, shiny and bright green; 'Fuerte', rather presentable with smoothish green skin; 'Hass', with wrinkled black rind; and 'Nabal', round with a smooth shiny-green skin. The skin is inedible in every case, but the creamy off-white flesh, sometimes yellow-green, is highly comestible—plump, oily and savoury. There is a large single stone, ovoid and completely inedible. A tiny new Israeli type is stoneless, in size and shape like a gherkin and known as a cocktail avocado. A giant Brazilian variety is also sometimes available, twice as big as standard avocados and with more stone than meat, but quite flavoursome.

Selecting the Best
Avocados are available all year round. Ripe fruits yield slightly to gentle pressure. If too soft they

Alligator Pear, Avocado Pear, Butter Pear, Midshipman's Butter, Mountain Pear, Poor Man's Butter, Soldier's Butter, Vegetable Marrow

Brazil: abacate; France: avocat, poire d'avocat; Germany: Advocatbirne; Holland: advocaat; Italy: avocado; Malaysia: apukado; Peru: patta; Spain: aguacate; West Africa: pear; West Indies: aguscate, alligator pear, avocado (pear), avocat, guacate, pear, zaboca, zabooka

Nutritional Values

The avocado is arguably the world's most nutritious fruit, having the highest protein content of about 2 per cent and a generous richness of B complex vitamins, as well as some vitamin E and minerals. There is from 5–30 per cent oil, but a low carbohydrate level, and no cholesterol.

Raw:

cal	165	Ca	12	A	250
pro	2	P	42	B$_1$	0.11
fat	16	Fe	0.6	B$_2$	0.2
car	6.4	Na	0.4	B$_5$	1.6
fib	1.8	K	604	C	14

will be overripe. Those on the firm side can ripen at home for a day or two. Bruised avocados indicate blackened flesh; a very glossy skin betrays unripe fruit.

Storage and Preparation

Ripe fruit will keep in the refrigerator for a few days but it is best not to refrigerate unripe ones. To ripen, keep in foil at room temperature. To prepare: cut in half lengthwise around the stone and pull the halves apart for two identical servings—a half is the usual portion. The stone is easily teased out of the half in which it is embedded if the fruit is properly ripe. For mashed pulp for purées and sauces, scoop out the flesh with a spoon. Make sure the very green flesh next to the skin is scraped out as this gives a good colour. The flesh should separate easily if ripe. Brush exposed surfaces with lemon or lime juice to prevent discoloration.

Culinary Uses

Though technically a fruit, the avocado is a savoury fellow and is best eaten as a salad vegetable—most simply, and possibly most satisfactorily, raw with a little vinaigrette or Worcestershire sauce, or diced in fresh salads. It is good in sauces, soups, dips, mousses and sandwiches. Avocado halves may be topped with American 'chili', sour cream, cheese, chopped onion, or anything acidic. Prawns or crabmeat in mayonnaise are popular fillings. For more adventurous preparations, we go to Mexico for *guacamole*, a creamy dip or topping, and to Austria for diced avocado and Kirsch, with a little vanilla sugar.

Herbal Properties

In view of its nutritional bounty and sensual gastronomic qualities, it is no surprise that the avocado is hailed as a *nouvelle cuisine* aphrodisiac.

Facts and Features

Native to Mexico and Central America (the name derives from the Aztec *ahuacatl*, testicle tree), the avocado now grows worldwide in the tropics and sub-tropics. Commercial cultivation, for food and cosmetics, dates from this century. Three botanical types are recognised: Mexican, characterised by small fruits; West Indian, with tough skin; and Guatemalan, with a woody skin. Intense hybridisation has produced many cultivars combining the best of three worlds. Avocado is one of the few exotic fruits that are never canned—a tannin contained in the fruit prevents this treatment. The stones can be easily persuaded to yield house plants. Wash the stone and suspend it half-floating in a jar of lukewarm water. Pot it in compost only when the stem has grown a good 15cm (6in) and nip out or cut back the central shoot. Trim the plant regularly for even exposure.

BABACO
Ecuador

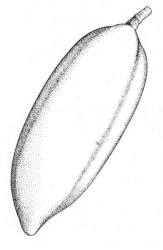

Carica pentagona
Fam Caricaceae

Nutritional Values
Babacos are low in sugars, containing about 6 per cent, but high in vitamin C—two slices are said to provide the average daily requirement.

The babaco is a striking yellow fruit of the papaya family. It is some 10cm (4in) wide and 30cm (12in) long, weighing around 1kg (2.2lb). Its pentagonal cross-section gives attractive star-shaped slices. The seedless juicy flesh and skin are entirely edible, leaving no waste. Slightly acid, but melting on the palate, babaco is one of those many flavours described as 'unique'; it is often likened to a *mélange* of strawberry, pineapple and papaya.

Selecting the Best
Best when ripe, indicated by a completely yellow skin. New Zealand is making efforts to market the babaco on a large scale, and the fruit is now available in UK markets from October to March.

Storage and Preparation
The babaco keeps exceptionally well for a soft fruit, up to 4 weeks in the open and longer in the refrigerator (best just above freezing point). Bad patches will not spread and you can cut it as required—there is no need to peel it. Eat when fully ripened. The juice can be squeezed out in a press for a refreshing drink.

Culinary Uses
This fruit is best treated simply, although it is usual for novel fruit such as babacos to be recommended for a profusion of uses, more in enthusiasm than in good taste. Cut it into inch-thick slices or dice perhaps in a fruit salad. You could stew it, use it in cakes or jams, or even with meats and savoury or barbecue dips. However, we know of no traditional recipes demanding its use although babaco juice has long been traditional in Ecuador, especially as an appetiser before breakfast.

Herbal Properties

The babaco is reputed to aid the digestion and, as it is a cousin of the papaya which is known for its digestive properties, this would seem likely.

Facts and Features

This curious newcomer to international cuisine was formerly only of local interest in Ecuador. Now it is well on the way to intense production in New Zealand where much effort has developed very efficient production methods. We can expect the babaco to make an impression on Western markets within the next few years.

BANANA
Southeast Asia

Musa acuminata
syn *M. sapientum*

Fam Musaceae

Adam's Fig, Apple of Paradise

Bananas, once an exotic novelty, are now commonplace but recently some of their more curious brethren have started to appear in ethnic shops and markets. Here are a few you might come across:

Lady's Fingers: One of the best varieties. Canary-yellow and thin-skinned, they are short and tubby. The flesh is whiter than ordinary bananas and firmer. The flavour is sweet and the texture rather floury.

Red Bananas: These come in various sizes, some about 13cm (5in) long, others much larger. The skin is a deep burgundy-red and the pinkish flesh is soft, sticky, and dry tasting but also sweet.

Baby Bananas: Green at first, turning yellow, these tiny fellows are unusually attractive to the eye. Only 5cm (2in) long, they are straighter than the usual banana. Their flavour when ripe is sweet and creamy—delicious.

Green Cooking Bananas: These grass-green bananas are stubbier than ordinary ones and may have more pronounced 'sides'. They are always cooked and their flavour is mild. (See also Plantain, page 137.)

Selecting the Best

The more unusual bananas are offered by Asian, West Indian and specialist shops. Make sure the skins are unbroken. Green cooking bananas vary in size and a few black streaks or patches are acceptable. Red bananas will yield slightly when fully ripe and yellow bananas are at their peak when speckled brown. 'Overripe' ones are ideal for sandwiches, dishes requiring puréed fruit, and banana bread.

China: kan chiao, tsiu; East Africa: ndizi (Swahili); France: banane; Germany: Banane; Holland: banaan; India: kadaly, kela, kula; Indonesia: pisang, tjaoo; Italy: banana, fico d'adama; Japan: banana; Malaysia: pisang; Middle East: moz; Spain: banana; West Indies: fig

Nutritional Values
No data are available for the more exotic bananas other than red, but it can be expected they will vary little from the common banana.

	COMMON green	COMMON ripe	RED raw
cal	110	90	90
pro	1.4	1.2	1.2
fat	0.2	0.2	0.2
car	28.7	23	23.4
fib	0.5	0.5	0.4
Cal	8	9	10
P		26	18
Fe	0.9	0.6	0.8
Na		1	1
K		370	370
A	950	170	400
B$_1$	0.04	0.05	0.05
B$_2$	0.02	0.06	0.04
B$_5$	0.6	0.7	0.6
C	31	10	(10)

Recipes:
Nasi Goreng, page 181; Undihu, page 198.

Storage and Preparation
Keep them at room temperature. Cooking varieties are peeled like plantains, or sliced unpeeled. In India the peel is sometimes cooked as a separate vegetable. Eating bananas peel easily; prepare them just before serving or sprinkle them with lemon juice to prevent discoloration.

Culinary Uses
Ripe yellow bananas, digestible and nutritious, are a familiar nursery food eaten mashed, in sandwiches, trifles, puddings, fruit salads, ice-creams, banana splits and milk shakes. They are also popular in breads, cakes and biscuits; baked and flamed with rum; or fried as a garnish to curries and *nasi goreng*. Other dessert bananas may be used in the same way or perhaps are best on their own, especially lady's fingers and the baby bananas. Red bananas are good cooked or raw and a favourite way to eat them in South America is grilled in their skins, preferably over charcoal, until they are black. They are then served immediately, slit and sprinkled with soft brown sugar and cinnamon. Green cooking bananas can be treated as plantains. These appear in many Indian mixed vegetable curries, side dishes and sweetmeats and are popular in Indonesian desserts. Very widely used in the Caribbean, they are stewed with meat or fish, cooked with sugar and cheese, and boiled and added to savoury salads.

Herbal Properties
Banana starch is used as a disintegrating agent in pills. (See also Plantain, page 137.)

Facts and Features
Native to the Old World tropics, the banana is one of the world's major economic food plants, with twenty recognised species and some three hundred varieties in cultivation. It grows now throughout the tropics and sub-tropics, having been brought to North Africa by the Arabs and to the Americas by the Spaniards. The Canaries and West Indies are important exporters, although the fruit is grown equally extensively for local consumption as a staple in Africa, the Americas and Asia. Bananas were a luxury item in the West until the late nineteenth century when banana boats were developed to ripen them en route. They are planted ornamentally where cold

weather denies fruiting. The fruits grow in 'stems' or bunches of up to two hundred 'fingers' or single bananas, grouped into 'hands' of ten to twenty fruits each, around a central stalk. The word 'banana' comes from a language of the African Congo. Previously it was called 'Adam's Fig' or 'Apple of Paradise', in reference to the mythical serpent supposedly hiding in a banana bunch in Eden. In Uganda a formidable banana beer is made, wherein no doubt the devil also lurks. Believe it or not, bananas are grown commercially in Iceland, the only European country to do this.

BASIL
India

Ocimum spp
syn *Ocymum* spp
Fam Labiatae

Abyssinian, Bush, Camphor, Common, Dwarf, East Indian, Garden, Hairy, Hoary, Holy, Italian, Lemon, Monk's, Purple-stalked, Sacred, Shrubby, Sweet, and Tree Basil; Fever Plant, Mosquito Plant, Tea Bush

Burma: lun (Holy); China: ue heung (Sweet); India: babui tul(a)si, manjrik, sada tul(a)si, subzah, surasa (Sweet); kala tul(a)si, surasa

At least four species of basil are used in Asia. They all have different flavours but are difficult to distinguish at a glance. The leaves vary from 2.5–5cm (1–2in) in length and 1–3cm (½–1¼in) in breadth, and are variously toothed, plain, hairy, smooth, green or purple-tinged. Sold in bunches some 15–25cm (6–10in) long, the stalks, ridged on one side, are green or tinged with purple, and smooth or hairy. There are sometimes small purple flowers. The bouquets and flavours vary according to the contained volatile oils—essentially a mixture of anise, clove, lily of the valley and camphor.

Selecting the Best
Available mainly from oriental shops throughout the year. Choose obviously fresh bunches of leaves. If faced with several varieties, a good sniff should determine the one you like best.

Storage and Preparation
To keep for several days stand in a glass of water, cover with a polythene bag and place in the refrigerator or a cool place. The leaves are used whole in salads or chopped finely or coarsely according to your purpose.

Culinary Uses
Sweet basil is associated particularly with tomato and pasta dishes and Asian basils make a most economical substitute. These are used in a great variety of ways in Indonesian, Chinese and Thai dishes. Deep-fried beancurd skin rolls are filled with basil minced with beancurd. Little clams and coarsely chopped basil are fried together. Many curries are flavoured with it. Dolf Riks, the celebrated restaurateur of Pattaya, remarks that in

(Holy); (ram) tul(a)si (East Indian); Indonesia: daun kemangi, daun selaseh, daun soorawoong; Malaysia: kemangi, pokoh, selasseh puteh (Sweet); kemangi (Hairy); ruku-ruku merah, selaseh hitam (Holy); ruku-ruku hitam, selaseh besar (East Indian); Thailand: bai horapa, bai mangluck, manglak euk, selasi (Sweet); bai mangluk (Hairy); bai grapao (Holy)

Nutritional Values
Basils are good sources of vitamins A and C. The oils contain methychavicol, linalool, cineole and eugenol.

cal	39	Ca	320	A	4,900
pro	4.2	P	40	B_1	0.01
fat	2.2	Fe	5.6	B_2	0.6
car	2.8	Na		B_5	0.5
fib	1.4	K		C	71

Recipe:
Thai Chicken Curry, page 189

Thailand each basil has its own particular application: bai mangluk is sprinkled onto soups and salads; bai grapao flavours curried beef and stir-fried fish and frogs' legs and bai horapa is used in chicken and other curries.

Herbal Properties
Basils are associated with gastric disorders, being stomachic, carminative and aromatic. Other applications include the treatment of malaria, catarrh, ringworm and earache. In India 'the powder of the leaves is used as snuff for expelling maggots from the nose' (Dastur).

Facts and Features
Basils are annual herbs originating in India and have spread throughout the world. Human attitudes to these plants are ambivalent. In the West, basil was believed to beget scorpions and feed on human brains. Keats' poem 'Isabella and the Pot of Basil' relates how Isabella entombed her lover's head:
      And cover'd it with mould, and o'er it set
      Sweet Basil, which her tears kept ever wet.
In India, basil is sacred to Vishnu; it protects homes and temples (a sound concept, as the contained aromatics all have anti-bacterial properties), fosters love and brings peace to the dead.

BEANS AND PEAS

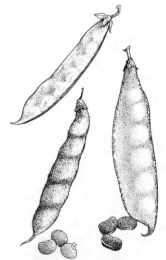

This section deals with the new peas and beans that are now imported daily for sale in Asian and West Indian outlets. Each has its individual characteristics, but they may with discretion be substituted or interchanged in conventional recipes. As with other pulses, these beans and peas are a useful source of vitamins A, B complex and C, and have an above average fibre content.

CHICKPEA
Tropical Asia
Cicer arietinum
Fam Leguminosae

Bengal Gram, Ciche, Coffee Pea, Common Gram, Dhal, Egyptian Pea, Garbanzo, Gram, Indian Gram, Yellow Gram

India: but mah, cha(h)n(n)a, kad(a)l(a)i, sanikalu (all with various spellings); Malaysia: kachang kuda; Middle East: hammes, hom(m)o(u)s, lalabi; Sri Lanka: konda kadala; West Indies: cha-na, chaqna, garavance, garbanzo, gram, pois chicke

Fresh chickpeas in their shells are now seen in Indian shops. These small, flat, hairy pods, about 2×1cm (¾×½in), have a short stalk and spiky calyx, and vary in colour from yellow through pink to light brown. Inside the pods are one or two seeds that have been likened to a ram's head and to a famous wart belonging to an ancestor of Cicero, whence the botanical name. The seeds are basically round with a point, knobbly, pale green to yellow and about 1cm (½in) in diameter. There is no aroma but the flavour of raw chickpeas is like that of green peas, rather nutty and not at all bitter.

Selecting the Best
Look out for signs of mould.

Storage and Preparation
Fresh chickpeas deteriorate rapidly and should therefore be hulled and cooked as soon as possible. Shell them like peas—they open easily with a satisfying pop.

Culinary Uses
The uses of dried chickpeas (*dhal*) in Indian, Arab and Mediterranean cookery are well known. However, it seems that green chickpeas are also well liked in India and are now under cultivation in the UK for the Indian community. They are cooked like peas, appearing in spicy side dishes and vegetable curries. Both raw chickpeas and chickpeas roasted in their pods are enjoyed as a snack with drinks.

COWPEA
Asia, Africa
Vigna unguiculata
syn V. sinensis
Fam Leguminosae

Blackeye Pea, Chori

China: tan kok (horn bean); India: chori (with various spellings and pronunciations such as chaula, chavli, chowlee, etc), lobia; Thailand: tua dam; West Indies: blackeye pea, cowpea, gub-gub

Recipe:
Spicy Beans and Potatoes, page 197

These are the long thin green beans seen in Asian shops. They are quite regular in size and shape, about 7–15cm (2¾–6in) long and about 5mm (⅕in) wide, with rounded sides. The end is curved and stubby. These are the younger versions; mature ones have pronounced seed constrictions and are bulbous and slightly longer. Their big brother is the yard long bean described below.

Selecting the Best
They should be firm and snappy.

Storage and Preparation
Very immature cowpeas (*choris*): their extreme thinness belies a certain toughness but it is only necessary to top and tail them. Mature cowpeas: may be cut into 2.5cm (1in) pieces.

Culinary Uses

With a very robust flavour for such a delicate-looking bean, *choris* adapt well to any uses for Kenyan fine beans and go particularly well in Mediterranean recipes with onions, garlic and tomatoes. They look prettier if kept whole. In China mature cowpeas are stir-fried until just scorched, and seasoned with soy sauce.

Hyacinth Bean
Southeast Asia
Lablab purpureus
syn *L. niger, Dolichos lablab, L. vulgaris*

Fam Leguminosae

Bana, Banner, Papri

China: pin tan, tseuk tau; India: avare, bana, papri, shim, val(or); Thailand: tua nang, tua pab; West Indies: bannabees, banner, bonabis, bonavis, bonavist, bunabis, butter bean, hyacinth bean, lablab bean, lubia, pois bourcosson, sa(e)me, sem, white bean

Hyacinth beans, more like pea pods in appearance, come in many sizes, from 5–20cm (2–8in) in length and 1–5cm (½–2in) in breadth. They are pale green, darkening towards one edge, with a leathery skin. There is a pronounced curled 'beak'. Like the pods, the seeds vary in size, often in inverse proportion to the pods, the 'eye' extending to at least a third of the way round the seed.

Selecting the Best

Choose them small and plump for shelling or large and flat for cooking whole.

Storage and Preparation

These are rather a curiosity, varying as they do so greatly both in length and in size of pea. Very small pods may be hulled and their large peas cooked on their own, while large, almost empty pods are topped, tailed, stringed and cooked whole.

Culinary Uses

These pods have an excellent flavour and the peas a mealy texture; they may be used to good effect in any pea or bean recipe.

Mangetout
Southeast Asia

Pisum sativum
var *macrocarpum*
var *saccharatum*

Fam Leguminosae

Snowpea, Sugar Pea

China: ho la(a)n tau, shieh do, shieh dow; Japan: chabo-endo

Mangetout—'eat all'—are flat, tender pea pods having only token peas within. They are usually about 10cm (4in) long, 2cm (¾in) wide, lime green in colour with stalk and calyx still attached. They are more delicate in flavour than the common pea and quite different in texture.

Selecting the Best

Available all the year from various parts of the world, they should be crisp—the smaller and flatter the better.

Storage and Preparation

Remove the tail and string in one deft operation. Leave whole. Mangetout need the minimum

Recipe:
Tempura, page 182

cooking time, just 1 or 2 minutes, or they will spoil. They are at their best steamed.

Culinary Uses
These sweet and tender pods rightly deserve their reputation as a 'luxury' vegetable and are delicious on their own with a knob of butter. They combine happily with ginger and garlic, bean sprouts and many Chinese stir-fried dishes. Mangetout are often included in Japanese *tempura*.

PIGEON PEA
Egypt
Cajanus cajan
Fam Leguminosae

Gunga, Tuwar

China: muk tau (tree bean); India: lilva (canned), (r)arhar, tur(a), tuvar(e), tuwar; Indonesia: katjang goode; Malaysia: kachang dal, kachang kayu; Thailand: tua-re; West Indies: congo pea, gunga pea, gungo, pigeon pea

Recipe:
Mattar Paneer, page 194

Pigeon peas are readily distinguished from other pulses by two features. The first is the marked separation of each pea in the pod by an oblique constriction, and the second is the colour, varying from dark green to purple but always with purple or maroon splotches and edges. A third distinctive feature is the long thin 'beak'. The seeds are green, round and flattened with a short 'eye'. When dried, like chickpeas they are known as *dhal* in India.

Selecting the Best
Pick even-sized full pods or frozen pigeon peas are quite readily available.

Storage and Preparation
Store and hull as you would ordinary garden peas.

Culinary Uses
These peas have a firm flavour and meaty texture, and figure in many dishes from the Caribbean, Africa and India. Jamaican Peas and Rice is best known, otherwise there are recipes for soups, stews and snacks. These latter are prepared from cooked and puréed peas. Indian vegetable *samosas* and *mattar paneer*, peas cooked with cream cheese, are traditionally made with pigeon peas.

YARD LONG BEAN
Asia, Africa
Vigna unguiculata spp
sesquipedalis
syn *V. sesquipedalis*
Fam Leguminosae

The famous yard long bean is a highly important foodstuff in China and most of the Far East. It grows as long as 100cm (40in) but is only about 1cm (½in) wide. Light or dark green, whippy and with a roughish skin, it is unmistakable in Asian food shops. The seeds are about 1cm (½in) long, pale yellow-green with a short 'eye'. They are actually super cowpeas (see above).

Asparagus Bean, Long Bean, Yard Bean

China: dao kok (horn bean), pat yuet tao (eighth moon bean), tua kok; France: haricot kilomètre; Italy: dolico gigante; Japan: jurokusasage; Thailand: tua faak yaow, tua fug yao; West Indies: bodi, boucouson, increase pea, six weeks, yard bean

Nutritional Values (all species)
Dried beans are well known as sources of some concentrated nutrients; young, fresh green beans have a fair sprinkling of these.

Selecting the Best
Usually sold in bunches. Choose smooth beans with little swellings. The darker variety are firmer.

Storage and Preparation
Wash, top, tail and cut into suitable lengths or leave whole and coil into the saucepan like spaghetti.

Culinary Uses
Yard long beans are common in China, Southeast Asia, and the Caribbean. Though crunchier, they may be used for a change in recipes for haricot or string beans. They appear in stir-fried dishes and Chinese omelettes, where the eggs are added to the fried fillings. Elsewhere they figure in spicy soups, salads and curries.

Raw, unless otherwise indicated:

	CHICKPEA (DRIED)*	COWPEA†	HYACINTH BEAN	MANGETOUT†	PIGEON PEA	YARD LONG BEAN
cal	360	34	35	43	118	37
pro	20	2.6	3.6	2.9	7.1	3.2
fat	5	0.3	0.2	0.2	0.6	0.2
car	60	7	8.6	9.5	21	6.1
fib	5	1.7	1.9	1.2	3.4	1.4
Ca	150	55	57	56	38	48
P	330	49	53	76	127	54
Fe	7	0.7	1	0.5	1.6	1
Na	25	3	2	—	5	5
K	800	196	285	119	552	230
A	50	1400	580	610	140	570
B_1	0.3	0.09	0.09	0.22	0.37	0.1
B_2	0.2	0.09	0.11	0.11	0.19	0.1
B_5	2	0.8	0.9	—	2.2	1.1
C		17	20	14	44	20

*fresh chickpea values not known—for comparison only
†cooked

BER
Africa, Asia

Zizyphus mauritiana
syn *Z. jujuba*

Fam Rhamnaceae

*Bair, Bedara, Bor, Chinese Apple,
Doere, Indian Jujube, Indian Plum*

*India: badri, ber, bier, boar, bora,
kul; Malaysia: bedara; Thailand:
phutsa, pusa; West Indies: bhyre,
collie plum, coolie plum, crab apple,
dumbs, dunks, (Indian) jujube, juju,
jurjue*

Nutritional Values
*Bers are an excellent source of
vitamin C.*

Raw fruit:

cal	60	Ca	26	A	50
pro	1.8	P	37	B$_1$	0.02
fat	0.1	Fe	0.8	B$_2$	0.04
car	14.5	Na	3	B$_5$	0.9
fib	0.6	K	270	C	66

Recipe:
Chat Masala, page 209

Bers look like small crab apples; they measure around 3cm (1¼in) long and are usually oval. Originally green or red with an apple-like flesh they mature to a dull orange, the toughish, thin rind covering crisp white and mildly sweet, though occasionally sour, flesh. There is a long, wrinkled white stone. The aroma and flavour are distinctly ciderish with a yeasty touch.

Selecting the Best
Available from Asian shops during the winter months. Select even-sized, unblemished fruits.

Storage and Preparation
Keep in the fruit bowl or salad drawer. To stone: slit the fruit down one side and prise out the stone, being careful not to break the flesh.

Culinary Uses
Mostly eaten raw, bers can be thought of as sweetish crab apples. They are sometimes stuffed with chillies and sweet spices and pickled in syrup. Dried or candied forms are occasionally available and used like dates. Crushed bers make a sweet-sour drink and green ones make jelly. In Sudanese cooking they go into sweet cakes.

Herbal Properties
Ber is beneficial in the treatment of sore throats and chest colds, and is used to improve the taste of some medicines. Renaissance herbalists knew of its properties, and the fruit was used in the original 'jujubes' or pectoral lozenges. In India it has many uses, including as a digestive and a blood tonic. In Africa the roots and tree bark are widely used in folk medicine.

Facts and Features
Indigenous to Asia and tropical Africa, the ber has a long history of cultivation in India and Malaysia. While under commercial development in Australia it escaped to thrive as a weed. It is a member of the large buckthorn family; both *Zizyphus* and 'jujube' come from the Arabic name *zizouf*. A larger-fruited variety, *Zizyphus jujuba*, has been grown in China for over four thousand years.

BLUEBERRY

North America and East Asia

Vaccinium spp

Fam Ericaceae

Bilberry, Huckleberry, Whortleberry

France: airelle, myrtille; Germany: Blaubeere, Heidelbeere; Italy: mirtillo; Spain: arandano

Nutritional Values
Blueberries have little food value.

cal	62	Ca	15	A	100
pro	0.7	P	13	B$_1$	0.03
fat	0.5	Fe	1	B$_2$	0.06
car	15.3	Na	1	B$_5$	0.5
fib	1.5	K	81	C	14

Recipes:
Blueberries Neuchâtel, page 199

These little round berries often reach 1cm (½in) in diameter. The bloomy skin is dark enough to pass for black; it is tight, smooth and edible; the delicious sweet blue flesh hosts many hard edible seeds. British varieties, recently much improved, are often called bilberries.

Selecting the Best
Imported blueberries are available in the winter; less expensive, home-produced ones appear in summer. Look for plump berries with a heavy bloom.

Storage and Preparation
Kept covered, unwashed, in the refrigerator, they will stay fresh for several weeks. Pick over the fruit to remove any stalks or leaves.

Culinary Uses
Blueberry pie is certainly the best-known dish associated with this fruit but there are a myriad of other uses for it both from northern Europe as well as from North America. The sweet cultivated berries are delicious on their own, with cream and sugar or with breakfast cereal. They are spiced or pickled, made into compôtes, fruit soups and sauces—the latter especially with duck—or stewed and served with pancakes or ice-cream. In baking they appear in tarts, pies, muffins and waffles as well as in such esoterically named dishes as slumps, grunts, buckles and cobblers (collapsing pie, sweet dumplings, buns, floating piecrust). They make good jam and wine too.

Herbal Properties
Blueberries are astringent, antiseptic, and laxative in some people and not in others, so care is required. They are used as a mouthwash, a relief in catarrhal infections and for cleansing the bowels.

Facts and Features
Native to the US and East Asia, blueberries are, like others of the heather family, extremely hardy and grow in areas generally unsupportive of crops. Many species of birds are highly partial to them. The Americans have had them in commercial production for over a century, and export the bushy evergreen to Europe, to grow as a superior, easier-picking strain.

BREADFRUIT
Polynesia

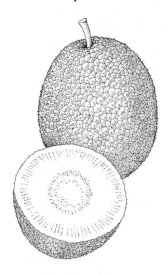

Artocarpus altilis
syn *A. communis, A. incisa*

Fam Moraceae

Chataigne (breadnut), God's Jack

Hawaii: ulu; Indonesia: kalooweh, kooloor (breadnut); so(o)ko(o)n; Malaysia: sukun; South America: fruto de año, fruto de name; Tahiti: uru; Thailand: sakay, sake; West Indies: arbol del pan, Canaan fruit, Captain Bligh, cow, pembwa (breadfruit); chataigne, katahar (breadnut)

Nutritional Values
Breadfruits are starchy, turning to sugar on ripening. They are good in vitamins B and C.

Raw:

cal	90	Ca	30	A	40
pro	1.5	P	32	B$_1$	0.1
fat	0.4	Fe	1.6	B$_2$	0.05
car	20–30	Na	15	B$_5$	0.8
fib	1.2	K	439	C	29

Recipe:
Carole's Breadfruit Casserole, page 191

Breadfruit is actually used as a vegetable rather than as a fruit. It is a compound fruit composed of fleshy pockets fused together around a central core. This has the effect of giving the rough warty skin a mosaic appearance. The fruit is spherical or oblong, 10–30cm (4–12in) in diameter, averaging 1.8kg (4lb) with larger ones weighing up to 4.5kg (10lb). The skin and flesh are green until ripe when the flesh turns yellow, sweet and fibrous and the skin yellow and mottled brown. The chewy pulp is moist with a slightly bread-like aroma when cooked, and has a sweetish flavour. It is quite tough to cut. Its close relative, the jackfruit, is described on page 87.

Selecting the Best
Buy firm fruit; soft ones are well on the way to rotting. Breadfruit tinned in brine is also available.

Storage and Preparation
Keep in the cool until required. Breadfruit is always cooked before eating. Peel and discard the central core before use. Cut up into chunks for casseroles, curries, etc. Bake whole for ½–1 hour until tender all through or slice and roast for 10 minutes.

Culinary Uses
Breadfruit is a staple in Polynesia and widely popular in the Caribbean, southern India and Sri Lanka, less so in Malaysia and Thailand. It is used somewhat like potatoes, and tastes like bread. It is boiled or fried, often with meat, cheese, and fish (especially tuna), or stuffed with something savoury. The ripe fruit, used as a dessert, can be mashed with milk and sugar, or go into pies, fritters, chips and even make a chilled soup. Breadfruit is an ingredient in hot and sour 'dry' curries with *dhal* and coconut, and in Thailand is made into *poi*, a fermented paste usually made from eddoes or yam.

Herbal Properties
No medical properties are known.

Facts and Features
Native to Sri Lanka, China and Malaya, breadfruit is important today in the West Indies, brought there from the South Pacific in 1787–8 by Captain Bligh of the infamous *Bounty*. The fruit, being substantial and bland, is a cheap

source of bulk, like bread in the West. It is frequently dried and ground down into biscuits. A yellow dye and a glue are extracted locally from the tree, the wood goes into African canoes and a kind of cloth is made from the bark. A seeded variety, the breadnut (or chataigne in the West Indies), has a prickly skin, little flesh and many edible brown seeds about 25mm (1in) in diameter. These are boiled or roasted like chestnuts, or curried.

CALABRESE (SPROUTING BROCCOLI)
Italy

Brassica oleracea var *italica* syn *B.o.botrytis cymosa*

Fam Cruciferae

Asparagus Broccoli, Broccoli Spears, Cauli-Broc, Green Broccoli, Green Broccoli Spears, Greenheaded Broccoli, Italian (Green) (Sprouting) Broccoli, Sprouting Broccoli

Calabrese first became popular in its frozen form, but is now readily available fresh. It is best described as a refined and superior version of its relative, the cauliflower. Cauliflower and purple broccoli are brassicas of the 'hearting' variety, that is having large heads of many densely-packed florets. Conversely, calabrese is a variety that 'heads' or 'sprouts', a few tops springing from a green succulent stalk which is itself highly palatable—much more so than cauliflower stalk. The florets are green with a blue tinge and often a delicate bloom. They are easily distinguished from other denser-hearting brassicas by their much more attractive 'beaded' appearance. However, the best feature of calabrese is its flavour—a compound of green beans and cabbage, but without the rather determined tone of the latter. The aroma of raw calabrese is slightly like that of cauliflower.

Selecting the Best
Good fresh calabrese has firm stalks and compact heads. Avoid any that are yellowing or starting to flower. Calabrese is usually sold trimmed so there is very little waste. Frozen calabrese is marketed under the name 'broccoli spears'.

Storage and Preparation
Calabrese merits the same respect as asparagus. Use it as fresh as possible, although it will keep for a few days in a polythene bag in the refrigerator salad drawer. Discard any tough leaves attached to the stalk but retain any tender little ones. Cut off stalk ends and clean the heads by swirling in cold water. Peel any tough-skinned stalks and cut a cross in the base to assist even cooking. To cook, place the calabrese, stalks down, in a saucepan of boiling salted water with the heads just above water level. Steam, covered, for about 8 minutes—no more. For

China: i taai lei kaai laan, sai lan fa, ts'in(g) fa ts'oi, yeung ye ts'oi fa; France: brocoli; Germany: Spargelkohl (broccoli); India: brocoli; Italy: brocoli calabrese

Nutritional Values
Calabrese is a good source of vitamins A, B_2 and C, with very little, if any, being lost in cooking.

cal	26–29	Ca	58–100	A	2,500–3,000
pro	3.1–3.2	P	62	B_1	0.07–0.09
fat	0.3	Fe	0.7–1	B_2	0.13–0.2
car	4.5–5.2	Na	10	B_5	0.6–0.8
fib	1.1–1.5	K	220–267	C	30–90

stir-frying, first blanch for 1 minute (this also helps preserve a good colour), refresh with cold water, divide into tiny flowerets and drain well before cooking.

Culinary Uses
Simplicity is the key to enjoying the fresh flavour of calabrese, minimally cooked to the right degree of crispness. Serve just with melted butter, or perhaps a sauce such as *maltaise*, *hollandaise* or *béarnaise*. Calabrese deserves a place as a first course with a delicate *avgolemono* sauce made with half chicken stock and half the calabrese cooking liquid. The Italians, who first produced this vegetable, clearly savour it *alla romana*—braised in wine or sautéed in oil and sprinkled with freshly-grated parmesan cheese. Serve it cold as a salad or *à la grècque*. A popular vegetable in China, it appears in stir-fried dishes, especially with squid and shellfish, and in Japan it is an ideal subject for *tempura* (see page 182)—deep-fried vegetables and prawns coated in a gossamer-thin batter.

Herbal Properties
No special properties are attributed to calabrese.

Facts and Features
Calabrese is native to Calabria in Italy, whence its name. It was introduced into France, by Catherine de Medici, in 1560 and into Britain in 1720. However, it is only within the last twenty years that it has become commonplace, first as a frozen vegetable and lately in the fresh state. It is worth growing in the garden. If your gardening book gives no specific instructions follow those for cauliflower.

CAPSICUM
Peru

Capsicum annuum var *grossum*

Fam Solanaceae

Once only green (unripe) or red (ripe) capsicums or sweet peppers were available, but the producers have now developed yellow, purple, black and white varieties. The white pepper is a longer version, more like a very fat chilli in shape but certainly not in flavour. The others retain the familiar bell shape.
Green: Slightly bitter, mild peppery undertones.
Red: Sweetish.
Yellow: Mild and sweetish.
Purple/Black: Sweeter, with more 'bite' than red.
White: Mild.

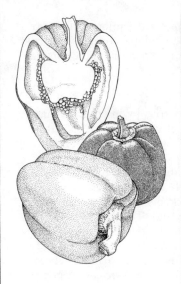

Bell Pepper, Bullnose Pepper, Caps, Paprika, Pepper(s), Pimento, Pimiento, Pumpkin Chilli (India), Sweet Pepper

China: dung lung tsiu (lantern pepper), tang lung tsiu (paper lantern pepper), tim tsiu (sweet pepper); France: pimenton doux, poivron; Germany: Ziegenpfeffer; India: kacha, Kashmire mirch, marich, mita-maris; Italy: peperone; Japan: kosho, piman; South America: aji dulce (Venezuelan); Spain: pimiento; Thailand: prik farang; West Indies: bell pepper, bonny pepper, burgeman, green pepper, piment, pimient, Spanish pepper, sweet pepper

Nutritional Values
Low in calories, sweet peppers are a good source of vitamins A and C, the red having ten times the amount of vitamin A as the green and twice as much C as cooked green pepper.

cal	12–31	Ca	6–13	A	400–4000
pro	0.9–1.4	P	16–38	B_1	0.04–0.08
fat	0–0.3	Fe	0.4–0.7	B_2	0.03–0.08
car	2–7	Na	9–13	B_5	0.3–0.9
fib	1.4–1.7	K	150–210	C	90–200

Recipe:
Rouille, page 202

Selecting the Best
Peppers are available all year round. They should be firm, bright and glossy, neither dull nor wrinkled.

Storage and Preparation
Kept in the cool, capsicums will last for a week or so, but deteriorate rapidly once cut. For stuffing, cut off the stalk and slice a lid from the top end. Alternatively, cut lengthways in half. Remove all seeds and membrane. If blanching is required, 3 minutes will do. It is unnecessary to skin capsicums, especially for crisp salads, but you might prefer to avoid the rather tough skin in cooked dishes. To skin: grill or scorch briefly over a flame and pop into a bag to steam for a few minutes. Scrape off the skin under the tap. Disappointingly, the purple ones turn green when cooked.

Culinary Uses
Popular worldwide, capsicums provide a natural receptacle for stuffing with meat, rice or cheese. *Pipérade, ratatouille*, and Hungarian goulash all feature the warm flavours and bright colours which liven up a meal in any season. *Rouille*, the hot spicy Mediterranean sauce, embodies the capsicum quintessence. It is simple to make and will transform a fish soup, especially a canned one. Green peppers have become characteristic in Chinese cookery, widely teamed with beef, while in Japan they are pickled, grilled or fried in *tempura* (see page 182) batter.

Herbal Properties
Apart from the properties associated with valuable vitamins, capsicums have been neglected in medicine. Their relative novelty is probably a reason but perhaps some secrets will eventually be discovered in the mists of the high Andes.

Facts and Features
Capsicums were virtually unknown in the UK before 1950, even to the sophisticated cook. But once the belt of rationing had been loosened—and with promptings from Elizabeth David—the green pepper became the 'in' vegetable, reaching a peak of popularity in the sixties. Today they are hardly exotic except for the producers' cunning in creating varieties of many colours. The name 'capsicum' derives from the Latin *capsa*, a box.

CARAMBOLA
Indonesia

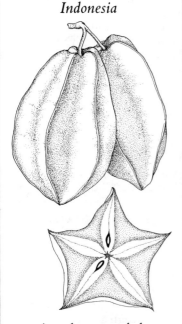

Averrhoa carambola

Fam *Oxalidaceae*

Blimbing, Caramba, Chinese Gooseberry, Country Gooseberry, Five Corner, Star Apple, Star Fruit

China: yeung toe, yuan toa; India: kam(a)ranga; Malaysia: blimbing manis; Thailand: ma-feung, mafueng; West Indies: Chinese starapple, coolie tamarind, five finger, pomme canelle

Nutritional Values
Carambolas are a fair source of vitamin A precursor, and good in vitamin C. They contain much potassium oxalate which inhibits calcium and magnesium absorption.

Raw:

cal	35	Ca	5	A	1,350
pro	0.6	P	18	B₁	0.04
fat	0.4	Fe	1.2	B₂	0.02
car	8.4	Na	2	B₅	0.3
	(sugar)				
fib	0.9	K	190	C	35

This fruit has a curious and attractive structure. It resembles a yellow, five-sided sausage, with five marked longitudinal ribs giving star-shaped slices. Frequently it is 8–13cm (3–5in) long, 5cm (2in) in diameter. The skin is thin, with a waxy sheen; the translucent flesh is yellow or orange, crisp, aromatic and juicy, reminiscent of loquat, but mild to acidic depending on variety. There are up to a dozen small flat oval seeds. Usually the whole fruit is edible.

Selecting the Best
Buy when ripe, or just before. Most varieties ripen to yellow or orange, though some may remain green-yellow. They are available sporadically throughout the year.

Storage and Preparation
Keep in a cool place and handle carefully as the fruit is fragile. It may be home-ripened for a few days. It is at its most attractive cut across into star shapes, but it may be necessary to cut off thick edges and corners. Remove the seeds from the slices as you would from lemons.

Culinary Uses
The clear juice is a pleasant soft drink; it makes a good daiquiri. The fruit is used stewed, preserved and pickled, its flavour increasing on cooking. Chutneys and jams are prepared using sour carambolas, but it remains one of those tropical fruits which seem best when treated simply—in a salad, with nuts, cheese, or coconut, or as a plain garnish for roast meats, spiced beef or pork. In Asia where it often occurs as a sweetmeat, preserved in honey or candied, there is one widespread use for it in cooking—with chicken.

Herbal Properties
Carambola juice is a good pre-prandial digestive.

Facts and Features
A popular fruit tree in oriental gardens, carambola is native to Malaysia and Indonesia. Now it grows throughout the tropics and has long been under cultivation in the US and Hawaii. It came to southern Europe at the end of the eighteenth century, but this environment is not particularly suitable. The botanical name is owed to Averrhoes ('Ibn Rushd), the mid-twelfth century physician and philosopher famed for his commentaries on Aristotle.

CASSAVA
Tropical America

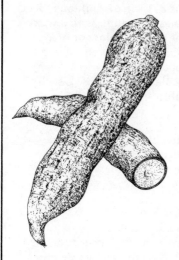

Manihot esculenta
syn *M. utilissima, M. aipi,*
M. dulcis, M. palmata

Fam Euphorbiaceae

Brazilian Arrowroot, Cassara,
Mandioca, Manihot, Manioc,
Tapioca, Tapioka, Yuca

China: muk shue, pok fung; East
Africa: muhogo, mogo (Swahili);
France: cassave, manioc; Germany:
Kassawastrauch, Maniok; Ghana:
agabli, bankye, duade, gbedi, gbeli;
India: kelala, marachini, mara valle
kilangu, maravalli, s(h)imul alu,
tikhoor; Indonesia: boodin, kaspe,
katela bodin, poohoong; Italy:
cassava, manioca; Malaysia: ubi
kayu;
Nigeria: abaca, akpara nkpa iwa
(bitter), akpe, doyar kudu, gbaguda,
ege, igari, iwa uneme, jigbo,
k'araza, rogo; Sierra Leone:
E-yoka, tangei; South America:
aipim, macaxeira, mandico, yuca,
yuca dulce; Spain: canabe, mandioca;
Thailand: man sam parang, mun
sumpalung; West Indies: aypu
(sweet), boniato (sweet), cassava,
manioc, tapioca

Cassava is the swollen root of a tropical plant. Usually cylindrical or tapering, it measures 15–45cm (6–18in) long and 3–15cm (1¼–6in) in diameter. The skin is coarse, usually brown, sometimes with small roots attached. Others have a pinkish tone or are much paler. Below the corky skin is a white rind covering the main core of starchy material, normally white but often yellow or red-veined. White cassavas are sweeter and softer than yellow types, which are faintly bitter.

Selecting the Best
Cassava is harvested all year. It is available in Indian and West Indian shops. Choose even-sized fresh roots of clean appearance. Frozen cassava from South America may also be obtained.

Storage and Preparation
Use as soon as possible. Wash the roots and peel away the bark-like skin and white rind with a sharp knife or potato peeler. Grate, chop or slice according to recipe. After grating, excess water should be squeezed out through a cloth.

Culinary Uses
Popular in South America, the Caribbean and East and West Africa, cassava is usually bought in processed forms such as tapioca for milk puddings; *farina* or *gari* for dumplings, cakes and biscuits; and *cassareep*, a spiced liquid extract essential to the West Indian dish, pepperpot. However, the fresh root, washed, peeled, boiled and pounded exhaustively with a traditional wooden pestle becomes *fufu*, famous in Africa—a bland starchy accompaniment to soups and stews. Grated cassava mixed with desiccated coconut and sugar makes good biscuits, but cassava chips are perhaps the best and easiest application for this vegetable.

Herbal Properties
In the thirties cassava was used as an invalid food. It is renowned for its prussic acid content. In many varieties this must be extracted by washing and cooking. There are tales, probably apocryphal, of starving European explorers in the jungle eating raw manioc and perishing just when they believed they had finally found sustenance. Far more likely are the reports that Indians tipped their arrows and blowpipe darts with the poison juice.

Nutritional Values

Cassava is a starch staple in many tropical countries, but is unfortunately poor in protein, particularly the essential amino acid methionine, and in vitamins other than C. Thus diets restricted to the vegetable invariably result in protein deficiency diseases such as kwashiorkor.

cal	145	Ca	33	A	0
pro	0.7–2.6	P	37	B₁	0.06
fat	0.3	Fe	0.7	B₂	0.03
car	35	Na	2	B₅	0.6
fib	1	K	390	C	20–36

Recipes:
Cassava Crisps, page 203; Fufu, page 193

Facts and Features

Cassava has spread rapidly from its home in South America to all tropic regions with a marked wet and dry season. It is easy to grow—merely plant pieces of stalk in any soil, even laterite, and a crop is soon forthcoming (8–12 months). A further important feature is that it can remain in the ground almost indefinitely as a store. In parts of Africa one sees cassava flourishing around every habitation. The plant consists of narrow noded woody stems up to 3.6m (12ft) high with lobed palmate leaves; all parts contain a latex. There are over a hundred cultivars. It is a source of industrial starch for the plywood, textile, adhesive, paper and foodstuff industries. Its best-known product is tapioca, made by heating the starch on iron plates where it agglutinates into tiny pellets. Chopped and sun-dried, cassava is a major export of countries like Thailand to the West for animal feed. The name derives from South American Indian Taino *caçábi.*

CELERIAC
Mediterranean

Apium graveolens var
rapaceum
Fam Umbelliferae

Celeriac has been called 'turnip-rooted celery', which is a fair description—except that it is neither 'turnip' nor 'root'. Bulbous, turnip-like by all means, it is actually the swollen stem-base of a type of celery. Very celery-like in aroma and flavour, its texture is closer to potato. A winter vegetable and, until recently, not that common, its appearance varies from neatly trimmed to quite shaggy. Some resemble brown beetroots with a profusion of rooty tendrils at the bottom, others are enclosed in a straggly embrace of rootlets. Finally, when all these appurtenances have been trimmed off, one discovers a globe, fairly knobbly, with brown and creamy-yellow patches.

Selecting the Best
Celeriac now appears all year round but is scarcer during the summer. Medium-sized, smoother roots are best. Pick those that seem the heaviest for their size, as lighter, older roots may have a hollow interior and woody texture.

Storage and Preparation
If wrapped in a polythene bag to retain moisture, celeriac should keep for a couple of weeks in the refrigerator salad drawer. Remember that this vegetable discolours rapidly once cut, so put it

Celery Rave, Knob Celery,
Turnip-rooted Celery

France: céleri-rave; Germany:
Knoll-Sellerie, Knollensellerie;
Italy: sedano-rapa; Spain:
apio-nabo; Turkey: kereviz; United
States: celery root

Nutritional Values
Full of flavour but low in calories,
celeriac is an ideal dietary vegetable.
However, its miserly mineral and
vitamin content makes it of little food
value.

cal	40	Ca	43	A	—
pro	1.8	P	115	B_1	0.05
fat	0.3	Fe	0.6	B_2	0.06
car	8.5	Na	100	B_5	0.7
fib	1.3	K	300	C	8

Recipes:
Celeriac Salad, page 191; Lamb
Cutlets with Celeriac, page 185

into acidulated water immediately after
preparation. Remove the knobbly skin with a
sharp knife and cut the celeriac into manageable
pieces before chopping, slicing or grating. For
eating 'raw' in salads we believe celeriac is
preferable blanched in boiling water (for no more
than a few seconds) and then refreshed
immediately in cold water. This removes its
slightly bitter taste. But if you prefer it
unblanched, grate it straight into the dressing.

Culinary Uses
It is a pity that celeriac's popularity is still largely
confined to France, Italy and Germany, as it is
both delicious and versatile. Perhaps its
somewhat suspicious outward appearance is too
forbidding, as is the greyness the flesh acquires if
it is not treated with lemon juice. Its best-known
use is in *céleri rémoulade*, cut into matchsticks and
mixed with mayonnaise well seasoned with Dijon
mustard. Apart from its use in divers salads,
celeriac is an excellent addition to soups and
winter casseroles. It goes particularly well with
lamb or beef. Puréed celeriac with or without
potato, and seasoned with salt, pepper and butter,
traditionally accompanies duck and game dishes
(see Jerusalem Artichoke, page 8). Again, it is an
ideal vegetable for oriental stir-fried dishes.

Herbal Properties
Celery-related plants are diuretic, carminative and
emmenagogic. It is inadvisable for anyone who is
pregnant or suffering from kidney disease to take
excessive quantities of them. They are beneficial
in skin diseases, and oil from the roots is believed
to restore sexual potency after illness.

Facts and Features
Celeriac is a member of the parsley family and,
like celery, has been developed from smallage
only quite recently. Indeed, it is mentioned in
neither Gerard, 1597, nor Culpeper, 1640. What
early references exist are vague to say the least,
but Alexandria, the Levant and Apulia (the 'heel'
of Italy) are all mentioned as sources of a weird
odorous bulb. The word celery derives from the
Greek *selinon*, parsley; where the '-ac' comes
from remains a mystery.

CHARD
Mediterranean

Beta vulgaris var *cicla*
Fam Chenopodiaceae

Leaf(y) Beet, Perpetual Spinach, Rhubarb Chard (var), Seakale Beet, Sicilian Beet, Silver Beet, Silver Seakale Beet, Spinach Beet, Sweet Chard, Swiss Chard (Beet), Thick-leaved Beet, White Beet

China: gwun dat tsoi (royal beetroot), kwan taat tsoi (royal beetroot), paak tim tsoi (white sweet vegetable); France: carde, cardes de b(l)ette (ribs of beet), poirée (à carde blanche); Germany: Beisskohl, Mangold (beet); Indonesia: bit; Italy: bieta, bietola da coste; Japan: to-jisa; Middle East: silq; Portugal: acelga; Spain: acelga, bleda

Nutritional Values
Chard is a useful source of vitamin A, with a smattering of other vitamins and minerals.

Cooked:

cal	18	Ca	73	A	5,400
pro	1.8	P	24	B_1	0.04
fat	0.2	Fe	1.8	B_2	0.11
car	3.3	Na	86	B_5	0.4
fib	0.7	K	321	C	16

Recipes:
Cream of Chard Soup, page 179; Rice and Lentil Rolls, page 196

Chard is in effect two vegetables in one, the leaves and stalks being used separately. The former are dark green, like a robust, ribbed spinach, but mild in flavour and therefore more palatable to children. The stalks are broad, white and succulent, reminiscent of celery in appearance. It is sometimes mistakenly called seakale. There is also a red variety from the United States, fairly called rhubarb chard, which is sweeter, smoother and more succulent.

Selecting the Best
Chard is available intermittently throughout the year. Choose specimens with even-sized, even-coloured leaves. The stalks should snap easily.

Storage and Preparation
Separate the leaves from the stalks and store in polythene bags in the refrigerator salad drawer. The stalks will keep the longer. If cooking leaves and stalks together, give the stalks a 4-minute start. Wash well, chop or shred the leaves, string the stalks like celery and cut into lengths. Stalks to go into salads are best blanched for 2 minutes. Avoid aluminium utensils.

Culinary Uses
Chard stalks are considered a delicacy in France and may be treated like asparagus or celery. A cream soup made with the leaves only was greatly favoured in the Middle Ages but chard soup is also most satisfactory with the stalks included. Serve chard plain, steamed and buttered or try stuffing the leaves with rice and lentils, Middle Eastern style.

Herbal Properties
The juice is decongestant; the leaves and stalks are acid neutralisers and purgatives: ' . . . boyled, it quickly descendeth, looseth the belly, and provoketh to the stoole . . .' (Gerard, 1597). Ignorant of vitamins, the old master is also scornful of its nutritive value.

Facts and Features
A hardy perennial of the beetroot family, chard was known to Aristotle, and the Romans introduced it to Britain and Europe. It is now favoured in the US and the Orient but has missed out India on its travels. The name derives from French *carde*, artichoke leaf stalk, also *chardon*, thistle. The qualifier 'Swiss' probably different-iates imports to France from local produce.

CHAYOTE
Mexico

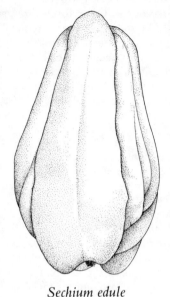

Sechium edule
Fam Cucurbitaceae

Chaci, Chaco, Chaka, Chocho,
Choke, Choko, Chowchow,
Choyote, Christofina, Christophene,
Christophine, Chuchu, Custard
Marrow, Guisquil, Mirliton,
Pepinello, Soo Soo, Squash,
Vegetable Pear, Xuxu

China: faat sau gwa, fa chon kwa,
fat shau kwa (all Buddha's hand
gourd or melon), hop jeung gwa;
Indonesia: gamas, labooh seeyem,
labooh tjena, ledjet, maneesah,
(walooh) djepan, waluh seeyem;
Malaysia: labu seeam; Polynesia:
chayote; South America: chayote,
guispui; West Indies: chaco,
christophene, christophine, chocho,
choco, squash, tallon, tallote

Nutritional Values
*Of little nutritional value, chayote is
90 per cent water.*

Raw:

cal	28	Ca	13	A	20
pro	0.6	P	26	B_1	0.03
fat	0.1	Fe	0.5	B_2	0.03
car	7.1	Na	5	B_5	0.4
fib	0.7	K	102	C	19

The chayote is a member of the squash family. Averaging 10–12cm (4–5in) in length, it is pear-shaped, often furrowed, with a characteristic cleavage and sometimes a peeping shoot at the larger end. The colour varies from yellow to dark green—generally it is pale green. The skin is thin, tight and leathery, sometimes covered with tiny spikes, soft but sharpish. The usually pale green flesh covers a flat, cream-coloured seed which is about a third of the length of the chayote. Chayote flesh is bland in flavour with a crisp and juicy texture rather like water chestnut; the seed is nutty and crunchy.

Selecting the Best
Available all the year round. They are at their best and most tender when small and pale. The large ones are good for stuffing.

Storage and Preparation
Chayotes will keep for 2–3 months in a cool place, but eat them before they begin to sprout or their shoots will spread with triffid-like rapidity. The skin is easily peeled with a knife or potato peeler, but may be left on the younger fruit. Likewise the edible seed may be left intact or removed for eating separately. They may be cooked whole, but are usually halved, sliced or diced.

Culinary Uses
Chayotes, appreciated for their subtlety of flavour, may be eaten blanched in salads, cooked through or even raw as an appetiser, sliced with a sprinkle of lime juice and salt. They are enormously popular in Mexico and the West Indies where they lend themselves to a wide variety of dishes, combining especially well with sweetcorn, tomatoes, fresh coriander and chillies. Try them cooked like courgettes or stuffed either with cheese and onion or minced beef and chilli together with their own mashed pulp. Chayotes are common in Chinese markets, favoured for their ideal stir-fry texture. Sweet dishes may include them—they are cooked like pumpkin in tarts and pies, and a traditional Mexican dessert is *chayote rellenos*, in which chayote shells are stuffed with a mixture reminiscent of spiced fruit cake.

Herbal Properties
A good healthy vegetable, chayote has no other special properties.

Recipes:
Chayote Rellenos, page 199;
Chayote Salad, page 192; Stuffed
Chayotes, page 197; Sweet and Sour
Wheels, page 188.

Facts and Features

Native to Mexico and Central America, chayotes were popular with the Aztecs. Their ease of cultivation has led to widespread production in the warmer countries and they appear in many cuisines, including those of India, China and Africa. Popular in the Caribbean, different coloured chayotes appear on every wayside stall; some white, others yellow, light green and dark green. Chayotes grow on a tough spreading vine, invariably trained on trellises for commercial production. A fine straw is extracted from the vines and woven into expensive hats in Réunion. In some parts of the world the tuberous root is eaten and young leaves and buds are used as a vegetable. The name derives from the Nahuatl *chayotli* and the West Indians call them 'christophine' after Christopher Columbus.

CHICORY
Europe

There are two chicories commonly available, a white and a red. (Others are described under Facts and Features.)

WHITE CHICORY

Belgian Chicory, Brussels Chicory, Witloof (white leaf)

China: kuen ip shang tsoi (rolled leaf lettuce); France: barbe-de-bouc (goat's beard)

This is a tightly-wrapped sheath of white leaves with soft tops, yellow to light green; a speciality of the Belgians, who accidentally discovered the secret of its production. Chicory shoots (*chicons*) are forced through a layer of sand or peat to produce the tight, blanched leaf bundles. The flavour is faintly bitter, juicy, and crisp.

RED CHICORY

Radicchio, Radiccio

Red varieties are the speciality of the Italians, who boast thousands of chicories. The one most common in British shops is *radicchio*, as it is also called in Italian. It is like a small red cabbage, with bright or deep red leaves with firm white ribs, and a tight, round heart. The flavour is like lettuce, but far more bitter.

Most red chicories are interesting in their response to day-length and temperature. Usually green at first, as the days shorten in autumn they turn red like the deciduous trees around them, and when temperatures fall very low in winter the normally spreading leaves turn inwards and close up to form a tight head. Three varieties are:
Rossa di Verona: spreading, with browny-red markings.
Radicchio di Treviso: described by some writers as like a brush with the root and stalk as a handle.

Cichorium intybus
Fam Compositae

Succory, Witloof (Chicory)

United States: endive, Belgian endive, French endive

Nutritional Values
Chicory has no nutritive value at all.

cal	15	Ca	18	A	—
pro	1	P	21	B_1	—
fat	0.1	Fe	0.6	B_2	—
car	3.2	Na	7	B_5	—
fib	—	K	182	C	5

Recipe:
Ham-wrapped Chicory in Cheese Sauce, page 185

Radicchio di Castelfranco: deep red, often likened to a rose.
All these have variations of colour and shape, and even the names are not rigorous.

Selecting the Best
White chicory is available all year. Choose even-sized, tight, white, yellow-tipped heads. Those with open, green-tipped leaves will be bitter. Radicchio should be compact. Make sure the outer leaves are neither wilting nor flabby.

Storage and Preparation
Wrap white chicory in foil or paper and keep in the salad drawer. This prevents it turning green or bitter. It is usually unnecessary to wash chicory. Just remove any brown parts. Cut it just prior to use. It is advantageous to blanch it for 10 minutes before braising. Radicchio keeps quite well in the salad drawer. It is usually ready-trimmed but if not, remove the root and outside leaves and wash briefly if necessary.

Culinary Uses
White chicory is esteemed in Europe, especially in Italy, Belgium and France. It makes an excellent winter salad. Sliced oranges, onion and chopped walnuts are often combined with it to make a splendid accompaniment to cold meat and game. Braised with butter and a little lemon juice, it is perfect with roast meat; add some cream for extra richness. A good luncheon or supper dish can be made with chicory wrapped in ham and cooked in a cheese sauce. It can also be stuffed, puréed or made into a soufflé.
   Radicchio is prized as a salad leaf in Italy. Its reputation has spread through France to England, where it now appears as a regular feature in side salads. Its attractive colour and slight bitterness contrast nicely with bland green leaves.

Herbal Properties
Chicory is digestive, diuretic and laxative. Culpeper suggests its use for liver complaints and 'for swooning and passions of the heart'.

Facts and Features
Chicory is native to Europe and its shoots have been harvested from Roman times as a salad vegetable. It is well worth growing; any good gardening book will describe suitable methods. In addition, other chicories include:

Bitter Lettuce, Blue Succory (after its flowers), Hard Ewes, Monk's Beard, Strip for Strip, Succory, Wild Lettuce

France: barbe-de-capuchin; Italy: barba di capuccine di campo

Wild Chicory   This chicory grows wild throughout Europe; the toothed shoots are harvested in early spring in Mediterranean countries, especially Italy and France. This is the common variety that is the forebear of cultivated chicories. The flavour is sharply bitter.

Green Chicory   There are several varieties which are more like lettuce, especially Sugar Loaf, the best known. The greener parts are more bitter than the white centres of bunched varieties.

'Coffee' Chicory   Varieties with large tap roots, like Witloof, Magdeburg and Brunswick, are grown for use as a coffee substitute, or additive, popular in France and Germany. Much ritual used to be attached to their harvesting in Europe, such as the use of gold or silver coins or going barefoot.

CHILLI
South and Central America

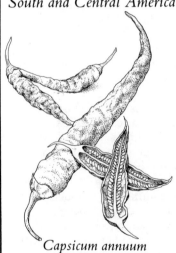

*Capsicum annuum
C. frutescens
syn C. minimum (C.f.)*

Fam Solanaceae

Bird Pepper, Bonnet Pepper, Pepper, Red Devil

Burma: nil thee; China: fan chiew, ngau kok tsiu (cow's horn pepper), tse tin tsiu (pointed-to-sky pepper), tsim tuk laat tsiu (pointed-bottom

Although chillies occur throughout the world in an amazing profusion of shapes, sizes, colours and pungencies, only a few of these have beaten a path to the average British shop. The most common are listed below. As a rule, it is safe to say that a chilli's hotness is in inverse proportion to its size: the smaller the hotter, and the more mature the more pungent they become. Young chillies are usually green, ripening to yellow, orange or red. More exotic varieties are white and some even become purple or black. The pointed tip is usually milder than the broader top while the seeds and internal membrane are the hottest parts.

Selecting the Best
Various chillies are available throughout the year. Always ascertain the hottest chilli when faced with a choice in order to avoid it if necessary. Be warned that the tiny chillies from Thailand and the squashed-looking bonnet peppers will be searingly hot. Whether wrinkled or smooth, chillies should be firm and shiny.

Storage and Preparation
Fresh chillies should keep for up to 3 weeks stored in the refrigerator in a paper bag. Check that none are going bad as deterioration will rapidly spread. They freeze quite successfully loose. Depending on the recipe, chillies are used

Type	Names	Shape/Size	Colour	Pungency
Indian	mirchi, mirich	thin, conical 7×1cm (2¾×½in)	green, red	very hot
'Chinese'	chiew, tsiu	plump, conical 7–12×2–3cm (2¾–5×¾–1¼in)	green, red	mild, like sweet peppers
West Indian	bird pepper, bonnet pepper	spherical 2–3cm (¾–1¼in)	yellow	very hot
Thai	priki nu	thin, conical 3–4×0.8–1cm (1¼–1½×⅓–½in)	green, red, white	extremely hot

This table is far from rigid—most types are international.

pungent pepper); France: piment, piment fort, pimentoiseau, piment rouge; Germany: Roter Pfeffer, Spanischer Pfeffer; India: marich, maris, mirchi, mirich; Indonesia: lombok, lombok hijan (green), tjabé; Italy: diavoletto peperonicino, peperoncini, peperone; Japan: togarashi; Malaysia: cabai hijan (green), chilli, lombok, tjabé; Mexico: chile; Middle East: uran filfil; Spain: chile, guindilla (cayenne), pimentón; Thailand: nil thee sein (green), priki fa (large red), priki nu (small hot), priki nu kaset (Serrano type); West Indies: bird pepper, bonnet pepper, chilli, finger pepper, Guinea pepper, hot pepper, Jumbie pepper, pepper, pimentoiseau, red pepper, spur pepper

whole, roasted and skinned, seeded, chopped or pounded. (Follow the instructions for the preparation of capsicums on page 28.) Always wash your hands after handling chillies and avoid touching eyes or other sensitive areas. The fieriest parts are the seeds and inner membrane, so remove these for a less incendiary flavour. To make a highly decorative chilli 'flower' to garnish rice or curries, take any long, thin chilli and cut from just below the stalk down to the tip, six or eight times, to make petals. Put into iced water until the petals curl upwards. You can dry your own chillies to make chilli powder.

Culinary Uses
Fresh chillies are associated primarily with Asian and Mexican cookery and are widely used in South America, the Caribbean and West Africa where many regional recipes call for enormous measures of the more dramatic chillies. Many curry pastes are based on chilli and are ridiculously easy to prepare with the aid of an electric blender or food processor and may be refrigerated or frozen for handy use. Chillies are also the base of many commercial products such as chilli seasoning, chilli sauce, 'red' pepper, paprika, cayenne, tabasco sauce, pimenton etc. They are an important feature of Chinese Sichuan cookery and appear in a seemingly infinite succession of sauces and sambals from Southeast Asia. Grilled fish steaks are excellent with a condiment of ground fresh red chillies, salt and lemon juice. Tunisian Couscous is served with the fiendishly hot chilli sauce harissa. We have encountered a Senegalese custom where a whole bonnet pepper cooked in the stew is extracted and given pride of place in the centre of the table. Guests requiring more heat simply press their forks into the chilli. Most daunting, however, is

Nutritional Values

Chillies are one of the most fruitful sources of vitamins A and C but because the hot varieties are eaten in small quantities this usefulness is somewhat dissipated. However, the mild varieties can be taken in larger amounts and their benefits properly obtained. As chillies ripen from green to red there is a dramatic increase in vitamin values.

Chilli pods excluding seeds:

	GREEN (IMMATURE)	RED (MATURE)
cal	37	65
pro	1.3	2.3
fat	0.2	0.4
car	9.1	15.8
fib	1.8	2.3
Ca	10	16
P	25	49
Fe	0.7	1.4
Na	—	25
K	—	564
A	770	21,600
B_1	0.09	0.1
B_2	0.06	0.2
B_5	1.7	2.9
C	235	369

Recipes:
Chilli Sambal, page 206; Sambal Bajak, page 208

the Indian chilli *pakora* (whole chilli fried in batter)—try one of these if you dare!

Herbal Properties

Chilli is antiseptic, digestive, carminative, irritant, rubefacient, stimulant and febrifugal. It is used as a counter-irritant to rheumatic, nerve and muscular pains, but in moderation, to avoid skin burns and blisters. Its antiseptic property is used in meat preservatives and sticking plasters. Being red and fiery it was once considered an antidote to scarlet fever and to the exquisite agony of gout.

Facts and Features

Chillies have been grown and used in South and Central America for millennia. Being so ancient and so readily hybridised, they have produced hundreds of different types that defy neat classification—there are over one hundred and fifty in Mexico alone. They were brought to Europe by Columbus in 1492 and soon the Portuguese had spread them round the world, the seeds possessing long viability. Chillies easily supplanted pepper (*Piper nigrum*) as the main condiment for the dull starchy diets common throughout the tropics. Their physical characteristics vary considerably, and apparently identical chillies of the same batch may be different in strength. Some chillies, especially 'wild' or escapes, are so hot that they can burn the hands and arms, let alone the mouth and digestive tract. In some cultures they are used as a means of torture.

CHINESE KEYS
Southern China

Chinese keys are a type of galangal (see page 68), a close relative of ginger, although their form is quite different—looking like an orgy of octopuses. There are two or three slightly knobbly 'heads' with many long fingers hanging downwards. The colour is light brown and there is a distinctive lemony-ginger aroma. The inner flesh is bright yellow with a creamy core; its aroma is far stronger. The heads or corms are some 2cm (¾in) round and are closest in semblance to ginger or galangal while the 'legs', or 'Chinese keys', are anything from 8–13cm (3–5in) long and about 1cm (½in) in diameter. Both parts are used.

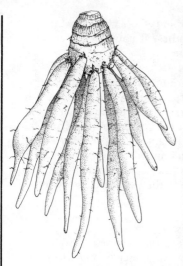

Boesenbergia pandurata
syn *Curcuma rotunda*
Gastrochilus panduratum
Kaempferia pandurata

Fam Zingiberaceae

*Lesser Ginger, Resurrection Lily,
Rhizome*

*China: soh shi (key); Indonesia:
temoo koontji, tumu kunci;
Malaysia: temu kunchi; Thailand:
kachai, krachai*

Nutritional Values
*Chinese keys are used only in small
quantities as a flavouring so have a
negligible nutritive effect. However,
through their contained essential oils
and other constituents they are an
excellent digestive.*

Recipe:
Bangkok Beef Curry, page 183

Selecting the Best
Chinese keys are only available in shops
specialising in Thai and Indonesian food. Select
smooth bunches that are not bruised or withered.
They are also available in dried slices or
powdered under the names 'rhizome' and
'powdered rhizome' respectively.

Storage and Preparation
They keep well for several weeks in a cool place.
Separate the fingers from the knobbly tops, and
gently scrape off the outer skin with a knife. Peel
or scrape the tops; pound or slice as with ginger.

Culinary Uses
Confusingly, Chinese keys are never used in
Chinese cookery but are found in recipes from
Thailand and Indonesia. 'Sweet and aromatic,
their distinctive bouquet furnishes authenticity to
the green curry paste used in various Thai curries,
particularly of chicken, duck and fish. They also
flavour soups and sauces, may be steamed as a
vegetable accompaniment, are pickled, and even
eaten raw when young.

Herbal Properties
Like galangal and ginger, Chinese keys are
carminative, stomachic, expectorant,
emmenagogic and analgesic. They are also a
potent aphrodisiac and a lunch flavoured with
Chinese keys is usually followed by an egregious
siesta.

Facts and Features
Chinese keys were introduced to the UK as
recently as 1984. Although common in parts of
Southeast Asia, the Chinese themselves use them
solely in medicine. In Thailand they are
considered a good luck charm: 'I am sure that
when you carry a bunch of *krachai* on a string
around your waist, it will protect you against
evil.' (Dolf Riks, *Sawaddi*, March 1983.)
Unknown to the ancient Indians, there is no
Sanskrit name. The scientific name *Kaempferia
pandurata* has been superseded by *Boesenbergia
pandurata*, much to the relief of the more pedantic
botanists.

COCONUT
Pacific

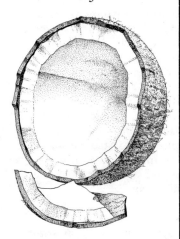

Cocos nucifera
Fam Palmae

Cocoanut, Pharaoh's Nut, Porcupine Nut

China: ping tang yea tze, tong long (coconut strips); ya chee; East Africa: nazi (Swahili); France: noix de coco; Germany: Kokonuss; India: nareul, narikel, nariyel, nar(r)ul, thainga; Indonesia: enjor, kalapa, ketajambil, klendah, krambil, tenga (Tamil); Italy: noce di cocco; Spain: nuez de coco; Thailand: hang kathi (thin milk), hua kathi (thick milk); maprao; West Indies: coco, narial, naryar

The largest nut in the world, the coconut is the single seed of an enormous fruit. Usually recognised by its brown fibres, it sometimes retains its green husk looking like a pale green melon. The edible part is the meat, a 1cm (½in) layer inside the shell. This white flaky substance is crisp and dry when ripe or 'old', otherwise it is soft and jelly-like and much prized locally. Mature coconuts contain a pleasing liquid known as coconut water ('coconut milk' means something quite different, see Storage and Preparation below) which can be heard on shaking the nut. The nut varies from 10–20cm (4–8in) in length, most being of moderate dimensions. In the wild, the nut is embedded in a fibrous husk, known as 'coir', that is removed in commerce.

Selecting the Best
Always shake coconuts and avoid waterless ones, or those with mildew around the 'eyes'. Various forms of desiccated and dried coconut are available, as is canned coconut milk or cream.

Storage and Preparation
Sound coconuts will keep for several weeks but once opened should be used immediately. First, drain the water: there are three little 'eyes' at the base of the coconut; one is quite soft. Pierce this and one other, pour off and retain the liquid. To open the nut, tap sharply across the middle with a hammer or hard object. Prise the flesh away with a knife—this can be done more efficiently if the coconut is warmed in the oven for 10 minutes. A special gadget exists to extract and grate the flesh simultaneously. For coconut 'milk', peel away the hard brown skin and grate the flesh across the grain or put through a processor. Add the coconut water and ½–1 cup of warm water. A rough proportion is 5 cups water to 4 of flesh. Alternatively, desiccated or creamed coconut can be used—80g (3oz) with 285ml (½pt) water. Knead, cool and strain or sieve through a jelly bag. 'Thin milk' is obtained by repeating the process with once-used flesh or using 30g (1oz) of creamed coconut. Coconut 'cream' is made by leaving the original milk to stand overnight—the cream rises to the top. These liquids freeze well, as do coconut chunks, keeping up to 2 years. Grated coconut keeps frozen for months or refrigerated for 2 days. Coconut milk and cream are liable to curdle with boiling: stir and do not cover.

Coconut is rich in fats and iron but
poor in vitamins. Only 2 per cent of
the oil is polyunsaturated.

cal	320	Ca	13	A	0
pro	3.5	P	90	B_1	0.04
fat	31.3	Fe	1.8	B_2	0.02
car	11.5	Na	23	B_5	0.06
fib	3.9	K	256	C	4

Recipes:
Sticky Rice, page 201; Thai
Chicken Curry, page 189

Culinary Uses

Coconut is less known in the West than the East
as an ingredient in main dishes. It goes into
poultry, fish and shellfish preparations, Indian,
Thai and Indonesian *sambals* and curries, where
the milk is often used to thicken and flavour.
Coconut is particularly common in Hawaiian
shrimp and chicken curries, with ginger, apples
and sultanas. The milk, called *santan* in Malay, is
an important ingredient in Malaysian cooking. As
a dessert it figures in fudge, cookies, cakes,
toffee, custard (replacing dairy milk), fruit
cocktails, baked apples and toasted coconut chips.
It is a feature of *halva*, Indian and Southeast Asian
rice puddings, soups and sweet breads in South
America and the Caribbean.

Herbal Properties

Coconut water is diuretic; the oil is a substitute
for cod liver oil, and is used as a remedy in lung
disorders. The flesh is a vermifuge, the sap juice
laxative.

Facts and Features

Native to Pacific tropical coasts, the coconut
takes six months to grow, and a year to ripen.
The major commercial palm of the tropics, it is
arguably the greatest money-spinning crop in the
world, copra (dried meat) and oil in particular
being exported by the Philippines, Malaysia, Sri
Lanka, Indonesia and Papua New Guinea, while
many other countries use their own home
products. The rich, syrupy sap, 'toddy', from the
flowering spathes is fermented and distilled to
make a powerful liquor, *arrack*, or boiled down to
produce palm sugar or *jaggery*. The outer husk
fibre, or 'coir' is widely used in ropes and
matting, while the leaves and trunk provide local
construction material. Oil from the copra forms a
base for soaps, margarine and cosmetics—the
residue makes cattle cake. The bark ash is a local
toothpaste.

CORIANDER
Mediterranean, Asia

Coriandrum sativum
Fam Umbelliferae

*Chinese Parsley, Cilantro,
Dizzycorn, Japanese Parsley*

*Burma: nannambin (leaves); China:
(y)uen sai, yuin si tsoi (leaves); East
Africa: giligilani (Swahili); France:
coriandre; Germany: Koriander;
India: dhania patta(r), dhania sabz,
hara dhania (all leaves); Indonesia:
daun ketumbar; Italy: coriandolo;
Japan: mitsuba; Malaysia: daun
ketumba(r) (leaves); Middle East:
kizbera (seed); Spain: cilantro,
culantro; Sri Lanka: kottamalli kolle
(leaves); Thailand: pak chee,
pakchee farang (foreign); West
Indies: cilantro*

Coriander leaves are often mistaken for broad or flat-leaved parsley but can be easily distinguished from that plant by two features. Firstly, the three-lobed leaf of coriander is more deeply cleft and, secondly, the smell is quite different—sometimes called 'fetid' by Western writers, coriander leaves are 'delicate' and 'fresh' according to Eastern cooks. The smell of coriander does take some getting used to, but a tolerance acquired will pay dividends in the kitchen. This aroma varies from mild to overpowering according to growing conditions and becomes highly pronounced as soon as the leaves or stems are bruised. The flavour inclines to sweetness and imparts a unique curiosity to savoury dishes.

Selecting the Best
Coriander is available all year. It wilts rapidly and irrevocably, so choose fresh-looking bunches with plenty of leaves per stalk. Many supermarkets now stock fresh coriander, but larger, cheaper bunches are available in Asian foodstores. Never substitute the dried seeds for the leaves as they have an altogether different flavour.

Storage and Preparation
A foolproof method for keeping the leaves fresh for at least a week is to place the unwashed bunch in a tumbler of water and cover the leaves loosely with a polythene bag. Use as required. A paste of the leaves and stalks with ginger, garlic and chilli is a useful standby for use in curries and will freeze satisfactorily. Coriander is cut into sprigs for decoration, and chopped, or pulverised for various recipes. It is not dried commercially, but drying by microwave oven has proved successful.

Culinary Uses
Coriander is essential in Indian, Thai and Mexican cookery. It is also important in China, Japan, Southeast Asia, South America and the West Indies, the Middle East and North Africa, Greece, Turkey, Cyprus, Spain and Portugal. This wide range of possible applications must in itself tempt one to experiment, however gingerly, with coriander's unfamiliar, even alien savour. Generally it is used as a garnish, both pretty and pungent. Coriander leaves are made into Indian fresh chutneys as well as going into curries and *dhals*. The root is a unique feature of

Nutritional Values
Coriander is usually used sparingly so its fairly adequate vitamin content is barely utilised.

cal	40	Ca	155	A	8,250
pro	2–3.3	P	55	B_1	0.14
fat	0.3–0.6	Fe	7.8	B_2	0.15
car	7	Na	—	B_5	1
fib	—	K	—	C	90

Recipes:
Coriander and Mint Raita, page 206; Spicy Coriander Relish, page 208

the Thai cuisine where its special flavour characterises soups and green curries. In Mexico, it garnishes a galaxy of dishes and is included in hot chilli sauces, soups and stews. Coriander goes happily with fish—much in evidence in Chinese dishes—and is sprinkled onto countless different salads, especially those including tomato, with which it shares a particular affinity.

Herbal Properties
Coriander leaves are anti–inflammatory. Gerard (1597) advises that coriander: '. . . boiled with the crumb of bread or barley meale, consumeth all hot swellings and inflammations: and with Beane meale dissolveth the Kings evill, wens and hard lumpes.' It is similarly used in India, as well as for the treatment of piles and headache. The fruit and seeds are antibacterial and have been used from ancient times for treating ulcers and the like.

Facts and Features
Coriander has been grown and used in Europe, the Middle East and Africa for millennia. It is mentioned by Hippocrates and Pliny, who named it *coriandrum* (*coris* meaning bug) after its bug–like odour or perhaps after the seed's curious resemblance to the European bed–bug, *Cimex lectularis*. It is also frequently referred to in the Bible. It was introduced to the New World by the Spaniards, where it was received with enthusiasm, except in Trinidad where the indentured Tamil sugarcane cutters discovered a local weed, *shado bene* (*Eryngium foetidium*, culantro, fitweed, stinkweed), which for most purposes has a bouquet and flavour identical to coriander. This plant had been a traditional ingredient of South American and Caribbean cookery from time immemorial, and grows more easily in the hot tropics. For the British herb garden, coriander is easy to grow: sow in spring for seeds, summer for leaves, in drills 1cm (½in) deep, 25cm (10in) apart. Seeds are harvested in 3 months when their aroma loses its fetor. The leaves can be plucked as required. Virtually no maintenance is necessary.

CORN SALAD

Europe and Middle East, Asia Minor

Valerianella locusta
syn *V. olitoria*
Fam Valerianaceae

*Cornel-salette, Fetticus, Field
Lettuce, Lamb's Lettuce, Lamb's
Tongue, Lettuce-valerian, Mâche,
Milk-grass, White Pot Herb*

*France: doucette, mâche,
valérianelle; Germany: Acker Salat;
Italy: erba riccia; Spain: canonigo,
valeriana cultivada*

Nutritional Values
*Corn salad has no significant
nutritional properties.*

cal	21	Ca		A
pro	2	P		B$_1$
fat	0.4	Fe		B$_2$
car	3.6	Na		B$_5$
fib	0.8	K		C

Corn salad leaves are bright green, shaped like a tongue, and come either in bunches of separate leaves or still on the stalk. They measure about 10–15cm (4–6in) long by 4–5cm (1½–2in) broad. The texture is best when soft and young but the flavour is not universally popular. Some describe it as nutty, others as astringent, some even as insipid. However, its flavour depends largely on where it is grown. Italian corn salad (*V. eriocarpa*), lighter in colour and slightly hairy, is used in much the same way.

Selecting the Best
Available autumn to spring, through winter, corn salad is at its best when small and young.

Storage and Preparation
Keep in the cool and eat as soon as possible after purchase. Cut the leaves from the stem, wash carefully to remove any hidden grit, and separate them.

Culinary Uses
Known as *mâche* in France, corn salad has long been a popular winter salad there as well as in Holland and Germany. Its soft and succulent leaves are good on their own or mixed with lettuce. Cubes of fried bacon are often added and beetroot is another popular partner. Corn salad may be cooked like spinach and Gerard (1597) mentions it as an ingredient of 'loblolly'—sailors' gruel.

Herbal Properties
There are no modern medicinal uses for corn salad, but it should not be confused with valerian—the powerful and poisonous sedative.

Facts and Features
Corn salad is indigenous from the west coast of Ireland to the Caucasus. Although one of its rural names is 'lamb's lettuce' it is not of the lettuce family, but sheep were supposed to show a particular predilection for it. It is easy to grow: sow in late summer in drills 15cm (6in) apart, or broadcast. Harvest whole plants or leaves as required. Protect with cloches in severe winters.

CRANBERRY

Europe, North America and North Asia

Vaccinium oxycoccus
syn *Oxycoccus macrocarpus*

Fam Ericaceae

Bounceberry, Crane, Craneberry, Crone

France: canneberge
Germany: Moosbeere
Italy: mortella di palude
Spain: arándano agrio

Nutritional Values

Raw cranberries contain:

cal	46	Ca	14	A	40
pro	0.4	P	10	B_1	0.03
fat	0.7	Fe	0.5	B_2	0.02
car	10.8	Na	2	B_5	0.1
fib	1.4	K	82	C	11

Recipes:
Cranberry and Blackberry Kissel, page 199; Cranberry and Orange Sauce, page 202

Cranberries are most familiar to us as jelly but, for the enterprising, fresh or frozen berries are now available. Pinky-red fruits with a pleasant appearance, they are the size of small grapes and they have a tart flavour, something like sour blackcurrants. The skin is thin and tough, the flesh dry and white with four cavities containing tiny brown seeds. The variety commonly used today, *Oxycoccus macrocarpum*, comes from America and is slightly larger than the original wild form.

Selecting the Best
Boxes of fresh cranberries are available from autumn to early spring. The fruit should look plump and bright.

Storage and Preparation
These berries keep exceptionally well: 2 weeks or more in the refrigerator. Freeze them whole, sealed in bags or containers. It should not be necessary to top and tail them. Some prefer to halve them before cooking. Sweeten them after cooking and don't overcook or they will taste rather bitter. When heated, they burst like pop-corn, so keep covered.

Culinary Uses
Although we are discussing the imported American cultivated cranberry associated with traditional American fare such as jelly, pies, tarts and sauces, the wild cranberry has long been popular in northern European cookery and the American fruit is ideal for dishes such as a salad of sauerkraut, cranberries, apple and celery to accompany cold pork or chicken; or *kissel*, a favourite Russian dessert. Otherwise there are countless ways to enjoy the fruit in breads, stuffings, ices and soufflés; and the sauce, as a glaze for barbecued and roast meat and duck; and as an accompaniment to traditional roast turkey or as a topping for cheese cakes or ice-creams. The juice is good in hot and cold punches. Cranberries make an acceptable wine and figure in liqueurs from Scandinavia.

Herbal Properties
In America, crushed cranberries and buttermilk are applied to the skin to relieve erysipelas (St Anthony's Fire). They are also recommended in breastfeeding and as a general tonic. American Indians used cranberries as a meat preservative.

Facts and Features

The cranberry was one of the original American fruits adopted by the thankful New England settlers, who copied its use from the Indians, as they did with the persimmon. Ancestral cranberry estates have harvested the fruit for centuries in the US and Canada, nowadays for world export. Good berries are supposed to be highly bouncy and in some areas are known as bounceberries. A member of the heather family, related to the blueberry, the cranberry owes its name to one of three facts: the flower's resemblance to a crane's head; the bird's habit of feeding on the berries; or because birds and berries live in close marshy proximity.

CROSNES
China, Japan

Stachys sieboldii
syn *S. tubifera, S. affinis*
Fam Labiatae

Chinese Artichoke, Chorogi,
Japanese Artichoke, Knot Root

China: kon loh (sweet dew); France:
crosne de chine, crosne de japon;
Japan: choro-gi, chorogi; United
States: hedge nettle

Pronounced 'crone', these little tubers that look like the limbs of a pygmy Mr Michelin have never taken on in the British kitchen, but ought to, as they are delicious and the French, who are supposed to know such things, adore them. Variously said to resemble maggots, twisted shells and pasta spirals, they are 3–5cm (1¼–2in) long and several millimetres in diameter, smooth skinned, and are basically white but, being a tuber, show some discoloration.

Selecting the Best

Available autumn to spring, crosnes are rarely on sale in Britain, but keep asking for them. They should be plump and not too flabby or discoloured.

Storage and Preparation

Use as soon as possible as they quickly lose their moisture. There is no need to remove the skin. Trim top and bottom and scrub under running water. Crosnes are usually left whole.

Culinary Uses

Classic recipes *à la Japonaise* usually mean any dish where Chinese artichoke is included, but curiously enough the oriental culinary uses of crosnes are barely documented. However, we find them delicious stir-fried with a little ginger and garlic. In France (where they are esteemed far above Jerusalem artichokes) they are first blanched then gently sautéed in butter as an accompaniment to roast meat or grills. They are made into fritters or served in various sauces, but it is important not to mar their delicate

Nutritional Values
No nutritional data are available except that crosnes are starchy tubers with an inulin content, hence their likening to artichokes.

flavour—just a light sprinkling of herbs is elaborate enough treatment.

Herbal Properties
If insulin (an indigestible sugar common in some plants) is present crosnes have possibilities for diabetic diets.

Facts and Features
The Chinese artichoke is related to the plant that once inspired the name 'all-heal', namely sweet betony (*Stachys officinalis*). It is a great pity its culinary aspects are not so well respected. Some writers blame this on its curious shape. Native to northern China and Japan, crosnes only appeared in France in the mid-nineteenth century, and naturally enough through the good offices of a French doctor in Beiping. They are supposed to have spread to the Americas but little information exists on this score. Up-to-date vegetable gardening books now include crosnes, so enthusiasts for this 'new find' are recommended to grow their own.

CURRY LEAF
India, Sri Lanka

Murraya koenigii
syn *Chalcas koenigii, Bergara koenigii*
Fam Rutaceae

If you are ever fortunate enough to go into an Indian shop when they are busy plucking fresh curry leaves from the stem, you will be immediately struck by the warm and aromatic fragrance that fills the air. This is the exotic touch you can put to many delicious recipes. The leaves themselves are actually leaflets that resemble bay leaves, but are thinner and less leathery. They are olive green, paler on the underside, but vary greatly in size, from 1–4cm (½–1½in) in length. The bouquet is tantalising with a strong undertone of capsicum while the flavour is aromatic and strongest in fresh leaves.

Selecting the Best
Curry leaves are found all year in Indian shops. Choose them as fresh as possible, when they are shiny, pliable and aromatic.

Storage and Preparation
While fresh, keep in a paper bag in the cool, otherwise store in an airtight container. Curry leaves are minced, torn or left whole according to the recipe. Often they are fried in ghee together with mustard seeds until they crisp and the seeds pop.

Curry Pak, Curry Patte, Nim, Nim Leaf, Sweet Nim Leaf

Burma: pyi naw thein; France: feuille de cari; Germany: Curryblatt; India: barsanga, gandhela, goranimb, kadhilimbdo, kadhinim(b), karia-phulli, karivempu, karuvepila, kat(h)nim(b), kurry patta, misht nimb, mitha neem; Indonesia: daun kar(r)i; Italy: foglia di curry; Malaysia: daun kari, karupillay; Spain: hoja de cari; Sri Lanka: karapincha; Thailand: bai garee, bai karee

Nutritional Values
Curry leaves are rich in vitamin A and calcium. However, the presence of oxalic acid inhibits the availability of the latter. They also contain seven essential and ten non-essential amino acids. Vitamin B_5 is well supplied but B_1 and B_2 are absent.

cal	93	Ca	810	A	12,600
pro	6.1	P	600	B_1	0
fat	1	Fe	3.1	B_2	0
car	16	Na	—	B_5	2.3
fib	6.4	K	—	C	4

Recipes:
Bean Raita, page 206; Bhuna Ghosh, page 183

Culinary Uses
Curry leaves are employed generously for culinary decoration. Extensively used in South India, Sri Lanka and Southeast Asia, they blend naturally with the characteristic flavours of those areas—hot chilli, mild coconut, sour tamarind and lime. They are included in chutneys, *rasam* (Indian pepper soups) and meat, poultry and seafood curries. Fried as described above, they add a special fragrance to *dhals* and vegetable dishes. Despite their name, curry leaves are not included in curry powders or pastes except those associated with Madras.

Herbal Properties
Curry leaves are anti-emetic, antiphlogistic, tonic, stomachic, anticathartic and germicidal. In India, young leaves are used to cure bowel disturbances and a toasted leaf infusion is given to ease vomiting. Their antiseptic properties are utilised in cases of skin eruptions and poisonous bites. Pruthi mentions their use in Ayurvedic medicine, while recent research on laboratory animals has proven curry leaves to enhance the manufacture of the blood cells that attack foreign organisms.

Facts and Features
Curry leaf trees are a common sight in the gardens and yards of southern India, many householders believing them to bring good fortune, besides supplying the aromatic leaves so intimately associated with the cookery of that region. They are less popular in other parts of Asia, but are often available where Muslim communities exist. The fruit is also edible; it has an orangey bouquet and a peppery flavour with a soothing aftertaste. Although curry leaf is not a regular ingredient of many curry powders, it is arguable that the word 'curry' did come from the Tamil name for the leaf and the tree, *kari*. In Indonesia *daun salam*, the leaf of an unrelated tree, *Eugenia polyantha*, is similarly used.

CUSTARD APPLE

There are several fruits from the botanical family Annonaceae which are called 'custard apple' and we list them roughly in order of their importance to the British market.

CUSTARD APPLE
Tropical America

Annona squamosa

Custard Apple of India, Scaly Custard Apple, Sugar Apple, Sweetsop

China: fan lai chi; France: pomme canelle; India: ata; Malaysia: buah nona, sere kaya; Thailand: noi nar; West Indies: anon, cashiment, pomme canelle, sugar apple, sweetsop

This is the most curious-looking of all the custard apples, having a yellow-green skin composed of many rounded fleshy 'plates' or scales which give it a somewhat prehistoric appearance. It is heart-shaped or oval, commonly 5–10cm (2–5in) in diameter and weighing up to 2kg (4½lb). When ripe the scales separate and part from the white, creamy flesh which has a rich, scented aroma. The flesh is very sweet and pleasant with a hint of banana, justly earning the 'custard' sobriquet. Enclosed in the grainy-textured flesh are black-brown inedible seeds, more numerous than in the 'West Indian' custard apple.

CHERIMOYA
South America

Annona cherimolia

syn A. tripetala

Cherimalla, Cherimola, Cherimoyer, Custard Apple

West Indies: cherimoya

Slightly larger than the custard apple described above, the cherimoya has a green, surprisingly fragile skin forming little V-shaped bumps. The firmish white flesh has a unique flavour, sweet and delicious, with an exotic acridity, and there are many black seeds. The cherimoya is reckoned by the Peruvians to be one of the finest fruits in the world.

SOURSOP
Tropical America
Annona muricata

Corossol, Prickly Custard Apple

France: corossol épineux; Indonesia: mandaleeka, nangka landa; Malaysia: durian blanda, nangka blanda, s(w)irsak; West Indies: corasol, corosol, guanabana, soursop
Recipe:
Soursop Sorbet, page 201

The soursop is the largest member of this group and is oval, heart-shaped or kidney-shaped. The skin is dark green with rows of curved leathery spines. The fruit can grow to 30cm (12in) in length and weigh up to 6kg (13lb). The juicy white flesh encloses many brown-black seeds and has a fresh, acidic aroma. The flavour is fruity, acidic and refreshing.

BULLOCK'S HEART
Tropical America
Annona reticulata

Anon, Corazon, Corossol, Custard Apple, Netted Custard Apple, Ramphal

France: coeur-de-boeuf; India: noona; Malaysia: nona (kapri); West Indies: bullock's heart, che boeuf, custard apple

Slightly larger than the custard apple, the bullock's heart is considered inferior in flavour and is not nearly as popular. It is rounded and heart-shaped with a drab brown or reddish skin which is almost smooth but marked in a netted pattern. The flesh is grainy, yellowish with brown tinges, and sweet.

ATEMOYA
Florida
Annona atemoya

The atemoya is a cross between the custard apple and the cherimoya in an attempt to obtain the best features of both fruits. It only partly succeeds. The skin is light green to yellow, a little knobbly like that of its second parent. The flavour is sweet and pleasant but the ubiquitous seeds are ever present. Visitors to Florida can bring these home as they travel quite well (providing import regulations are adhered to).

Selecting the Best (all species)
Firm annonas will have to ripen at home. It is best to buy them when they are slightly soft. The skin can be very fragile—don't buy fruit which looks as if it will burst.

Storage and Preparation
Store in the dark if necessary for a few days to ripen. When soft, the fruit can be refrigerated for

Nutritional Values (all species)

The custard apple is calorific and useful in iron and vitamins B and C, the other annonas less so.

Fresh fruit:

	CUSTARD APPLE	CHERIMOYA	SOURSOP
cal	75–100	94	65
pro	1.8	1.3	1
fat	0.2–0.6	0.4	0.3
car	18–25	24	16.3
fib	1.6–3.4	2.2	1.1
Cal	27	23	14
P	20	40	27
Fe	0.8–1.8	0.5	0.6
Na	—	—	14
K	—	—	265
A	trace	10	10
B_1	0.08	0.1	0.07
B_2	0.12	0.11	0.05
B_5	0.5–0.9	1.3	0.9
C	22–35	9	20

a short while. It is impracticable to peel these fruits—cut them in half and spoon out the flesh. Rub through a sieve for purée, or simply discard the seeds. This last method is best done by hand, if rather messy. A food processor is ideal for achieving perfect smoothness.

Culinary Uses

All annonas are best eaten raw and fresh, simply spooned out of the rind. Alternatively, the flesh can be strained of seeds—when ripe it is virtually a purée itself—and used as a dessert sauce, mashed with cream, banana or other pulpy fruits, or used in custard, ice-cream, trifles and other fruit-flavoured desserts and confections. The soursop makes an especially delectable sorbet. Sieved, and watered down, custard apples make a tempting sherbet or milkshake, with the possible addition of a pinch of sugar, citrus juice and salt.

Herbal Properties

None known.

Facts and Features

There are over 600 species of annona in the tropics and sub-tropics, the edible varieties characterised by the lumps or spines formed in the fusion of separate ovaries into an 'aggregate fruit'. The commonest, though perhaps not the finest, is the custard apple, growing in hot gardens throughout the world. The cherimoya, widely considered the best species, is native to Peru, where prehistoric terra cotta vases have been discovered modelled on the fruit's unusual shape. It is now cultivated in Asia, Australia and especially Israel. The atemoya is gaining popularity in southern Florida. A few other species are edible and hybridisation will doubtless produce others.

DATE
Middle East

Phoenix dactylifera
Fam Palmae

Finger Apple

France: datte; Germany: Dattal; India: khajur, kharjuri, khujjoor, sendhi; Indonesia: korma; Italy: dattero; Middle East: balah, khorma; Portugal: tamara; Spain: datil

Nutritional Values
Being a desert staple, dates are highly calorific but have little vitamin content. The carbohydrate is mostly sugar (60 per cent). They are useful in iron and potassium.

Dried:

cal	275	Ca	60	A	50
pro	2.2	P	60	B$_1$	0.09
fat	0.5	Fe	3	B$_2$	0.1
car	73	Na	1	B$_5$	2.2
fib	2.3	K	650	C	0

The date is a fruit like a fat little sausage, 2.5cm (1in) in diameter and 2.5–5cm (1–2in) long, containing one long grooved seed. The dates known in the West, mainly from Arab lands, are of the dried or pressed variety, but recently fresh specimens, mainly from Israel, have appeared in the markets, and are, we believe, a much more satisfactory alternative. They ripen to a very dark brown with a tough, shiny, parchment-like skin and pale, soft, moist flesh.

Selecting the Best
The Israeli harvest is in the autumn, although fresh or 'soft' dates are available throughout the year. Look for plump, glossy fruit.

Storage and Preparation
Dates cannot safely be kept frozen but will stay fresh for several days in the refrigerator. To stone dates, winkle the stone out with the end of a small spoon or push straight through from one end to the other. To skin them, pull out the stalk and pinch the other end, to slip the flesh out.

Culinary Uses
Dates are perhaps best known as sugary, candied sweets in long boxes, eaten at Christmas or used in cookery in puddings, cakes and chutneys. Apart from eating it raw, the most popular way of treating a fresh date is to stuff it. All kinds of stuffing have been proposed, from cream cheese to bacon and poultry pieces. We find the Middle Eastern custom of serving chilled, fresh dates with yoghurt particularly delicious and if an extra flavouring seems appropriate, cardamom has a marked affinity with dates. In India dates are liked in chutney, alone or combined with limes or mangoes.

Herbal Properties
Fresh dates are nutritious, laxative and aphrodisiac; a drink made from them is good for intoxication and its side effects. An Indian custom is to use smoke from burning seeds to relieve painful piles.

Facts and Features
Dates have proliferated astonishingly in generally uninspiring conditions, which makes them highly important in local subsistence diets, especially in Arab countries. Over 350 varieties are commercially recognised. Such profusion, and

5,000 years of history, complicates the task of identifying their origin—which is probably around western India or the Persian Gulf. At their best in the arid sub-tropics, especially North Africa and India, they are now under production also in Spain, California, and Israel, the major supplier of fresh dates. Palms may yield up to twelve 'bunches' of 10kg each, dry weight, per harvest, also making attractive mini houseplants in more temperate zones. Like other palms the date palm yields a mass of other useful products such as building materials, dyes, fuel and alcohol. The European names derive from the classical botanist Theophrastus (second or third century BC) whose Latin name we still use, and which means 'the finger-sprouting palm'.

DRUMSTICK
India

Moringa oleifera
syn M. pterygosperma

Fam *Moringaceae*

Ben (Oil) Tree, Horseradish Tree, Indian Asparagus, Oil of Ben Tree, Susumber

India: mungna, sainjna, saj(j)ana, shevgi, shingh fali, shingh ki phaliyan, shojinedanta, sigru; Indonesia: kelor, marongghi, mooroongaki (Tamil); Malaysia:

Drumsticks, often called 'susumber', are the unripe pods of a small tropical tree. These slender legumes measure anything up to 50cm (20in) in length, with a diameter around 1cm (½in). Like many pods, they vary greatly in size. The skin can be tough and woody, and highly inedible. The nine lengthwise ridges and grass-green colour give it some resemblance to a section of garden hose. Inside, there is a light-green mucilaginous pulp and a row of seeds each in a winged triangular membrane, comparable in size to garden peas. The raw seeds have a pleasant hottish savour. When boiled, both seeds and flesh taste strongly of asparagus.

Selecting the Best
Look out for the healthy-looking specimens generally available in Indian shops. Drumsticks are also sold canned.

Storage and Preparation
Keep in the cool and use as soon as possible. Wash the drumsticks and string them like celery, or scrape with a knife or peeler. They are usually cut into 2.5–5cm (1–2in) lengths. Because of their strong character, some cooks prefer to parboil the drumsticks for 10 minutes before proceeding with a recipe. The cooking water is discarded.

Culinary Uses
The pods can be simply boiled like beans, and eaten like asparagus—the pulp and seeds being sucked out of the fibrous skin. In India,

keloh, kelor, muringak(k)a(i);
Mexico: coatli; Thailand: malum;
West Indies: ben nut tree, horseradish
(tree), si-jan

Nutritional Values
Little is known of the food value of
this vegetable. The seeds, however,
contain 38 per cent oil and a
glycoside is present. The leaves
contain vitamin C in useful amounts.

Recipe:
Indian Asparagus, page 203

drumsticks are favoured with duck and often included in *avial*, a mixed vegetable curry. The cooked pith is ground into a paste with chillies, onion, tamarind, ginger and coriander leaves to make a distinctive chutney. Pickled drumsticks are common throughout Asia, and the oil from the seeds is popularly used to dress West Indian salads. Some Burmese and Philippine dishes call for the pods and leaves, and the flowers also find their way into various local Indian recipes.

Herbal Properties
The leaf juice is antibacterial; the remaining parts of the plant seem to cater for any disease one cares to name. The leaves are used to treat scurvy, catarrh, eye infections, and flatulence in children; the stem bark is a heart stimulant, rubefacient and abortifacient; the root bark is a stimulant and diuretic, and applied to all varieties of aches and pains. The gum relieves head and toothache while the root has as many effects as the other parts together. Finally, the flowers are aphrodisiac, but apparently you must boil them in milk.

Facts and Features
Native to India, the horseradish tree reaches up to 10m (33ft) and is widespread throughout the tropics, especially West Africa, the southern US, Mexico and the West Indies. The tap-root and secondary roots, which are swollen like carrots, are eaten in Africa. They are a substitute for horseradish, especially among the British in India. The dried seeds, 'ben seeds', go into curries, and yield the ben oil used in cosmetics, clockwork, lamp oil and cookery. The oil–cake left after pressing is a good fertiliser. All parts of the tree seem to find a use in India: even the flowers and twigs are cooked, and the rest is medicinal. The tree produces a gum used in printing calico, and the branches constitute a charm against witchery.

DURIAN
Malaysia

Durio zibethinus
Fam Bombacaceae

Civet Cat Fruit, Civet Nut

Indonesia: ambetan, duren, durin, kadu; Malaysia: durian; Thailand: thurian; West Indies: erizo de arbol (Cuba)

Nutritional Values
No data are available.

A remarkable and seemingly forbidding fruit, the durian is likely to remain only a curiosity in the West, if an unforgettable one. Olive-green or yellow, it is covered with hard sharp spikes, not unlike a green hedgehog. Very large and oval, up to 30cm (12in) long and 20cm (8in) wide, it weighs some 4.5kg (10lb). Inside a thick and woody rind, smooth pale-yellow flesh divides into three to five segments, each containing some seven large brown seeds. When just ripe, the flesh is soft but firm, although the fruit is often kept to the verge of decomposition, when the interior may be described as 'custard-like'. 'Highly aromatic' is the phrase used by some books to denote the drainy smell, one fortunately unrelated to the taste of the flesh—the varying descriptions 'unique and delicious', 'strawberries and cream with a suggestion of almonds' portraying the broad spectra of human senses.

Selecting the Best
Durians split when overripe so examine them carefully. It is best to ask the shopkeeper as to ripeness. Shops specialising in Southeast Asian produce will sell durians from November to February and again from June to August.

Storage and Preparation
Keep the durian well away from anything else, preferably outside, as its smell will prove highly offensive! To extract the custard-like flesh, cut the durian in half or quarter it with a bread knife and scoop out the flesh with a large spoon.

Culinary Uses
Asian connoisseurs recommend that the durian be eaten fresh and without accompaniments. In view of its expense in the West they are probably right. Also noted are its uses in cakes, jams and ice-cream, or as preserved pulp. The seeds are edible, best roasted or boiled. Among the specifically Malaysian uses are: 'Penang cakes', made from durian, flour and sugar; *lempok*, preserved pulp with rice and sugar; *tempoyak*, durian with prawn paste and salt. Unripe fruits may be cooked as a vegetable, very popular in Indonesia.

Herbal Properties
Hardly surprisingly, this curious fruit is seen as an aphrodisiac.

Facts and Features

Native to Malaysia and Indonesia, the durian has been cultivated for centuries in that region, but, except for Thailand, rarely elsewhere. In spite of strenuous efforts, it refuses to budge from its original environment. 'The colde it liketh it not,' Cosmo, 1512. Small bats are thought to pollinate the flowers by night, when the stigma is receptive, durians being generally sterile. In Thailand the durian is so prolific that fruits have to be culled when they are about grapefruit size. Propagation is by marcotting (rooting a branch or shoot in a pot on the tree before taking the cutting). Fruits are often collected in bags hanging on the branches. Canned durian finds some use in ice-cream and confectionery for expatriate devotees.

EDDOE AND DASHEEN (TARO), TANNIA, ELEPHANT FOOT YAM

Fam Araceae

EDDOE AND DASHEEN
Southeast Asia

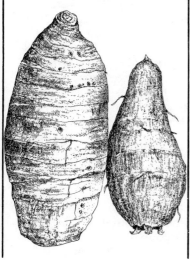

These starchy tropical vegetables, although of different botanical species, are of similar composition and can all usefully be substituted one for the other. This has given rise to immense confusion over their names. Simply, eddoes and dasheens are both varieties of taro (*Colocasia esculenta*), whereas tannia and elephant foot yam are two quite separate species. All the corms or tubers of these plants are brown, hairy, scaly and round. In the ground lies a central corm around which grow cormels (smaller tubers), the number and size of each differing among the plants.

Eddoe: These are both corms and cormels, depending on which the shape varies from spherical to elongated. They can weigh between 30g (1oz) and 455g (1lb). The flesh is often snowy-white, but yellow, pink and orange types occur. They are readily digested and the flavour is much like the common potato, but to some appears attractively nuttier.

Dasheen: These are large, cylindrical and ringed; they can grow up to 30cm (12in) in length and 15cm (6in) in diameter. The rings are quite pronounced and there are several 'eyes'. The flesh is usually white or yellow and is easily digested. Cooked, it becomes rather stodgy.

Tannia: The tubers are flask-shaped and vary in size from 10cm (4in) to 25cm (10in) in length and between 10cm (4in) and 15cm (6in) in diameter at the widest part. They have a scaly, hairy outer

Eddoe: *Colocasia esculenta*
var *antiquorum*
Dasheen: *Colocasia*
esculenta var *esculenta*

*Most of the following names appear
to be interchangeable between
dasheen and eddoe. There are many
other variations.*

*Chinese Potato, Cocoas, Egyptian
Ginger, Elephant's Ear, (Old)
Cocoyam, Taro*

*China: oo tau (black head), woo tau,
ya, yu tao; Greece: kolokassi; India:
arbi, arum, arvi, chamk(a)ora
(variety), ghuiyan, kachalu, kachu;
Indonesia: beti, empoo, entik, tales,
taro de Chine; Japan: (sato)imo;
Malaysia: keladi, tallas; Middle
East: kolkas, qolq(u)as; Philippines:
abalong, gabi, lubiñgan, pising;
South America: malanga, ocumo;
West Indies: Barbados eddoe,
Chinese eddoe, chou bouton, chou de
Chine, coco, cocoyam, curcas,
dasheen, eddoe, guagui, madère,
malanga, slip and dip, white eddoe*

TANNIA
America

Xanthosoma sagittifolium

*(New) Cocoyam, Poi-plant,
Tan(n)ia, Tan(n)ier, Tanyah,
Xanthosoma, Yautia (Malanga),
Yellow Yautia*

peel and rose-coloured inner skin. The flesh is
variable, basically white, sometimes yellow, but
often pinkish with brown speckles. Sliced, it is
quite sticky. The flavour is similar to the taros
but the starch is less digestible.

Elephant Foot Yam: This is not nearly as
common as the others and quite different in
appearance. Its name probably gives the best
description. It is round, up to 25cm (10in) in
diameter, knobbly around the edges,
hemispherical with a depression on the top. Like
most tubers it is hairy and scaly. The flesh is
white and the flavour starchy.

Selecting the Best (all species)
All can be found the year round. Elephant foot is
usually only available from Indian shops. When
buying the large corms or smaller cormels, select
those of even size and ones that look full and
sound. Larger corms lend themselves to braised
and slow-cooked dishes as they are somewhat
drier and coarser.

Storage and Preparation
Keep them as you would potatoes. Elephant foot
keeps particularly well. It is wise not to eat any
raw as some varieties contain harmful irritants
which can affect the throat but which vanish on
cooking. Taro and tannia can be cooked with or
without their thick skins. For unskinned use, first
scrub under the tap and after cooking in boiling
water remove the skin with a knife and proceed
with recipe.
   To remove the skin from these vegetables,
certain steps must be taken to prevent them
turning a little slimy or the hands becoming itchy
from any acrid substances. Either oil the hands or
wear gloves to handle. Taro should be scrubbed
and dried, then the thick skin removed with a
sharp knife. Wedge shapes are obtained by
knocking or breaking off pieces with a heavy
instrument. Slices or cubes may be cut for use in
certain recipes and here an hour's soaking in
salted acidulated water may lessen the stickiness,
but this is quite optional. Dry well before cooking.
Tannia is easily grated to make fritters etc.

Culinary Uses
These tropical vegetables have long been used by
settlers from Europe as a substitute for the
potato. With this versatility they appear at home
in many different cuisines from all round the

Indonesia: kimpool, kong kong taro;
South America: mangareto, ocumo;
West Indies: badoo, belembe, chou,
chou caraibe, mafaffa, malanga(l),
tanier, tata(e), taya, tayobe,
tayonne, tayo tyo, yautia bravia

ELEPHANT FOOT YAM
Southeast Asia

Amorphallus campanulatus
syn *Arum campanulatum*

Elephant Bread, Elephant Yam,
Suran, Sweet Yam, Telinga Potato

China: mo yu; India: arsaghna,
balukund, jimikhand, kidaran, ol,
olkachu, olkuchu, suran,
zaminkand, zimikand; Indonesia:
ilis-ilis, kand godda, sobek, sooweg,
telinga potato, waloor; Japan:
konjac, konniaku; Malaysia: chena,
karak-kavanai; Philippines: anto,
oroy, pañgapoñg, puñgapuñg;
Polynesia: daga, koe, teve

globe. In Cyprus, *kolokassi* is very popular and is cooked with pork or chicken flavoured with onions, celery and wine or lemon juice. In Egypt it is preferred with lamb. We find the small cormels delicious roasted like potatoes round a joint of meat—succulent and nutty. Tannia is most commonly eaten in the West Indies, Africa and South America, grilled, fried, puréed or made into soups. It is pounded into *fufu* in West Africa. Barbecued whole, it acquires a delicious smoky savour—don't eat the skin. Yautia or tannia sweet fritters are served with roast meat or chicken, and the vegetable is found in many recipes from China, Japan and India. Suran or elephant foot yam is much loved in India where, when cubed and fried, it is likened to meat and curried accordingly.

Herbal Properties
These tubers are irritant and fortifying, but little is known of any medicinal use for them in the Pacific or amongst the Indians of South America.

Facts and Features
Taros and elephant foot yam are native to India and Southeast Asia while tannias are native to America. There has been a cross-over, albeit only recently compared to the speed with which other food plants have spread around the globe. The tannia is supplanting taro in West Africa because the corms make a better *fufu* (see page 193). It is used extensively in Polynesian *poi*. The plants of all types are closely similar and need an accustomed eye to tell the difference. Fleshy stalks carry very large ribbed, heart-shaped, velvety, edible leaves (see Arvi, page 9) reaching 2m (6½ft) long; they are a familiar sight in the lowlands and moist areas of the tropics—resembling gardens of giant lilies. The flowers of elephant foot yam and of some related species of taros and tannias give off a vile smell of ordure. Other relatives are also grown for tubers, for leaves, or both. The stalks are also eaten and can be seen in bundles for sale on the sidewalks of Bangkok and other Asian city streets. Captain Cook was probably the first Englishman to breakfast on taro but the Chinese included it in the *Shuo-wen* dictionary some 1,600 years earlier. The name dasheen is a corruption of '*de la Chine*' and 'coco' (cocoyam) stems from 'cockow (cuckoo) pint'. Taro is the name widely used in the Pacific.

Nutritional Values (all species)

All types are a rich, and in many tropical lands, a staple source of starch. Eddoes and dasheens are more easily digested than tannias because the starch grains are small; however, tannias are more nutritious. Most types may contain calcium oxalate which needs to be destroyed by cooking. Taros are rich in mucilage. The starch grains of elephant foot yam vary considerably; it also contains calcium oxalate.

Recipes:

Pork with Kolokassi, page 186; Suran Curry, page 198; Yautia Fritters, page 205

	TARO	TANNIA	YAM
cal	97–105	133	79
pro	1.4–3	1.3–3.7	1.2–5.1
fat	0.1–0.4	0.2–0.4	0.1–2.1
car	13–29	17–31	18
fib	0.8–1	0.6–1.9	0.8
Ca	23–40	20	50
P	61–140		20–34
Fe	1–1.7	1	0.6
Na	7–9		
K	514–550		
A	20–40	0	434
B_1	0.09–0.13	0.1	0.06
B_2	0.02–0.04	0.03	0.07
B_5	0.4–1.1	0.5	0.7
C	4–5	6–10	

ENDIVE

East Asia, Egypt, Mediterranean

Cichorum endivia var *crispa, latifolium*

Fam Compositae

Frisses (Frizzies), Moss Curled Endive, Stagshorn Endive (all

Closely related to chicory, there are two types of endive: curly- and broad-leaved.

Curly-leaved: It looks like a cross between a lettuce and a dandelion. Broadish stalks carry along most of their length irregularly waved and frilly divided leaves, which are much curled and wrinkled. The plant is basically quite bitter, so growers blanch the centre to reduce its bitterness. Thus the centre is pale yellow but the outer parts are a striking green.

Broad-leaved: This type, most commonly called batavia in the UK, is more like a lettuce but with curly, slightly serrated edges to the leaves. As with curly endive, the centres are usually blanched. The flavour is less bitter than the curly variety, and the outer leaves are a lighter green.

Selecting the Best

Choose salads that are crisp and fresh looking.

Storage and Preparation

Store unwashed in the salad drawer in a polythene bag. They will keep well for over a week. Cut away bruised or extra-tough outside leaves and tear off as many leaves as required. After washing, tear, cut or shred leaves.

curly-leaved); Batavia, Escarole,
Scarole (all broad-leaved)

China: foo kui (bitter endive);
France: chicorée frisée (curly-leaved),
chicorée scarole (broad-leaved),
endive; Germany: Endivie; India:
kuru salad; Indonesia: andewi; Italy.
indivia, scarola; Spain: endibia;
United States: chicory, curly endive
(both curly-leaved); chicory, endive,
escarole (all broad-leaved)

Nutritional Values
*Like chicory, endive has little
nutritional value. Vitamin A value
is reasonable and there are small
quantities of B complex.*

Cal	20	Ca	40–80	A	3,300
pro	1.7	P	54	B₁	0.07
fat	0.1	Fe	1.7–2.8	B₂	0.14
car	4.1	Na	14	B₅	0.5
fib	0.9	K	290–380	C	11

Recipes:
*Curly Endive and Bacon Salad, page
192*

Culinary Uses
Endives are enjoyed in both Europe and the
United States. Curly endive, being the stronger
flavoured, is mostly mixed with other salad
leaves. *Salade niçoise* often contains it and it is
now popular as a starter combined with cubes of
bacon and garlicky croûtons. Strongly seasoned
dressings are appropriate. Batavia lends itself to
plain or mixed salads but may also be braised like
lettuce or blanched and mixed with a creamy
nutmeg-flavoured béchamel sauce.

Herbal Properties
Like chicory, the bitter principle aids digestion
and is beneficial in liver complaints.

Facts and Features
A quite ancient vegetable, endive was discussed
by Ovid, Pliny and Dioscorides. Its origin is
obscure; some offer Egypt, others suggest Sicily.
Again, India and the East Indies have been
mentioned, but the latter may reflect a confusion
between Batavia, Holland and Batavia (now
Djakarta), Java. Today the plant grows
worldwide, but not too happily in the tropics.

FALSA
India and East Indies

Grewia asiatica
Fam Tiliaceae

*India: dela, dhamin, karunda,
phalsa, phulsa*

Falsa are small round fruits rather like tiny crab
apples with a star-shaped, finely-pointed calyx.
They measure 10–15mm (⅖–⅗in) in diameter.
Varying in colour from green through red to
dark purple, the skin is thin and shiny. The
flesh is green or pink, crisp, juicy and thirst-
quenchingly sour. Embedded in the flesh are one
or two small pips.

Selecting the Best
Falsa are available in early summer from Indian
food stores. Make sure they are neither wrinkled
nor bruised.

Storage and Preparation
Use as soon as possible as bruised fruit will
quickly turn rotten. Wash well. Leave whole, or
halve if large, for pickling. Halve or roughly
chop for eating as a snack. For juice, crush the
fruit with a potato masher, add a quarter of its
volume of water, steep for 15 minutes and strain
through a cloth.

Culinary Uses
Their tart characteristic makes them popular as a

Recipe:
Falsa Pickle, page 206

snack, sprinkled with *chat masala* (see page 209) and lemon juice. They are pickled with spices in mustard oil and made into soft and alcoholic drinks and sherbets.

Herbal Properties
Grewia fruits are acidic, astringent and cooling.

Facts and Features
There are many *Grewia* species throughout the tropics of Africa and Asia, all bearing edible fruits. They belong to the same family as the plants that provide commercial jute and their own bark is also a source of fibre for ropes and cordage. In India, the strong elastic wood is used for bows, spears and shoulder-loading poles.

FEIJOA
South America

Feijoa sellowiana
Fam Myrtaceae

Brazilian Guava, Feijoya,
Pineapple Guava

West Indies: guavasteen (Cuba)

Nutritional Values
The feijoa is quite rich in vitamin C, 28mg per 100g, and like most fruit is low in calories—34mg per 100g.

Now imported from New Zealand, the feijoa is a fair-sized round or oval fruit about 8cm (3in) in length. It has a thin, waxy, green or grey-green skin and a white to yellow grainy flesh containing small black seeds coated in red gelatinous pulp. Everything is edible except the tough skin. The fruit is a close relative of the guava and we agree with the New Zealand producers that the flavour is tangy. It has been compared to passion fruit.

Selecting the Best
The fruit is ready when the flesh begins to soften. The New Zealand season is March to May whilst in Florida it is August to October.

Storage and Preparation
Feijoas will store for only a short period in the cold (3°C) so eat as soon as possible. Always remove the peel.

Culinary Uses
General advice tells us to use it like guavas. This means that there are no special uses for it, although it is sometimes preserved to go with meats in New Zealand, or as jam or jelly. Have it with ice-cream or in fruit salads; but perhaps it is best on its own.

Herbal Properties
No special properties are known but they are likely to be similar to those of guava.

Facts and Features
Often mistaken for one of the guava family, the

feijoa is in fact a single genus. Originally from South America, it is now cultivated in Australia, New Zealand (where it is very popular as a fruit) and the US, especially California, where it is planted as an ornamental bush and home fruit producer. Named after the botanist Don da silva Feijoa, the fruit reached Europe in the 1890s and has since escaped to the wild in the South of France. Under cultivation the fruit falls before ripening. It is harvested early and kept to mature, reaching the stores at its peak.

FENNEL (FLORENCE FENNEL)
Italy

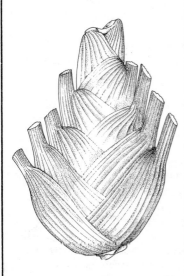

Foeniculum vulgare var *dulce*
Fam Umbelliferae

Finicho, Finocchio, Finochia, Hitchin

France: fenouil de Florence, pied de fenouil; India: anise; Italy: finocchio dolce; United States: anise, sweet anise

Florence fennel or finocchio is one of the most spectacular vegetables in the greengrocer's array. Some writers state that its flavour surpasses all other vegetables, thus matching its distinguished appearance. Swathes of succulent sheaths, one enclosing another, form a swollen, bulb-like base from where they converge into celery-like stalks which are festooned with the wispy leaves typical of herbal fennel. The stalks are usually cut off at 5–8cm (2–3in). The base and stalks are white with green tinges and the feathery leaves are a pleasing light green. The whole vegetable is 10–13cm (4–5in) wide and can weigh up to 500g (1lb). It gives off a strongish aroma of anise or liquorice.

Selecting the Best
Fennel is available all the year but more commonly in the summer. Unfortunately it is difficult to judge the quality of fennel at a glance but yellowing denotes age while greener bulbs suggest a flavour too determined for some. However, Waverley Root quotes Colette as writing that female plants are tastier than male plants and can be distinguished from the latter by their flatter roots.

Storage and Preparation
Fennel will keep well for a few days in the salad drawer. Cut off the hard woody top stalks and any coarse, stringy or pithy parts. Keep these for stock, fish *court-bouillon* or soup, and snip the feathery green herb into salads. Fennel is left whole, or halved, quartered or sliced across before being used raw, or steamed, boiled or braised. For use in salads, place slices in iced water for ½ hour to ensure extra freshness. Cooking time varies, according to size and quality, from 10–30 minutes.

Nutritional Values
Fennel is very low in calories so is a useful adjunct to dietary meals.

Recipe:
Fennel with Parmesan Cheese, page 193

Culinary Uses

This is a vegetable extolled by some and snubbed by others, but it must be said that the aniseed flavour is much stronger when fennel is eaten raw. It is mostly associated with Italy but is also popular in France and North Africa. A little finely-sliced fennel adds subtlety to a mixed salad and it often partners cucumber or radish. A justifiable favourite is halved and cooked fennel, dotted with butter, smothered in freshly grated Parmesan cheese and baked until golden brown. It may be served *au gratin, à la grecque, à la niçoise* or as a substitute for celery or chicory. It also makes a delicious soup. The Arabs stuff fennel as they would aubergines or tomatoes.

Herbal Properties

No properties are known for the vegetable but if there are any they are likely to be fairly similar to those of the seeds. The seeds are carminative (their most well-known property), stomachic, stimulative, digestive and aphrodisiac.

Facts and Features

Fennel is particular to Italy where it is as common as cabbage is in Britain. It has never been seriously cultivated in this country, primarily because its flavour seems too sweet and exotic to British taste. However, this attitude is being adjusted as the Great British Palate is subjected to more and more interesting fruit and vegetables in modern times. Fennel was introduced here sometime around 1750, cultivated mainly at Hitchin in Hertfordshire, whence one of its names, and into America at the turn of that century. It is easy to grow but likes a sunny position. Sow in April in light fertile soil, in drills 50cm (20in) apart, and thin out to 25cm (10in). When the stem bases start to swell, cover with soil and tamp down. Harvest as required.

FENUGREEK (METHI)
Asia, Southern Europe

Trigonella foenum-graecum
Fam Leguminosae

Bird's Foot, Foenugreek, Goat's Horn, Greek Hay, Helbeh

Ethiopia: abish; France: fenugrec Sénegré, trigonelle; Germany: Griechisches Heu; India: mayti, mentee, methi sag; Indonesia: vendayam, venthiyam (Tamil); Italy: fieno grecco; Malaysia: alba, uluva, ventayan; Middle East: helbeh; Sri Lanka: uluhaal

Fenugreek is an aromatic leaf vegetable and herb easily recognised by its spicy fragrance and its leaves which grow in threes. The leaves, which are about 2 × 3cm (¾ × 1¼in), are rounded with slight serrations and mid-green, only slightly paler on the underside. The stalks are a lighter green, hollow and about the thickness of a knitting needle. Its flavour is warm with a faintly bitter undertone.

Selecting the Best
Asian and Middle Eastern food shops offer fenugreek (under the name 'methi') all the year round. It is usually sold in bunches about 20–25cm (8–10in) long and weighing around 225g (8oz). These should be upright with nice flat leaves. Avoid leggy or drooping stalks.

Storage and Preparation
Fenugreek is best used as soon as possible; otherwise keep in a polythene bag in the salad drawer. If the leaves have wilted, they will perk up remarkably on immersion in cold water for 30 minutes. Coarse or tough stems should be removed and the leaves and remaining stems washed and patted dry with kitchen paper. Chop up with a knife or pull off sprigs by hand according to the recipe.

Culinary Uses
Fenugreek is undoubtedly one of the most neglected vegetables outside India. This is a mystery since it is deliciously piquant, good value and easy to grow. Furthermore it is very good for you. Fenugreek appears in almost every style of Indian dish: with other vegetables, particularly potato and cauliflower; spicy side dishes; *pilaus*; fritters; *raitas*; breads; and *methi ghosh* (meat) so popular in Indian restaurants. It is also enjoyed in Iran where it is appreciated as a herb for omelettes and sauces and is especially popular served fresh in a mixed herb platter with parsley, mint, chives, coriander and watercress, accompanied by *pitta* bread and *feta* cheese. Try a few sprigs in a green salad as you would water-cress and substitute it for spinach and watercress recipes. You will be well rewarded.

Herbal Properties
In India the leaves are used to relieve swellings and burns, as a digestive, in treating leucorrhoea and as a hair tonic. The seeds have a multitude of

Nutritional Values

Fenugreek is one of the most nutritive plants known to man. If spinach made Popeye the strongest man in the West, a fenugreek-eating Indian Popeye would be twice as muscular. Fenugreek surpasses spinach (and watercress, another very nutritive plant) in nearly every component—containing almost twice as much food energy and iron which was supposed to be that animated matelot's source of strength. Furthermore it has very little of the oxalic acid which in spinach inhibits the absorption of calcium and magnesium.

cal	49	Ca	360	A	6,450
pro	4.4	P	51	B_1	0.05
fat	0.9	Fe	17.2	B_2	0.3
car	6	Na	76.1	B_5	0.7
fib	1.1	K	51	C	54

Recipes:
Fenugreek and Onion Fritters, page 204; Keema Methi, page 185; Methi Potatoes, page 195

uses in the East, where they are considered aphrodisiac, and in the West they are recognised as a source of diosgenin, a substance used in oral contraceptives. Roasted seeds are eaten by harem women to acquire plumpness.

Facts and Features

Fenugreek is native to southern Europe and Asia where it has been grown as a crop for its leaves, pods and seeds for millennia. It has also been used as a cattle fodder, and cattle like the seeds as well. For cultivation a mild Mediterranean-type climate is preferred and fenugreek is fairly tolerant of frost. Sow in spring in a light limy soil in drills 25cm (10in) apart. Thin the seedlings, then after 30 to 45 days a first cutting can be made when the plants are about 15–20cm (6–8in) high. Two or three cuttings in all can be made. Allow some plants to go to pod and seed. The leaves of older plants become bitter.

FIG
Asia

Ficus carica
Fam Moraceae

The fig has the reputation of being the most carnal of fruits; it is soft and smooth, fleshy and juicy, red and purple. It can be egg-shaped or pear-shaped. There is a great variety of skin colours, according to cultivar—black, brown, purple, white, gold and green. Figs vary in size from 4–8cm (1½–3in) in diameter. The soft succulent flesh is actually composed of many tiny flowers fused together, which have ripened within the skin. This meat is usually highly sugary, dark red, lightening at the edges, giving a sunburst effect, and peppered with tiny seeds. There is a small hollow central cavity, encrusted with dried flower remnants and seeds.

Selecting the Best

Figs are available from early summer to autumn. They are best when ripe enough for the skin to split, but can be bought before rupturing and kept until splitting-ripe. Dried figs are a large part of commercial production.

Storage and Preparation

Delicate fruits, these bruise easily. They are

China: mo fa go; France: figue; Germany: Feige; Greece: sykon; India: doomar, doombur; Italy: fico; Japan: ichijiku; Middle East: seen, teen; Spain: higo, higuera

Nutritional Values
Figs, especially dried ones, have a high sugar content, but little other nutritional merit.

cal	80	Ca	50	A	80
pro	1.2	P	25	B_1	0.05
fat	0.4	Fe	0.6	B_2	0.05
car	20	Na	2	B_5	0.4
fib	15	K	190	C	2

Recipe:
Fig and Apple Preserve, page 210

preferred when slightly above room temperature and should not need peeling unless the skin is tough. Steam or boil dried figs to reconstitute them.

Culinary Uses
Apart from the odd, exotic two-tone cocktail, fig and lychee for example, figs do not take kindly to fruit salads. Distinctive and solitary, they are at their best with cream, citrus peel, or nuts, or stuffed with some combination of these. They can be simply sprinkled with pepper, just as some cooks treat strawberries. With cereal, or stuffed with cottage or cream cheese, they make a welcome difference to breakfast. Like melon, they team up well with Parma ham or salami. They are also good with aperitifs and liqueurs alike. Figs can be pickled with a sweet spice pickling mixture, baked, preserved, or caramelised. Dried, they are used in bakery, confectionery and ice-cream.

Herbal Properties
The main medicinal use of figs is as the famous laxative 'syrup of figs'. Otherwise the fruit is emollient and demulcent. Roasted figs were once often used in poultices for ulcers and boils. 'The milke . . . openeth the veines of the hemorrhoids, and looseneth the belly, being applied to the fundament' (Gerard, 1597). Figs are a domestic remedy for coughs and give a caffeine substitute in the form of 'fig coffee'.

Facts and Features
One of the mulberry family, the fig is native to Asia Minor, from whence it reached India and China at an early date. More recently, it was widely spread throughout Europe by the Romans. The fig is one of those biblical fruits that is mentioned sporadically from Genesis to Revelations. There are some 700 varieties, highly variable in quality. Major areas of cultivation are the Mediterranean, North Africa, and Turkey, the original producer of Europe's favourite fig, the 'Brown Turkey'. The 'Smyrna' varieties are said to be the best, and arriving in California in the nineteenth century, these were combined with others to form the now famous 'Calimyrna' strains. The Germans make a lederhosen-thigh-slapping fig brandy called *Feigenbranntwein*. The word 'fig' has acquired some unbotanical meanings over the centuries—amongst these, to fig is to pickpocket or to make an obscene gesture.

GALANGAL
GREATER GALANGAL
India, Southeast Asia

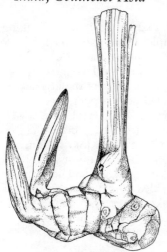

Languas galanga
syn *Alpinia galanga*,
Maranta galanga

Fam Zingiberaceae

*Black Ginger, False Galangal,
(Greater) Galingale, Siamese
Ginger*

*China: gaoliang-jiang; India:
kulanjan; Indonesia: ladja, laos;
Malaysia: lengkoowas, lengkuas;
Thailand: ka(h), kha*

LESSER GALANGAL
China
Languas officinarum
syn *Alpinia officinarum*

Fam Zingiberaceae

*Aromatic Ginger, China Root,
Chinese Ginger, Colic Root, East
Indian (Catarrh) Root, Galanga,
Gargaut, India Root, Siamese
Ginger*

*China: sa leung geung, sha geung
fun*

There are three galangals, two of which are
described here and the third, which is very
different, under Chinese keys (see page 39).
Greater galangal is a most unusual-looking root,
rather like a cross between a flamingo's leg and a
golf club. Good quality rhizomes (roots) consist
of a bulbous part, ivory in colour, tinged with
orange, with darker bands at intervals, at the base
of a leafy stalk. The colour is a vivid pink where
this stalk joins the rhizome and sometimes pink
shoots spring from the ends of the latter, which is
itself sometimes divided. The root is more or less
cylindrical, between 2 and 3cm (¾–1¼in) in
diameter and about 4–6cm (1½–2½in) in length.
Scraped versions are creamy-white, which
emphasises the 'eyes' common to all rhizomes.
The 'flesh' is ivory-white, highly aromatic and
recalls ginger. The flavour is hot, gingerish with
a sweetish tone.

Lesser galangal, not as common as greater, is
larger, more bulbous, more hairy and scaly and
mostly browny-orange in colour. Its flesh is
yellower and the flavour is deemed superior to
the greater galangal, being more pungent and
aromatic.

Selecting the Best
Galangal should be available all year from
specialist Chinese, Thai and Indonesian shops.
These roots should look plump and neither dried
out nor withered. Both varieties can also be
obtained in powder form or in dried slices.

Storage and Preparation
Galangals will keep for at least a week stored in a
cool place but the sooner used the juicier they are.
As they are not so easy to come by, it is a good
idea to freeze them just as they are in a polythene
bag and break off pieces as and when required.
The skin is quite easy to scrape or peel off and the
flesh is then sliced, chopped or minced.

Culinary Uses
Like its cousin, Chinese keys, galangal is typical
of Indonesian and Thai food, but more delicate in
flavour and more often used. Sauces, pickles,
curries of fish, meat, poultry or vegetables
contain it. It is particularly delicious combined in
a spicy marinade for barbecued chicken and in
tom yam (see page 180), the most famous Thai
soup.

Galangals are used as flavourings in small quantities and therefore have little nutritive effect.

Recipes:
Green Curry Paste, page 209

Herbal Properties
The essential oil in the rhizomes acts as a decongestant and respiratory germicide as well as a digestive aid. This oil contains some camphor, 20–30 per cent cineol, and pinene, perhaps some eugenol, and 48 per cent methyl-cinnamate. The rhizome also contains a resin. In India, galangal is used as a breath purifier and general body deodorant. A paste is used for skin infections. The root is a powerful aphrodisiac and is incorporated in a French toothache antidote.

Facts and Features
Although galangals had been introduced into Europe in the Middle Ages it was not until 1867 that the botanist Hanse connected one type of rhizome to the plant of lesser galangal of China. The greater galangal is native to India and Southeast Asia, whence the Arabs brought it to Europe, where it is mentioned in mediaeval writings. Its most provocative use was in the Middle East, inserted in stallions' rear ends to instil speed.

GARLIC
Central Asia

Allium sativum
Fam Alliaceae

Despite some variety of size and shape, from the pingpong-ball-sized Euro-varieties to the tiny purple oriental specimens, garlic is always unmistakable; the odour of the crushed cloves will confirm its identity. There may be up to twenty ivory-coloured cloves tightly packed in their parchment cubicles, but there is an Asian form with only four or five. The Spanish rocambole is another miniature variety. California, however, characteristically boasts a giant cultivar.

Selecting the Best
Garlic is always available. Look out for juicy new-season bulbs. Garlic from the Far East is usually only to be had from specialist shops. Always choose fresh, plump garlic, large for its particular variety. Good garlic is hard to the touch. Avoid bulbs showing small green shoots. Buy them singly or in pairs—only buy the strings if you are going to use them frequently. Manufacturers have seized upon garlic's ubiquity and indispensability to market it as paste, powder, granules or mixed with salt as the useful 'garlic salt'.

*Clown's Treacle, Poor Man's
Theriac, Poor Man's Treacle*

*Burma: chyet-thon-phew; China:
suen tao, taai suen; France: ail;
Germany: Knoblauch; Greece:
skortho; India: lahsan (various
spellings), thom; Indonesia: bawang
bodas, bawang puteh, ullipundu
(Tamil), vellaippundu (Tamil);
Italy: aglio; Japan: ninniku;
Malaysia: bawang puteh, velluli;
Middle East: toom, tum; Spain: ajo;
Sri Lanka: sudulunu; Thailand:
krat(h)iem; Turkey: sarmisak; West
Indies: garlic, l'aile*

Nutritional Values
*If we believed everything that has
been written about garlic then it
should be eaten with every meal for
both its nutritive and medicinal
properties. Notwithstanding its more
fantastic and fanciful attributes,
modern research has proven many
times that garlic remains an
extremely valuable food. We heartily
recommend its inclusion in as many
dishes as possible.*

cal	140	Ca	30	A	trace
pro	6	P	200–310	B₁	0.2
fat	0.1	Fe	1.3	B₂	0.08–0.23
car	30	Na	19	B₅	0.5
fib	1	K	529	C	9–15

Recipes:
*Nasi Goreng, page 181; Skorthalia,
page 202*

Storage and Preparation
A cool dry place is best for storage; either hang the garlic in strings or in a small wire basket for the air to circulate. It should keep for several months. Oak-smoked garlic from France is now available keeping fresh for as long as a year. Pull off as many cloves as you need, peel and put through a garlic squeezer or preferably leave the skin on, smash the clove with the flat of a heavy knife or cleaver, discard the skin and chop as finely as you wish. A sprinkling of salt will absorb the juices and stop the pieces slipping about. In Asian cookery garlic is often ground to a paste, with or without ginger, but without water. This may be frozen to advantage. A tasty garnish for curries and rice dishes is made by deep-frying minced or sliced garlic until pale golden. The drained, cooled pieces can be transferred to an airtight jar for future use. Take care not to burn garlic or it will develop an acrid taste.

Culinary Uses
The uses of garlic are legion. In one form or other, it has always been a familiar ingredient throughout the culinary globe, from ancient cuisines onwards. Although many cooks are familiar with the dishes it characterises, prejudice, like the aroma, lingers on. Indulge in it with impunity—it will do you nothing but good. Small amounts are virtually indetectable yet will 'lift' dishes of meat, fish and vegetables. However, generous amounts are thrown into the lusty Mediterranean-style cookery in soups, pâtés, sausages, pasta dishes and salad dressings. Greek *skorthalia* and Spanish *aïoli* are pungent sauces, irresistible to the garlic-lover. Spike a joint of lamb with slivers of garlic before roasting for a mouth-watering aroma. Long, slow cooking results in a mild, almost nutty flavour, and therefore garlic soup and even *poulet aux quarante gousses d'ail*, chicken cooked with forty cloves of garlic, should not be a daunting prospect. Equally beloved in Asian cookery, garlic forms the basis of most curries and is essential in stir-fry cooking and in countless sauces and pickles. Pickled garlic is consumed in Southeast Asia and Japan as we would eat pickled onions—an excellent accompaniment to alcohol.

Herbal Properties
Although the chemistry of garlic was unknown

to the ancients they were well aware of its unique properties and applied it in innumerable ways. Modern research has come some way to explaining its chemistry and active components, the most important being the pungent principle allicin, which is bactericidal. Allicin is produced when the enzyme alliinase reacts with the precursor allin, each of these being locked in separate cells in the garlic and only released when the cells are ruptured by crushing or bruising.

There is recent evidence that garlic is effective in the following ways: in reducing hypertension; as a bactericide (in Russia, allicin is known as 'Russian penicillin'); as a fungicide, effective in thrush; used against certain cancer tumours, ulcers and wound infections (in World War I garlic juice was used extensively); in treating stomach and chest problems; and in assisting the absorption of vitamin B_1 (thiamine). Garlic has always been recommended as an aphrodisiac, in sterility and impotence but it is suggested that both partners take the recommended prescription.

Facts and Features
Apart from a minor North American form, no wild garlic has ever been discovered. Garlic is one of the earth's few 'non-wild' plants because of its long history of cultivation. Naturally enough, such a food has inspired hundreds of legends, stories, superstitions and fantasies. Arab mythology relates that the first garlic sprang from the footprint of the Devil as he left Eden. More positively, the beneficial effects of the vegetable were known at the dawn of history, the Pyramid Age in Egypt, where the health and productivity of tomb workers were maintained with a balanced diet including plenty of garlic. The plant is a member of the lily family, characterised by their bulbs, and the name 'garlic' comes from Old English 'gar-leac', spear-onion, possibly in reference to the sharpness of its taste.

GHURMAH
India

Peucedanum dhana var
dalzellii

Fam Umbelliferae

Indian Carrot

*India: bhoj raj, garmah, koland,
mann tirio*

Nutritional Values
*Nothing is known of the ghurmah's
nutritive properties but since it is
quite 'carroty' it can be expected to
have some vitamin A.*

The ghurmah is an Indian vegetable-condiment
that now makes a fairly regular appearance in
Indian shops. It consists of the roots of a
parsnip-type plant but, unlike parsnip, several
roots protrude from a single stem base. The roots
are irregular, roughish, brown and hairy, similar
to Chinese keys (see page 39) which, however,
are more regular, smoother and lighter in colour.
Ghurmahs are up to 20cm (8in) in length and 2cm
(¾in) in diameter at the widest part, tapering to a
very fine hair root. The flesh is white but quickly
darkens on exposure to the air; it has a pungent
aroma. The flavour is pungent and carroty with
mango and turmeric undertones.

Selecting the Best
Ghurmahs are available from Indian food shops
from time to time. Select plumper roots with the
least blemishes.

Storage and Preparation
Keep in a cool place for up to a week. Separate
the roots and peel or scrape the skin to reveal the
white flesh. This is easily done. Drop them into
acidulated water to prevent discoloration.

Culinary Uses
The ghurmah is used mainly in central India
where it is pickled, treated as a condiment like
ginger or turmeric and cooked in mixed
vegetable curries. It may be successfully adapted
to carrot recipes, adding an unusual lemony
pungency. Sprinkle with a pinch of *garam masala*
(see page 213) before serving. It can also be eaten
raw: grated in a salad it will add a certain
piquancy.

Herbal Properties
The ghurmah is eaten as a tonic and febrifuge.

Facts and Features
The ghurmah is native to India and is related to
the parsnip and carrot. It is a perennial herb
found in the humid areas of India that stretch
from Bombay through Hyderabad to Calcutta. It
is now imported to the UK and is fairly common
in Indian shops, being one of the many fruits and
vegetables for which efficiency of transportation
and new expatriate demand have helped create a
viable market.

GINGER
Southeast Asia

Zingiber officinale

Fam Zingiberaceae

Cochin Ginger, East Indian Pepper, Gingiberis, Jamaica Ginger, Jamaica Pepper

Burma: gin(sein); China: geung, jeung, keung, sang keung (green); East Africa: tangawizi; France: gingembre; Germany: Ingwer; Holland: gember; India: ada, adruk (green), ale, a(r)d(h) rak(a) (green), so(o)nth(a) (dry), udruk (green); Indonesia: atjuga, chukka (Tamil), (d)jahe, djhai, ingee (Tamil), inji (Tamil); Italy: zenzero; Japan: beni-shoga (red pickled), mioga, shoga; Malaysia: aleea, djae, halia (green), inji; Middle East: zenjabil; Polynesia: cagolaya ni vavalagi; Sabah: halia; Spain: jengibré; Sri Lanka: inguru; Thailand: k(h)ing (green); West Indies: gingembre, ginger

Fresh or 'green' ginger, now commonly available, is an irregularly-shaped rootstock. It is knobbly, and no two pieces are identical; the closest likeness is to a hand with arthritic fingers—indeed, the root is known as a 'hand' of ginger. The size varies from 5–20cm (2–8in) in length and 1–3cm (½–1¼in) in diameter. The flesh is pale yellow (sometimes greeny) enclosed in a light to dark brown skin, sometimes scaly or hairy. The aroma is warm and pungent and on snapping off a piece a lemony rosemary-like bouquet is produced (rosemary has many identical constituents). The flavour is fiery.

Selecting the Best
Ginger is widely available all year round. Smooth-skinned, plump 'hands' of pale colour are the best. Refuse withered or gnarled roots. Young tender ginger, small and pinkish, is much sought after for making pickles and relishes.

Storage and Preparation
Wrap in cling film, foil or a plastic bag and store in the refrigerator where it will keep in good condition for a week or more. Alternatively wrap and freeze. The skin is always removed; either scrape it away with a knife or use a potato peeler. Quantities of ginger are usually stated in slices and inches. Slices are cut diagonally about the thickness of a five pence piece. An inch is a rough guide depending on the diameter of the root. Pieces may be chopped, minced or grated. When grating, the fibres are retained in the grater and can be discarded.

Culinary Uses
An absolutely essential flavouring in Indian, Chinese and Southeast Asian cookery, fresh ginger has not been widely available in the UK until recently. Though ginger is familiar preserved or as a dried spice in sweet dishes, pickles and 'beer', the fresh root has altogether different applications and must become an indispensable ingredient to the adventurous cook. Apart from its use as a flavouring it is deemed a 'de-fisher' and also a 'sweetener' for cooking oil—a small piece is fried and then discarded before the cooking proceeds. Ginger, together with garlic and chilli, forms the nucleus of ten thousand curries from India to Indonesia. A primary flavouring for Chinese stir-fried dishes, it is also elemental in Japanese cookery where it

Ginger is used only in small quantities and in any event has little to recommend itself nutritionally, except for the strong volatile oil it contains, which is an excellent digestive.

Fresh root:

cal 48	Ca 23–44	A 0–10
pro 1.5	P 36	B_1 0.02
fat 0.9	Fe 2	B_2 0.05
car 9.2	Na 6	B_5 0.7
fib 1	K 264	C 3

Recipes:
Ginger Beer, page 212; Gingered Lamb Cutlets, page 184

appears in many fish dishes, marinades and often simply grated raw as a side dish. Gingered prawns make a marvellous starter or impressive snack to savour with drinks, and grilled lamb or pork chops prepared in a gingery marinade are deliciously different. Try tossing cooked carrots in butter to which a squeeze of lemon juice and a little freshly grated ginger has been added.

Herbal Properties
Ginger is carminative, rubefacient, stimulant and expectorant. There is modern evidence that ground ginger is a car-sickness remedy. Since time immemorial ginger has been used as an aphrodisiac, both internally and externally. In *The Perfumed Garden* it is included in a host of applications from curing premature ejaculation to increasing the proportions of the male organ. In the Melanesian islands it is employed 'to gain the affection of a woman'; conversely in the Philippines it is chewed to expel evil spirits. '. . . That canded, greene or condited Ginger is hot and moist in qualitie, provoking Venerie . . .' (Gerard, 1597).

Facts and Features
Ginger is so ancient that it has always been known as a cultivated plant. Its origin is believed to lie in Southeast Asia, where it has been grown for millennia, as it has in India. It arrived in Britain in the tenth century, long before the Spaniards took it to tropical America where it still flourishes. Before that ancient Rome and Greece appreciated and esteemed it. The best ginger comes from India and Jamaica but Kenya now produces a comparable quality. Japanese ginger is pungent, but lacks the true ginger aroma. Ginger is a well-known flavouring of alcoholic and soft drinks; it is used in perfumery and veterinary medicine, but is best known in the food industry.

GOURDS

This section deals with oriental and tropical gourds which for convenience can be divided into two groups: bitter and mild. These are all available from Asian shops but doodhi and tindori are now in some supermarkets.

BITTER GOURDS

There are three types currently available in the UK; all are closely related and belong to the same group or genus.

CHINESE BITTER MELON, INDIAN BITTER GOURD (KARELA)
Tropics

Momordica charantia

Fam Cucurbitaceae

African Cucumber, Balsam Apple, Balsam Pear, Bitter Cucumber, Bitter Gourd, Carille Fruit

Nature has wrought many wonders in the world of squashes, gourds and melons but her masterpiece of eccentricity must be the bitter melon. Knobbly like some prehistoric crocodile, its flavour is peculiarly bitter, and when ripe it is orange with spectacularly crimson seeds. The Chinese and Southeast Asian variety is rounder and plumper than the Indian karela, which is more pointed and more bitter. Both come in several shades of green from pale lime to deep, and average about 18cm (7in) long by 5–8cm (2–3in) wide. Other species, Thai for example, are stubbier, rounder but pointed and commence

China: *fu kwa*; India: *buno kakrol,*
karela, karvel; Indonesia:
pare(e)(a); Japan: *kiuri*; Malaysia:
peria; Philippines: *ampalaya*; Sri
Lanka: *karawila, pakal, pavakai*;
Thailand: *mara*; West Indies: *baan,*
bitter bark, carilla, cerasee, foo-gah,
maiden apple, maiden's bush,
miraculour vine

Recipe:
Bitter Melon with Beef and Salted
Black Beans, page 184

KANTOLA
Tropical Asia
Momordica dioica
Fam Cucurbitaceae

Apple of Jerusalem, Balsam Apple,
Marvellous Apple

India: bhat kerala, kakrol, kakur,
kantola; Indonesia: *palupakkai*
(Tamil), tumpai (Tamil);
Malaysia: *teruah*; Sri Lanka:
tumba-karawila; Thailand: *fak kao*

life white before turning darkish green; they are
often called balsam apples or pears. Usually eaten
before ripe, the interior is pithy with many
rubbery seed capsules. The taste of the ripe red
flesh, in striking contrast to its bitter origins, is
quite sweet.

Not unlike a very hairy and stubbly gooseberry,
the kantola is slightly bitter, although much less
so than its warty cousins described above. Some
characteristics are similar: it turns sweet on
ripening and the seeds change from green
through cream to pink or red. From 1–3cm
(½–1¼in) wide and 2–5cm (¾–2in) long,
kantolas are light lime-green, spiny and light in
weight. Inside the fleshy capsule are over twenty
seeds, soft when young but hardening as they
mature.

Selecting the Best (bitter gourds)
Bitter melons and karelas are available all year
from Chinese and Indian shops respectively;
kantolas, from Indian shops, are available during
the summer. Canned versions are also obtainable.
Chinese bitter melons are best when pale and
even in shape. Indian karelas are preferred
unripe—firm and dark green. Kantolas should be
full and fresh-looking.

Storage and Preparation
These keep in a cool dark place for several days.
To prepare bitter melons and karelas for cooking,
slice across or slit lengthways and scrape away
mature seeds—young seeds may be eaten. Salt
flesh liberally, set aside for 2–3 hours, rinse well
and pat dry. To reduce bitterness still further, the
outer skin may be scraped and salted too. The
Chinese blanch bitter melon for 3 minutes instead
of salting. Kantolas are left whole and either
blanched for 3 minutes or soaked in brine for 4–5
hours. It is important to scrub kantolas gently
under running water to remove all dirt.

Culinary Uses
Bitter melons look unusual and attractive and
may, after preparation, be cooked as courgettes.

A little sugar is sometimes an advantageous addition. The Chinese love them, whether stuffed, braised, steamed or stir-fried, invariably teamed with black beans and garlic. Karelas, very popular in India, are found in divers curries, pickles and *sambals*. Again they may be cooked as courgettes, especially in mixed vegetable courses. A favourite dish is whole karelas stuffed with onions and spices, with or without meat, secured with thread and slowly fried until cooked. Many karela recipes have found their way to the West Indies where they are also much relished with salt fish. Kantolas are cooked in much the same way as karelas but are kept whole.

MILD GOURDS

Five of these are described here but as the gourd family is so vast and constantly changing, it is quite certain you will find some in the shops that do not quite fit these descriptions. It is impossible to be absolutely accurate about gourds since there are literally thousands of variations on their theme.

ANGLED LOOFAH
India
Luffa acutangula
Fam Cucurbitaceae

Angled Gourd, Chinese Okra, Luffa Gourd, Ribbed Gourd, Ribbed Luffa, Ridged Cucumber, Ridge Gourd, Silk Gourd, Silk Melon, Silk Squash, Silky Gourd, Strainer Vine

China: se gwa, si gwa, sze kwa; India: hireballi, (jhinga) tori, jhingli, jungli tori, kali tori, katturaya, katukoshatki, kritabedhana, nasdar tori, nasili tori, peerkankai, toorayi, turia; Indonesia: gambas, katjoor, kimpoot, langker, oyong; Malaysia: ketola sagi, oyong, petola; Sri Lanka: (dara) vetakola; Thailand: booap

Recipe:
Stir-fried Angled Loofah, page 197

Like a cucumber with sharp ridges, the angled loofah is unmistakable. Green, 15–60cm (6–24in) long and 2.5–5cm (1–2in) in diameter, it has ten distinct ribs. The valleys between the ribs are often wrinkled. Some loofahs are straight while others are curved; there is a tremendous variety as is common in the gourd family but these fellows are easily identified. The ribs and skin are quite tough but the inner flesh is creamy-white with slippery seeds, either black or ivory-coloured.

DOODHI
Africa

Lagenaria siceraria
syn *L. leucantha, L. vulgaris*
Fam Cucurbitaceae

Bottle Gourd, Calabash Gourd,
Club Gourd, Doodi, Doody, Dudi.
Trumpet Gourd, White-flowered
Gourd, Zucca Melon

China: mo kwa, oo lo kwa, po kwa,
wu lo kwa; India: doodhi, ghia,
lauki; Indonesia: blontjeng,
kookook, laboo lente, walooh kentee;
Malaysia: laboo aer, laboo pootih;
West Indies: bottle gourd, gouge,
gourd, gourdie, sweet gourd

Doodhis are the young fruits of the bottle-gourd—the famous calabash of the tropics. They vary considerably in shape, being spherical or club-shaped, sometimes curved or, as the name suggests, bottle-shaped: that is with a neck or constriction. Usually pale green, some are yellowy or creamy. Most are smooth-skinned but some show visible ridges. As with shape, size is also variable, but averages 9–10cm (3½–4in) in diameter for the round variety and about 20cm (8in) for the club type. The thin skin is tough, with a rind up to 10mm (⅖in) thick. The flesh is white and spongy with flat cream seeds. There is a faint aroma of cucumber or squash.

FUZZY MELON
possibly China or Java

Benincasa hispida var
chieh-qua
syn *B. cerifera* var
Fam Cucurbitaceae

Hairy Melon

China: chit kwa, mo kwa; India:
petha; Indonesia: bleego-; Japan:
tongan; Philippines: kundol

This Chinese vegetable appears in many shapes and sizes, but can be distinguished from other similar cucurbits by its dark-green skin and the millions of minute hairs on its surface. Many of these get brushed off in transit but be careful of those remaining: they are a sharp nuisance, so handle this melon gingerly. It is generally cylindrical with a slight central narrowing; diameter varies between 4–10cm (1½–4in) and length between 15–30cm (6–12in). The flesh and seeds are rather similar to doodhi.

TINDA
India

Citrullus lanatus var
fistulosus
syn *C. vulgaris* var *fistulosus*
Fam Cucurbitaceae

Indian Squash, Round Gourd,
Squash Melon, Tinde, Tindo,
White Gourd

India: dilpasand, tinda

Tindas are small green-yellow spherical vegetables resembling baby apples. They average 5cm (2in) in diameter. The ivory-coloured flesh contains pale seeds. There is no aroma.

TINDORI
India

Trichosanthes dioica
syn *T. dioeca*

Fam Cucurbitaceae

Pointed Gourd

*India: padval, palbal, palwal,
parval, parwal, patal, patol, permal,
pulwul, putal, tendli, tindli*

Tindoris or parwals, as the larger versions are
called, look like gherkins. The smaller are 5cm
(2in) long and 2cm (¾in) in diameter, while the
larger measure up to 7cm (2¾in) long and 4cm
(1½in) in diameter. They are light or dark green,
often with pale stripes. Usually pointed, they are
thin skinned with a moist, pale-green flesh
containing many seeds around the central core.
The raw flavour is somewhat like cucumber but
some varieties are slightly bitter.

Selecting the Best (mild gourds)
Choose angled loofahs that are small or
medium-sized and firm—large gourds tend to be
spongy and slightly bitter. Doodhis should be
smooth and unblemished, and feel heavy. As yet,
fuzzy melons are available only from Chinese
shops. Select small firm ones—the younger and
fuzzier the better. Take great care when handling
as their hairs are as sharp and irritating as fibre
glass. Tindas are obtainable from Indian shops.
These tender little gourds should yield slightly.

Storage and Preparation
Mild gourds are good keepers, staying fresh for
at least 2 weeks in the salad drawer. Angled
loofahs need not have all their skin removed
unless toughness is suspected. Just peel or pare off
the ribs, giving a pleasing striped effect. For
stir-frying, 'roll cut' by slicing diagonally, rolling
over a quarter turn and slicing again to produce
wedge shapes. Otherwise cut across into 1cm
(½in) rounds. It is unnecessary to discard the
seeds from young gourds. Again, doodhis are
neither peeled nor seeded if young and tender.
They are cut as required; or peeled, grated,
cooked, cooled and squeezed dry for *koftas* and
raitas. A little extra oil is needed when stir-frying
shredded doodhi. To rid a fuzzy melon of its
hairs, scrub with a brush under the cold tap or
remove the skin with a knife or potato peeler,
always heeding the hairs. Tinda hairs are rubbed
or scraped away but the peel is left on. They are
halved or quartered and, for stuffing, are either
cored like an apple or the top is cut off and the
flesh scooped out. Don't overcook them.

Culinary Uses
Angled loofahs can safely be treated as
courgettes. They are popular in China, Southeast
Asia and southern India. In China, they are most
commonly stir-fried or made into soups, while in

India they are found in vegetable curries and chutneys. Doodhis are most versatile. Follow recipes for marrow, when you will find the doodhi's creamy delicacy rewarding. It is much appreciated cooked as a vegetable and in *raitas*, pickles or even sweetmeats. Fuzzy melon is not much known outside Chinese and Indonesian cookery but is well worth trying. It readily absorbs other flavours and when cooked is deemed superior to cucumber. Stuff with your favourite mixture or stir-fry with grated ginger, adding a dash of sherry before serving. Despite their size, tindas are enjoyed stuffed, particularly with a spicy onion and tomato mixture or with meat. Although rather fiddly to prepare, they look most attractive when served. Tindoris, crisp and crunchy, are good in salads; and sliced in vinegar are excellent with bread and cheese. Very popular in Indian cookery, they are fried with spices as a side dish; curried, often with potatoes; made into hot pickle and (for parwals) stuffed like tindas.

Herbal Properties (all gourd varieties)
Bitter melons have been ascribed innumerable curative properties. These cover the whole body from eye infections downwards ('. . . leaf juice is a liniment for relief of burning of soles of the feet.' Dastur, 1962). Applications are remedies for constipation, leprosy, skin eruptions, gout, anaemia, stomach disorders, urinary discharges, thrush, painful menstruation, boils, and liver and spleen diseases. Not to be entirely outdone, the fuzzy melon is efficacious as a remedy for prickly heat—just rub with a fresh slice and relief is immediate. All parts of the angled loofah are used in India for various purposes; generally it is a tonic.

Facts and Features
Throughout India and the Far East bitter melons are a familiar sight in the market and street stalls. In some parts the young and tender leaves and shoots are also eaten like spinach.

The angled loofah is thought to be of Indian origin. Its cousin, the smooth loofah, is more famous and grows twice as long. The young fruits are eaten but it is best known for its fibrous sponge interior—the bathroom loofah—and until the advent of plastics was extensively used in industrial filters. In World War II all GIs from Iwo Jima to the Ardennes wore protective bands of loofah in their steel helmets.

Nutritional Values (all gourd varieties)

Generally, gourds have little nutritive value but some do have special features. Small karela (bitter melon) varieties have excellent iron content. Typically, the bitter types appear more endowed with minerals and vitamins than the milder ones.

Raw:

| | BITTER | | MILD | | | | |
	LARGE	SMALL	LOOFA	DOODHI	MELON	TINDA	TINDORI
cal	25	60	21	12	10	20	20
pro	1.6	2.1	0.6	0.4	0.4	1.4	2
fat	0.2	1	0.2	0.1	0.1	0.2	0.3
car	4.2	9.8	3–4.9	2.5	1.9	3.4	2.2
fib	0.8	4.2	0.5			1	3
Cal	20	50	16–40	20	30	25	30
P	70	140	40	10–47	20	24	40
Fe	1.8	9.4	0.6–1.6	0.2–0.7	0.8	0.9	1.7
Na	17.8	2.4	2.9	1.8		35	2.6
K	152	171	50	87		24	83
A	210	210	56–150	0	0	23	255
B_1	0.07	0.07	0.04–0.07	0.03	0.06	0.04	0.05
B_2	0.09	0.06	0.02	0.02	0.1	0.08	0.06
B_5	0.5	0.4	0.3	0.3	0.4	0.3	0.5
C	88	96	6	1–6	1	18	29

GROUNDNUT
South America

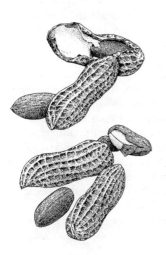

Arachis hypogaea
Fam Leguminosae

Earth Almond, Earth Nut, Goober, Grass Nut, Mandubi, Manil(l)a Nut, Monkey Nut, Peanut, Pindar, Underground Kidney Bean

Fresh groundnuts (or peanuts) come in their original shells which are actually fibrous pods with neat rows of dimples. The pods are 2–5cm (¾–2in) in length and a fairly regular 15mm (⅗in) in diameter. Being fresh they are usually quite dirty but this does not matter. Black ones are rotten. Inside the pod lie one to four nuts, with their skins cream through pink to brown in colour. The raw groundnut itself is crisp, moist and ivory-coloured, and very familiar to us in its roasted form. The flavour is much like raw peas or beans, but when boiled it is more like a kidney bean with nuttier overtones, and when roasted far more delicate than the commercial peanut.

Selecting the Best
Raw, freshly-dug groundnuts are available from Asian shops and markets and are easily distinguishable from roasted ones by their dirty appearance. Avoid any showing signs of mildew.

Storage and Preparation
Keep in a dry cool place or refrigerate for a few days; but note that fresh groundnuts do not keep well, especially if they are damp—when they soon rot. The shells are easily cracked open between finger and thumb and the nuts can be shaken out. To remove the outer skin at this stage pour on boiling water to cover. Leave for 5

*Burma: mye-be; China: fa sang;
India: mung phali, nila kadala, veru
sanaga; Indonesia: katjang, otok
tjena, suuk; Malaysia: katjang
(goreng); Thailand: tua din, tua li
song; West Indies: groundnut,
peanut, pistache, pistacio*

Nutritional Values

*Next to the soybean, the groundnut
(or peanut) packs the most food
values. Although it has no vitamin
A or C it contains more vitamin B$_5$
than any known foodstuff apart from
yeast; other B complex vitamins
occur in respectable quantities. It is
rich in protein (up to 30 per cent)
and oil (up to 50 per cent). The shell
represents about 27 per cent wastage.*

Raw (with skin):

cal	564	Ca	69	A	—
pro	26	P	401	B$_1$	1.14
fat	47.5	Fe	2.1	B$_2$	0.13
car	18.6	Na	5	B$_5$	17.2
fib	2.4	K	674	C	0

Recipe:
Tsire Powder, page 209

minutes and the skins will readily slip off. To
roast the shelled nuts, spread onto a baking tray
in a low oven until they are dry, golden in colour
and the skin papery. If desired the skin can be
rubbed off by hand and then blown away with a
hair drier. Groundnuts can also be fried in a little
oil until golden; but whichever method is chosen
overcooking will make them bitter. A West
African method is to soak the shelled nuts in hot
water for an hour before grilling them under
moderate heat until done. This gives the nuts a
more floury texture. Boiled nuts will take about
25 minutes to cook.

Culinary Uses
Although ready-roasted groundnuts (peanuts)
and jars of peanut butter are on every grocer's
shelf, the raw nuts prove more versatile for
snacks and purists will insist on them in the
preparation of Southeast Asian and African
dishes. Plain boiled, they have an altogether
different flavour and texture from the roasted
nuts—more like chestnuts or beans. After frying
or roasting, toss them in a little oil and a blend of
spices—*garam masala* (see page 213), Chinese five
spices or salt and chilli powder—for a change
from the ubiquitous cocktail nut. Hugely popular
in West and East Africa, groundnuts are eaten as
a snack, stewed with poultry, meat and fish,
made into cookies and sweets and ground with
spices to flavour grilled kebabs. Famous
Indonesian sauces such as *gado-gado* and *satay* are
based on groundnuts—rich, hot and spicy—and
the nuts appear in various *sambals*, and stir-fried
dishes throughout Southeast Asia and China.
Surprisingly, in India, the largest producer of
these nuts, recipes are few and confined to
sweetmeats and sherbets. Conversely, Americans
are the largest consumers of groundnuts,
devouring them in sandwiches, brittles, cookies,
pies, ice-cream and, vicariously, in Virginia
ham—from pigs fattened on groundnuts and
sweetcorn.

Herbal Properties
The groundnut plays only a small part in
traditional medicine, though in China the oil is
used for massage, reduction of inflammations and
swollen joints. The dried skins of roasted nuts are
a throat irritant. (Groundnuts are dangerous for
small children, who are unable to digest them and
also liable to choke on them.)

Facts and Features

Groundnuts are indigenous to South America but have never been known in their original form; they have been dated in Inca tombs from 1000BC. Their journey to civilisation was oddly circuitous—the Portuguese brought them to Africa and there the slave traders took them back to the Americas. Apart from being one of nature's most beneficient foodstuffs, groundnuts are also one of her curiosities in the way in which they are produced. After the flower is fertilised the stalk extends downwards until it can bury the ovary at its tip in the ground. Immediately the groundnut pod develops horizontally a few inches under the soil—hence its name. Nigeria and India top the production league while the US heads the consumption charts with 50 per cent used in peanut butter alone. Anticipating the Japanese invasion, the British in Hong Kong developed a 'siege biscuit' made from groundnuts, according to Herklots. The groundnut contributed to a huge waste of the British taxpayer's money in the infamous Groundnut Scheme of the 1940s in Tanganyika.

GUAVA
Tropical America

Guavas are tropical fruits that vary greatly in colour, size and shape, depending on species and variety. What characterises them all is a musky pervasive aroma. In fact it is as well to know you have a guava in the room, or else you could suspect the cat! There is a grainy yellow or pink flesh and an abundance of flat, hard, stony seeds. The substance of the flesh, and indeed the flavour, is confined to the hollow, firmer area beneath the skin, known as the shell. This is filled with a pulp, which is also edible, that bears the seeds. The commonest and most representative is often called the lemon guava. It is round, 2.5–10cm (1–4in) across. Its flavour is sweet, slightly acidic and 'dry'.

Selecting the Best

Formerly only available canned, fresh guavas are now usually found in the shops during the latter half of the year. Pick firm, intact ones that are unblemished.

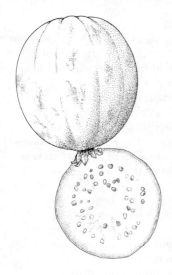

Psidium guajave (common guava)
P. littorale (strawberry guava) syn *P. cattleianum*

Fam Myrtaceae

China: *fan shek lau;* France: *goyave;* Hawaii: *ulaula (red), waiawi (yellow);* Holland: *gujave;* India: *lal sufriam (red), peyara, sufriam (white);* Indonesia: *djamboo;* Malaysia: *jambu batu, jambu biji;* Portugal: *goiaba;* West Indies: *gougave, goyave, guava, guayaba, guayabita cereza*

Nutritional Values

The common guava is the richest source of vitamin C in fruit, having up to five times that of citrus fruits and twice as much as kiwifruit.

cal	60	Ca	25	A	280
pro	1	P	35	B₁	0.06
fat	0.6	Fe	0.8	B₂	0.04
car	16	Na	4	B₅	1.2
fib	5.5	K	290	C	250–300

Storage and Preparation

Store away from other foods. Guavas can be frozen but ferment rapidly on the shelf. They should be peeled and the seeds are sometimes discarded.

Culinary Uses

Guavas are eaten raw, or cooked in a variety of ways. The flesh is often boiled down as a purée (with sugar, lemon juice and sweet spices such as allspice, ginger and cinnamon) to make the internationally-known guava butter or paste. Sometimes called guava cheese, this preparation is especially popular in South America, Florida and the West Indies. Use guavas like apples in crumbles and other apple dishes, like strawberries in shortcake, or fold into tapioca pudding to elevate this humble dessert. Guavas make good soufflés, sorbets, jellies and other preserves, especially pickles and ketchup, to go with cold meats. Fresh, they mix charmingly with cream cheese, honey or ice-cream. *Cascos*, made from the preserved shells, is a favourite in the West Indies, and the Filipino cuisine manages successfully to unite guavas and fish.

Herbal Properties

The skin contains tannin, and is used in the Philippines to treat diarrhoea in children. In Africa the ripe fruit and leaves are used as a laxative. The leaves are also chewed to relieve toothache. In India they are employed in local tanning.

Facts and Features

Native to tropical America, and coming to Europe by way of China, guavas are famed throughout the tropics, and are now equally common in the sub-tropics, prolific enough to be considered a weed in some areas. Various species are grown in Australia, India, the West Indies, Africa and Hawaii. The name in the English language derives from the Haitian *guayaba*. Members of the clove and eucalyptus family, the guavas produce ornamental plants which can be trained. One particular species, the strawberry or purple guava, commonest in Brazil, is said to outclass the lemon guava, with its wine-coloured skin and flesh, strawberry aroma and superior flavour. Guavas grow on an attractive tree, which attains up to 10m (30ft), with smooth peeling bark, fragrant white flowers and tough carvable wood.

GUNDA
India

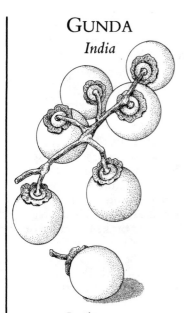

Cordia myxa
syn *C. dichotoma*

Fam Boraginaceae

Assyrian Plum, Australian Plum, Indian Cherry, Sapistan Plum, Sebasten, Sebestan, Sebesten, Selu

East Africa: muringa; India: bahubara, bahuvaraka, baragund, bohooari, chokargond, (chota) laso(o)ra, gondi, gunda, lesoora, lusora, nekra; Indonesia: naruvili (Tamil); Iran: pistan; Malaysia: cheruviri, viri; Middle East: sepistan

Nutritional Values
No nutritional information is available.

Recipe:
Gunda Pickle, page 207

Gundas are green drupes about the size of a large cherry. They ripen to yellow but are usually pale green with some brown mottlings when sold as vegetables or pickling fruit. They have a large brownish calyx and are often clustered three or four per stalk. Inside the thin skin is a layer of pale flesh, then a hard, curiously-shaped stone surrounded by very sticky opaque mucilage. The flesh is quite sweet and the jelly is similar to cucumber but very astringent.

Selecting the Best
Gundas are available only from Indian shops and should be firm and unblemished. Usually still attached to small branchlets, they should be green and unripe if bought for pickling.

Storage and Preparation
As with all pickling fruit and vegetables, use as fresh as possible. Detach the fruit from the stalks, discarding the calyx and any bruised parts. Wash well. Slit and remove the stones carefully.

Culinary Uses
Gundas are primarily used in Indian pickles, whole and sometimes still containing their stones. When thus highly spiced, gundas could be mistaken for olives which they resemble in size, shape and texture. An alcoholic drink is concocted from the fruit. Don't eat it raw when unripe—it is highly astringent. In India the ripe fruit is eaten just as any dessert fruit. The kernel is edible and closest in flavour to the filbert.

Herbal Properties
The gunda is anthelmintic, astringent, demulcent, diuretic, expectorant and laxative. '. . . ten drams . . . of the pap or pulpe hereof being taken inwardly, doth loose the belly' (Gerard, 1597). In India and the Middle East it is given to treat diseases of the respiratory and genito-urinary systems. In parts of Africa it is applied in paste form to accelerate abscesses.

Facts and Features
There are two *Cordias* in India, much alike, and some confusion persists over their names, both being called sebestan or gondi by authoritative writers. These are *Cordia myxa* syn *C. dichotoma* and *C. rothii* syn *C. gharat*. The former is smaller and sweeter, and the stone adheres to the surrounding mucilage. Gundas grow on a

low-spreading deciduous tree with broad leaves and a crooked trunk in the warmer parts of India, Africa and the Americas. The wood is light and used for many purposes including making fire by friction. The leaves make Burma cheroots.

HORSERADISH
Southeast Europe

Armoracia rusticana
syn *A. lapathifolia,*
Cochlearia armoracia

Fam Cruciferae

Great Raifort, Horse Plant,
Mountain Radish, Red Cole

France: moutarde des Allemands,
raifort sauvage; Germany:
Meerrettich; Holland: peperwortel;
Italy: rafano; Japan: wasabi;
Portugal: rabao de cavalho; Spain:
rábano picante, taramago

Nutritional Values
Horseradish is not important
nutritionally as it is consumed in such
small quantities, but it does contain
appreciable amounts of vitamin C,
especially in Indian-grown varieties.

Horseradish is a slightly tapering root, yellowish-brown in colour, with a few heavy rootlets and several swollen shoot bases at its top. It can grow to huge depths but averages 30cm (12in) long and 2cm (¾in) in diameter when sold in shops. Smoother-surfaced roots lacking rootlets indicate cultivated varieties. The whole root has little aroma but once broken, scraped or crushed it gives off a strong odour similar to that of watercress. This irritates the nostrils and eyes more so than onions. The flavour is also like watercress but far more pungent and sharp.

Selecting the Best
Fresh horseradish is best when thick and fairly even, being more pungent and easier to prepare.

Storage and Preparation
The whole root will keep fresh for 2 weeks or more in the salad drawer but it is probably more convenient to freeze the grated root in polythene bags and use as and when required. First trim off any little rootlets and scrub or scrape under the cold tap to remove any traces of earth. Finely grate by hand and discard the central core, or use a food processor, cutting out the core first. (The latter method is kinder to the eyes.) Horseradish may also be stored by grating it directly into vinegar. White vinegar is best as red wine or cider vinegar will discolour the root.

Culinary Uses
Popular in Eastern and Northern Europe, in salads, soups and cheeses, horseradish is best known as a relish and the fresh root will enable you to create sauces far removed from the often harsh and vinegary commercial offerings. Mix grated horseradish with whipped cream, sour cream or yoghurt, adding salt and spices as desired. This can accompany roast beef, grilled fish and cold meats, or top baked potatoes and open sandwiches, or form a tasty dip. Try a mild sauce with asparagus—popular in Germany—with smoked eel or trout, or rye bread and *pastrami*. A sharper flavour is produced

cal	87	Ca	140	A	—
pro	3.2	P	64	B_1	0.07
fat	0.3	Fe	1.4	B_2	—
car	20	Na	8	B_5	—
fib	2.4	K	564	C	80–300

Recipe:
Smoked Fish Platter with
Horseradish Sauce, page 181

by adding vinegar or lemon juice to the creamy horseradish preparation and this, blended with a hot béchamel sauce, makes a traditional accompaniment to boiled beef. Blended with butter and chilled it makes a refreshing change from garlic butter to accompany grilled steak.

Herbal Properties
Horseradish is diaphoretic, digestive, diuretic and stimulant. In Gerard's time it was considered anthelmintic, emollient, abortifacient and a remedy for 'strangulrie' (hernia). Modern research has demonstrated its antimicrobial activity against certain micro-organisms.

Facts and Features
Its origin is more or less guesswork but believed to be southeast Europe and/or Asia Minor. Like mustard its pungency is dependent on the interaction of substances locked up in separate cells until these are ruptured in the presence of water. The substances involved are the glucoside sinigrin and the enzyme myrosin which with water yield allyl mustard oil. As a plant, horseradish is almost a horticultural pest with its notorious propensity for revival and multiplication. The minutest root particle left in the ground will grow and thrive. Japanese horseradish, or *wasabi* as it is named in its powdered form, is *Wasabia japonica*, while Indian horseradish comes from the tree *Moringa oleifera*, drumstick (see page 54).

JACKFRUIT
India

Often confused with breadfruit (see page 25) the jackfruit is much larger, sometimes measuring 1m (3ft) long, and weighing up to 40kg (90lb). It is is the largest cultivated fruit. The comparatively small ones weigh 8kg (17½lb). The shape is irregular—oval or oblong—the green skin ripening to brown, densely studded with hexagonal spines. The fruit contains up to 500 large white triangular seeds up to 4cm (1½in) long, each in a pocket of succulent flesh (aril) that has a curious pungent aroma, musty and sweet. The flavour of the seed pocket is compared with banana, pineapple and peach. Its colour is a pleasantly soft orange or yellow. The fibrous flesh holding the covers is white or yellow and similar to that of breadfruit.

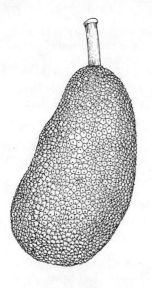

Artocarpus heterophyllus
syn *A. integra, A.
integrifolia*

Fam Moraceae

Jack, Jak, Jakfruit

*China: bo lo muk; India: ka(n)thal,
phanas; Indonesia: nan(g)ka;
Malaysia: chakka, nangka;
Portugal: jaca; Thailand: kanoon,
kha-nun; West Indies: chataigne
coolie, jac jaca, jackfruit, monkey
apple*

Nutritional Values
*Jackfruit is high in carbohydrates and
contains several minerals but hardly
any vitamins.*

Raw:

cal	98	Ca	22	A	—
pro	1.3	P	38	B_1	0.03
fat	0.3	Fe	—	B_2	—
car	25.4	Na	2	B_5	0.4
fib	1	K	407	C	8

Selecting the Best
Jackfruit are available intermittently from Asian food shops, imported from East Africa or South America. Seek advice as to the ripeness of the fruit as this, like the size, varies enormously and will dictate how you may use it. As a guide, a strong aroma is emitted from the ripe fruit.

Storage and Preparation
Keep in a cool place. It is sometimes a problem to know how to attack the more forbidding-looking fruits. Circumspection is often in order, as a highly staining and sticky juice exudes from the skin. To obviate this, rub the knife and your fingers with oil before preparation. The skin is always discarded. The young peeled fruit is cut up, nuts included, for cooking or separated into flesh, arils and nuts. The flesh and arils are eaten raw or cooked according to ripeness but the nuts must be boiled and the water discarded before roasting or otherwise.

Culinary Uses
Jackfruit is eaten mostly in South America, the Caribbean, India, Indonesia and Thailand, either raw as a fruit or cooked as a vegetable or sweetmeat. The juicy fresh arils from mature jackfruit are highly prized as a snack in Indonesia and we found them delicious. Peeled, tender fruits are sliced and curried and regarded as a meat substitute in India. Pickles and *poppadums* are made from the flesh; the arils are pounded to a paste with coconut, rice, sugar and cardamom and steamed in banana skins to make a delectable sweet. In Indonesia and the West Indies jackfruit is teamed with crab or chicken. The seeds are roasted like chestnuts and mashed or ground for various Sri Lankan and Indian recipes. A Thai recipe calls for a jackfruit, sliced lengthways, seeds removed and the pockets filled with ice-cream—an exotic feast.

Herbal Properties
The leaves provide a remedy for various skin diseases and a snake-bite antidote.

Facts and Features
Probably native to India, the jackfruit grows in various climatic regions, notably the wet tropics. It is cultivated most extensively in Southeast Asia, almost as a staple, also in Indochina and the South Pacific.

JICAMA (YAM BEAN)

Central America

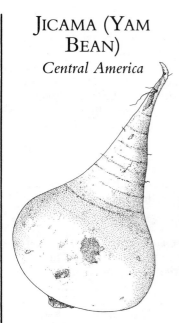

Pachyrrhizus erosus
syn *Dolichos erosus, D. bulbosus, P. angulatus, P. bulbosus*

Fam Leguminosae

Chopsuey Potato, Manioc Pea

Burma: pre-myit; China: saa got, sha kot (sand creeper), fan ko; India: s(h)a(n)kalu; Indonesia: bangkoowang, bangkuang, beeto(k), besoosoo, hooi heeris, tani uttan kai (Tamil); Malaysia: bengkuang, (kachang/ubi) sengkuang; Mexico: jicama (de agua); Philippines: bunga, frijol ñame, sinkamas; Polynesia: (wa)yaka; South America: ajipa, nupe(ra), xiquima; West Indies: jicama, patate-cochon

The jicama could be described as an underground fruit disguised in vegetable clothing. It is a large juicy tuber, shaped rather like a spinning top though some varieties are cloven into four segments. In British shops jicamas may vary between 10–15cm (4–6in) in diameter, and have a light-brown, thin, papery covering over a tougher creamy skin. The base has a fibrous root and the top a pointed remnant of stalk. The flesh is moist and ivory-coloured but does not oxidise in air. The texture is crisp and juicy, like an apple, and there is a slightly fruity flavour, faintly reminiscent of a pear. The jicama should prove to be a most rewarding discovery.

Selecting the Best
Jicamas are found in Chinese food shops. Pick firm ones about the size of a large turnip when they are young and tender.

Storage and Preparation
In a cool place jicamas stay fresh for up to a week. If only part of the tuber is required the remainder will not discolour or deteriorate, if wrapped, in the salad drawer. Cut off the slightly fibrous base and remove the papery skin and inner peel with a knife or by hand. This peel is always discarded. The flesh is simple to slice, shred or grate as desired.

Culinary Uses
Jicamas are popular in South America, the West Indies and, especially, in Mexico. Highly adaptable vegetable-fruits, they make an excellent addition to salads of either kind, their crisp and juicy texture more than compensating for any insignificance of flavour. In Mexico a traditional and highly recommended way to serve them is cut into small squares and speared onto toothpicks with a squeeze of lime and a shake of salt and chilli powder. They are grated and made into sweets with coconut, and may even be treated like potatoes. However, this latter method, although agreeable, does not do justice to jicamas' special qualities. They are favoured in Chinese cookery, as they retain their characteristic crispness when stir-fried; try substituting jicamas for water chestnuts or bamboo shoots. In Nyonya cookery—a blend of Chinese and Malay—they are a major ingredient of spring rolls.

Nutritional Values
Jicama tubers are a starch and sugar source with the equivalent vitamin C content of the common potato. They are generally considered a highly nutritious vegetable.

cal	40–45	Ca	15–20	A	0–trace
pro	1.2	P	16	B_1	0.4
fat	0.2	Fe	0.4–1.1	B_2	0.03
car	9.5–12.8	Na	—	B_5	0.2–0.8
fib	0.7	K	—	C	14–23

Recipes:
Jicama Salad, page 194; Jicama Sweetmeats, page 210

Herbal Properties
The young tuber has no special properties but as it matures it grows very starchy and a glycoside develops. The roots and mature seeds contain rotentone and coumarin and are toxic, insecticidal, laxative and anthelmintic, but very dangerous in uncontrolled doses. In Java, powdered seeds are used for skin problems such as prickly heat.

Facts and Features
The yam bean or jicama is neither a yam nor a bean. This name derives from the fact that the climbing plant is of the bean family and has a swollen root somewhat like a yam. It is indigenous to Mexico and Central America and is now distributed throughout the world. The Spaniards took it to the Philippines from where it crossed to China and the rest of tropical and sub-tropical Asia, though a none too wet climate is preferred. Young pods are sometimes eaten but mature ones are poisonous. There is another yam bean, also called the potato bean, *Pachyrrhizus tuberosus*, whose tuber is larger and whose pods and seeds are toxic. It is limited to South America and the Caribbean. *Pachyrrhizus* is Latin for 'thick root'.

KIWIFRUIT
China

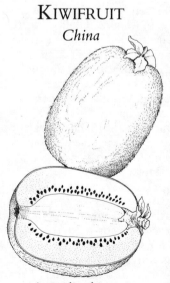

Actinidia chinensis
Fam Actinidaceae

Kiwifruit are now a common sight on fruit stalls. The rounded oblong fruits, about duck-egg size, are a browny-green with short hairs and when cut in half reveal a beautiful arrangement of colours. The cream core is surrounded radially with little black seeds which merge into the main ring of bright emerald-green juicy flesh. The whole fruit has a faint aroma and when cut there is quite a tantalising hint of banana and gooseberry; the flesh has a gentle aftertaste of grape or strawberry acidity. The seeds give the luscious flesh an attractive crunchy effect. The skin is papery and best discarded, or used as a meat tenderiser (see Culinary Uses).

Selecting the Best
Kiwifruit are now available all the year round. Buy when still firm and unblemished but if required immediately they should yield slightly when gently pressed. Sliced kiwis are also available in cans or freeze dried.

Chinese Gooseberry, Kiwi, Kiwiberry, Kiwi Fruit

China: yang tao; France: groseille chinoise, kiwifruit, le kiwi, souris végétale (vegetable mouse); Germany: Chinesische Stachelbeere, Kiwifrucht; Italy: frutta di kiwi, uva spina di Cina; Spain: fruta di kiwi, grosella chino

Nutritional Values
Kiwis are very rich in vitamin C, having twice as much as lemons.

cal	56	Ca	37	A	—
pro	1	P	23	B_1	—
fat	0	Fe	0.9	B_2	—
car	12	Na	9.5	B_5	
fib	—	K	340	C	105

Recipes:
Ma Ho, page 204

Storage and Preparation
In cool storage, kiwifruit keep for as long as 6 months, so unripe fruit may safely be bought well in advance. To speed up ripening, place kiwis with a banana in a polythene bag in a drawer until they are slightly soft to the touch. Although the skin is edible, generally speaking the fruit is peeled with a sharp knife or peeler and either thinly sliced across for a really pretty effect or cut lengthways into wedges. Even simpler, halve the fruit across and scoop out the flesh with a teaspoon. It is worth noting that the fruit does not spoil or discolour if prepared in advance. Puréed kiwi with a touch of sugar and lemon juice will keep for 3 days in the refrigerator. Try not to crush the seeds as they become rather bitter. If raw kiwifruit is to be combined with gelatine you must use a vegetable setting agent such as agar-agar as the fruit contains an enzyme which will cause the gelatine to break down.

Culinary Uses
Because of their attractive appearance, slices of kiwifruit are often used to decorate flans, cakes and puddings and are now as popular as passion fruit in the filling for a pavlova. They are an excellent addition to fruit salad, contrasting beautifully with any orange-coloured fruit. Of course they are delicious just eaten on their own or with a squeeze of lemon. Kiwifruit may also be made into ice-creams, sorbets, jams and pickles and go well with yoghurt and cream cheese. Kiwis also go well with meat and poultry and provide a cooling side dish to accompany hot curries. *Ma Ho* or Galloping Horses, the famous Thai snack, is usually made with tangerines but for a change try slices of kiwifruit. Last but not least, use the skins to tenderise a steak by laying them flesh side down on the meat for an hour or so before cooking, or, if you can afford it, use the puréed flesh.

Herbal Properties
Surprisingly, even the Chinese with their obsession with natural healing do not appear to have used *Actinidia chinensis* for anything, and it has been left to modern Europeans to discover that it contains the meat tenderising enzyme actinidin. Thus it is a good digestive and has laxative properties. The New Zealand Kiwifruit Authority says it is a source of proleolytic acid which serves to remove cholesterol and improves the circulation of the blood.

Facts and Features
The growth of the kiwifruit industry represents another example of the enterprise and determination of New Zealand's farmers to capture world markets. The boom years saw dairy farmers converting pasture to orchard and land prices more than doubled. The vine was prolific and profits rose in sympathy. Appropriately enough the Bay of Plenty area of the North Island is the main growing region. A liqueur based on kiwifruit is made and, not so amazingly in this day and age, a kiwi-flavoured toothpaste. Originally known as Chinese gooseberries, kiwis are indigenous to China but are not gooseberries and should not be confused with the carambola (see page 29) which is sometimes called by that name. To avoid McCarthy-inspired prohibitions in the USA of anything Chinese, New Zealand decided to shorten the name and make it eponymous. New Zealand may have a current monopoly of supply but countries such as France, Israel, Kenya, Italy and Spain are fast catching up and even southern England is trying its hand. The Chinese gooseberry was introduced to the West from the Yangtse valley in the early 1900s but its rapid growth as a commercial fruit occurred in the 1970s.

KOHLRABI
Europe

Kohlrabi is the swollen stem of a cabbage-type plant. It is typically round, about the size of a cricket ball or slightly smaller, pale green or purple with scars where the leaf stalks have been removed. Sometimes the stalks and leaves are left on, giving it an attractive appearance. The flesh is always white and crisp with a good, characteristic bouquet of brassica-style plants. Raw, the flavour is more like a sweet cabbage, the turnip association being purely in shape. Cooked, the flavour is rather more assertive.

Selecting the Best
Kohlrabis are quite widely available from greengrocers and supermarkets. Buy them as small as possible—Italians like them egg-sized. If the stems have been cut off, avoid kohlrabi with deep scars. If the leaves are still attached these should be fresh and green.

Brassica oleracea var
gongylodes
syn *B. caulorapa, B.o.* var
caulo-rapa communis

Fam Cruciferae

*Cabbage Turnip, Hungarian
Turnip, Knol-kohl, Stem Cabbage,
Turnip-rooted Cabbage*

*China: gaai laan tau, kaai lan tau;
France: chou-rave; Germany:
Kohlrabi; India: ganth gobhi; Italy:
cavolrapa*

Nutritional Values
*Kohlrabi's best feature is its vitamin
C content—it has more than citrus
fruits and three times more than that
of potatoes and tomatoes. Only a
third is lost in cooking. It is also a
reasonable source of minerals, calcium
and potassium. Composition values
vary between countries.*

Raw:

cal	25–30	Ca	20–50	A	10–36
pro	1–2	P	35–50	B₁	0.05
fat	0.2	Fe	0.4	B₂	0.07
car	3.8–6.6	Na	8–112	B₅	0.3
fib	1.2	K	37–490	C	60–85

Storage and Preparation
Refrigerate in a plastic bag, but not for more than
a couple of days. Trim off any stalks and leaves.
The stalks can be chopped and cooked with the
kohlrabi and the leaves cooked separately like
spinach. It is unnecessary to peel really tiny
kohlrabis but larger ones have a tough outer skin
which should be removed before or after
cooking. They are left whole, halved, quartered
or sliced as desired and are usually steamed,
boiled or par-boiled. They take 20–30 minutes to
cook.

Culinary Uses
Kohlrabi's popularity used to be confined to
Germany but has now spread as far as the United
States, India and China. Young kohlrabi is
enjoyable eaten raw in salads or as an appetiser.
Otherwise it is made into soup, served stuffed, *au
gratin*, in a cheese sauce or in any way you might
treat celeriac or turnip. It has an affinity with
basil. In India they like the leaves cooked and the
vegetable is often pickled.

Herbal Properties
Kohlrabi has no known properties.

Facts and Features
Kohlrabi has failed to gain much popularity in
Britain; it was only ever known as an animal feed
on any commercial scale, otherwise as an
occasional garden vegetable. The name derives
from German *kohl*, cabbage, and *rabi*, turnip. It is
a fine vegetable and well worth a place in the
garden, being easy to grow and frost resistant.
Sow in April–May in rows 40cm (15in) apart,
and thin out to about 20cm (8in). Water well and
weed as necessary. Harvest when 'bulbs' are
about the size of a cricket ball, the younger the
more tender and flavoursome. Old ones tend to
be hard.

KUCHAI (CHINESE CHIVES)
East and Southeast Asia

Allium tuberosum

Fam Alliaceae

Cantonese Onion, Chinese Leeks, Chinese Onion, Cuchay, Garlic Chives

China: gau tsoi, kau wong (blanched), kiu tsoi, nin fa, taai ip; India: bunga-gundeena; Indonesia: kucai; Japan: nira; Malaysia: kucai; Thailand: gutchai, kuchai

Nutritional Values
Used in larger quantities than ordinary chives, kuchai are low in calories but a helpful iron and vitamins B_2 and B_5 source.

cal	17	Ca	10–55	A	550
pro	2.2	P	9–41	B_1	0.03–0.06
fat	0.4	Fe	0.5–1.1	B_2	0.05–0.13
car	2.6	Na		B_5	0.4–1
fib	0.6	K		C	9–15

Recipe:
Chinese Chive Knots, page 203

Strikingly long, kuchai or Chinese chives are sold in two forms—bunches of leaves or bunches of the flowering stems. The leaves are about 40cm (15in) long and 8mm (⅓in) wide, flat or slightly cusped, and are mid-green with faint ridges. They are coarser than ordinary chives. The flavour varies from mild onion to strongish garlic. The flowering version is slightly longer, the stem being solid and angular. The flowers are usually unopened and are similar in flavour to the leaves but far more attractive in appearance. Blanched chives are sometimes available in Chinese shops.

Selecting the Best
Oriental food shops stock kuchai and they are occasionally to be seen in the more enterprising supermarkets. They come tied in quite large bunches weighing about 115g (4oz) as they are used not only as a garnish but as a vegetable as well. The leaves should be a good green, dry and not flabby.

Storage and Preparation
Kept quite dry, wrapped in paper in the salad drawer, they should keep for a couple of days after which they will rapidly deteriorate. Wash and dry them before preparation. Finely chop for garnishing like ordinary chives; in oriental cookery they are usually cut into 4–5cm (1½–2in) lengths and briefly cooked.

Culinary Uses
Kuchai have a stronger and more garlicky taste than ordinary chives and therefore will add extra flavour to Western-style dishes. They are particularly good in salads, scrambled eggs and as a garnish for potatoes. In China, Southeast Asia and Japan they are enjoyed cooked in soups, noodle dishes, and with meat and shellfish. An especially interesting Chinese snack is made by binding a number of leaves into knots or bundles, coating these in batter and deep-frying them—delicious with plum or *hoisin* sauce. A reputedly healthful dish, and a very pretty contrast of white and green, is achieved by stir-frying bean sprouts and kuchai together. Use four times the amount of bean sprouts and cut the kuchai to the same length as the bean sprouts. Spring onion tops are a reasonable substitute for kuchai.

Herbal Properties
With its garlicky flavour kuchai contains compounds similar to those of garlic and will have comparable properties (see page 70).

Facts and Features
Kuchai or Chinese chives have been grown in the Far East for centuries and are probably native to that region. They grow in dense clumps and are propagated either by seed or by dividing existing clumps. The Chinese prefer them blanched and achieve this in various ways with pots, tiles and mats to exclude sunlight. The Japanese eat the flower heads salted.

KUMQUAT
China

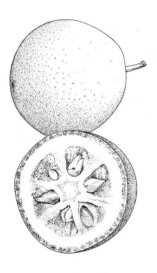

Fortunella japonica (round kumquat)
syn *Citrus japonica*
F. margarita (oval kumquat)
syn *C. margarita*

Fam Rutaceae

Cam-quit, Cumquat, Hedge Lime

China: gum quot, jin jiu, kam quat, kum quat; France: chinois, koumquat; Germany: Geldorange, Japanisch Orange, Kleinfruchtige; Italy: kumquat; Japan: kinkan;

Once, understandably, thought to be related to the orange, kumquats are not in fact citrus fruit but of a different species. These small fruits have plenty of orange characteristics, but not their size—they are only 2–5cm (¾–2in) across. They are orange in colour often with a green sun-starved patch. The thin shiny skin has those little pits which give citrus fruits their roughness, and the flesh is segmented. There are often several seeds crowding the flesh, yet you eat the whole fruit: everything. The commonest variety is 'Nagami' (*F. margarita*), with oval, orange fruit, 2.5×4cm (1×1½in). In flavour the kumquat packs the whole citrus spectrum into its tiny package—the sweetness of tangerine, the sharpness of lemon and grapefruit and the bitterness of sevilles. The round variety 'Marumi' (*F. japonica*), also appearing in UK shops, is orange, about 2.5cm (1in) in diameter, and quite sweet, but its pips are best discarded.

Selecting the Best
Available nearly all year from specialist greengrocers and supermarkets, kumquats should be full, firm and shiny. Greenish ones will ripen at home.

Storage and Preparation
At room temperature kumquats will keep for a few days. Otherwise store in the refrigerator for about a week. For using raw, remove stems, wash and slice across or lengthways. Remove seeds if desired.

Culinary Uses
Some maintain that the kumquat is best

Malaysia: *limau pagar*; Spain: *naranja Japonesa*; West Indies: *kumquat, kumkwat*

Nutritional Values
Kumquats are almost as good a source of vitamin C as oranges.

Whole raw fruit:

cal	65	Ca	33	A	20
pro	0.9	P	41	B₁	0.06
fat	0.1	Fe	0.3	B₂	0.03
car	5.3	Na	6	B₅	0.2
fib	1	K	260	C	43

Recipe:
Kumquat Preserve, page 210

consumed raw. Others affirm that it is best preserved, as the many recipes for pickles, marmalades and candy attest. Certainly, sweet-spice pickling mixtures call forth its piquancy, and as a relish it can quite comfortably accompany many meats and fowls. Seafood will perk up upon the addition of a few wedges. As sweets kumquats can be bathed in caramel and cream, dipped in fondant as *petits-fours*, or go into a flan with honey and liqueur. More elaborate recipes occur periodically in the glossy magazines. If you fancy them with alcohol, vodka is the appropriate poison.

Herbal Properties
No special properties are recognised for kumquats.

Facts and Features
Native to China, the fruit was known in Renaissance Europe but was not widely used. The name derives from Cantonese *kam quat*, 'gold orange'. It is now cultivated in Japan, Malaysia, Israel, East Africa, Australia and the US. All varieties make good pot plants, which are important for the Chinese New Year. The kumquat has recently been successfully crossed with citrus fruits, resulting in the citrangequat, the limequat and the orangequat. The calamondin is a natural kumquat hybrid of Chinese origin, extensively used in the Philippines (where it is known as calamonding) in place of limes and lemons.

LEMON GRASS
Southeast Asia

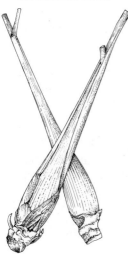

Cymbopogon citratus
syn *Andropogon citratus,*
A. schoenanthus

Fam Gramineae

Camel's Hay, Citronella (Grass),
Fever Grass, Geranium Grass, Oil
Plant, Sereh

Burma: sabalin; China: heung maau
tso (fragrant thatch grass); France:
herbe de citron, jonc odorant;
Germany: Zitronengras; India:
bhustrina, ghandhtrina, herva chaha,
sera; Indonesia: serai, sere(e),
sere(h); Italy: cimbopogone, erba di
limone; Laos: bai mak nao;
Malaysia: serai, sere betool, sere(h)
(makan), sere sayoor; Philippines:
tanglad; Spain: hierba de limon; Sri
Lanka: sera; Thailand: takrai

Nutritional Values
It is only as a flavouring that lemon
grass is important since the rootstock
and leaves are seldom eaten in
Europe.

Recipes:
Tom Yam Soup, page 180

With an abundance of lemons and limes in Southeast Asia serving to give that region's food its characteristic flavour, we find lemon grass of equal importance. As its name implies, it is a lemon-perfumed grass. Thicker and more substantial than our familiar grasses, rising from a bulbous base it grows in tight bunches of leaves. These are cut off about 15–23cm (6–9in) and often sold in bundles. They are apt to be called 'lemonade glasses' in the more humorous oriental stores. The blades are quite crisp and dryish; buff with pinkish to red or purple and green tinges. The bouquet is sweet and lemony and the flavour similar, with gingerish undertones.

Selecting the Best
Fresh lemon grass is now available from time to time in some supermarkets, otherwise it is found in oriental speciality shops, in packs of three or more. Although the outside leaves are quite papery the stalks if fresh should show signs of greenness. The dried form is easier to obtain, but as a last resort use lemon peel.

Storage and Preparation
Wrap the stalks well as their flavour will penetrate other foods. They keep for 2 weeks or more in the salad drawer. However, as they are unlikely to be used regularly, it is a good idea to freeze them. Pull off the papery outside and trim the root. Usually recipes call for one or two stalks. The bottom 12cm (5in) is used and the rest discarded. For use as a flavouring for stocks and soups bruise the stalk with the flat of a large knife or cleaver. Leave whole and remove before serving. Otherwise finely slice the lemon grass across, or pound it in a pestle and mortar. It may be liquidised or processed together with other ingredients. Soak dried lemon grass for 2 hours before use—a tablespoon of pieces is equal to one fresh stalk.

Culinary Uses
Lemon grass is an essential flavouring in Southeast Asian cookery and important too in Sri Lanka and south India. Also abundant in these regions are coconut, chillies, limes and members of the ginger family and it is with these that lemon grass is most often combined. Its distinctive lemony fragrance typifies a profusion of savoury dishes including soups (especially the legendary *tom yam* from Thailand), salads, grills

and curries. It is often used in the form of marinades and curry pastes and is included in sauces and pickles. Rice cooked in coconut milk instead of water with a stem of lemon grass is an agreeable variation as a curry accompaniment. Like ginger, lemon grass is a 'de-fisher' and is important in fish dishes for this reason as well as for its spicy delicacy. In India it is infused in the water in which dhal has been boiled for a hot drink or soup and in Java the heart of the stem is eaten raw to accompany the rice table.

Herbal Properties
Lemon grass contains the volatile oils citral and geraniol, and as an infusion is carminative, diaphoretic, stimulant, refrigerant, diuretic and stomachic. It is mildly insect-repellent and is common in modern lotions, sprays, balms and candles manufactured for this purpose. Queen Victoria enjoyed lemon grass tea, which is also helpful for children's stomach upsets. In India, in paste form or oil, it is applied on ringworm. It has many further properties utilised in folk medicines of Asia. Fresh lemon grass will revive a fainting person if held under the nose.

Facts and Features
Lemon grass is widely grown in tropical Asia and has spread to Africa and America. It rarely flowers, being propagated by root division. In Indonesia the finding of a flower brings such good fortune that it must be kept secret otherwise it invites rapid theft. Citral oil is extracted on a commercial scale from lemon grass and is an important raw material in the soap and perfume industries. It is possible to grow lemon grass in Europe. Pick out some stems with roots attached and allow these to grow in water. Plant outdoors in the summer and pot indoors in the winter, and with luck they will survive.

LIME
East Indies, Northern India

Citrus aurantifolia
syn *C. acida, C. limetta,*
Limonia aurantifolia
C. hystrix (wild or kaffir
lime)

Fam Rutaceae

Adam's Apple, Bartender's Lime,
Key Lime, Mexican Lime, Sour
Lime; Porcupine Orange (wild or
kaffir lime)

France: lime, limette, limon;
Germany: Limette, Limon; India:
leboo, neboo, nimboo; Indonesia:
dehi (Tamil), djerook neepis,
djerook petjel (all common lime);
djerook pooroot, keruk lima (both
wild lime); Italy: cedro, lima,
limetta; Japan: rime; Malaysia:
djerook teepis, limau kesturi, limau
nipis (all common lime); djerook
pooroot, limau purut (both wild
lime); Philippines: calamansi,
dayap; Spain: lima; Thailand:
manao (common lime); magrut,
makrut (both wild lime); West
Indies: citron, lime

Both the fruit and leaves of the lime are used in cooking. Limes are like small lemons, but rounder and usually lacking the little nipple. Commonly there are two kinds available—the larger West Indian type, green and about 5cm (2in), snooker ball size, and Indian which are yellow and about 4cm (1½in), squash ball size or smaller. All limes ripen to yellow. The peel is thin and the flesh in good varieties is firm, juicy and pale green, even when the skin is yellow. Seedless varieties exist although others can be very seedy. The juice radiates a fresh spicy aroma; it is sour but subtly different from lemon. Lime leaves, from a different citrus tree, *C. hystrix*, are easy to identify as they come in pairs joined lengthways. They are dark green on the upperside, paler underneath. They emit an aromatic fragrance, especially when crushed. The fruit of this tree has a rough, warty skin, and is used for its zest and juice; it is not yet seen in Britain.

Selecting the Best
Limes should be available all year. For Caribbean limes, select large smooth-skinned, deep-green fruit and avoid those that appear dry or wizened. Small Indian limes are usually yellow; again, reject shrivelled ones. Lime leaves should be clean, bright and only slightly curled.

Storage and Preparation
Limes stay healthy under refrigeration for up to 8 weeks. The fruit can be used as an alternative to lemon—indeed, it often takes preference in the tropics. Use two-thirds the amount specified for lemon juice. Tip: warm the lime and roll firmly on a table-top a few times before pressing or squeezing—this yields the maximum amount of juice. Use a lemon zester, potato peeler or grater to pare the rind or zest. A lovely garnish, lime can be cut in wedges or fluted slices and twists. Small Indian pickling limes are washed and either cut into slices or quartered without severing them right through. Lime leaves should be used as soon as possible, whole or broken, and with discretion as they are very pungent.

Culinary Uses
Lime is used to heighten the flavour of tropical fruit—banana, avocado, melon and so on—and in sorbets, pickles, jellies, sauces for puddings, mousses, and drinks, such as lime julep. Squeeze

Nutritional Values

Like all citrus fruits, limes are a good source of vitamin C. There are no data for lime leaves.

Raw fruit:

cal	30	Ca 30	A 10
pro	0.6	P 18	B₁ 0.03
fat	0.2–1.4	Fe 0.5	B₂ 0.02
car	8	Na 2	B₅ 0.2
fib	0.4	K 102	C 40

Recipes:

Lime Sambal, page 207; Salted Limes, page 208; Tom Yam Soup, page 180

over vegetables—like lemon juice, lime prevents discoloration—and use in iced tea. Whip it up with eggs and cream. Lime perks up a vinaigrette and adds spice to white meats. It has a curious 'cooking' action on thin fillets or cubes of fish: in the South American dish *seviche* the fish is 'cold poached' in lime juice and topped with a vinegared mixture of tomatoes, peppers and onions. In Southeast Asian cookery, limes are very important indeed, the juice often teamed with coconut, ginger and lemon grass. It is in this region that the wild or kaffir lime is used for its zest and strongly aromatic leaves; distinctive in Thai cookery it appears in soups, *sambals* and fish and meat dishes. Fresh Indian limes are much appreciated in the Middle East where they are also used dried, to invigorate stews, or dried and powdered as a spice. In Indian cookery they have an important place, not least salted and used in pickles and side dishes.

Herbal Properties

All parts of the tree are used in African folk medicine: the leaves are said to cure fever, eye complaints and gonorrhoea; the roots are eaten to relieve headache and expel worms; the fruit juice is taken for dysentery, and used as eye drops and as an antiseptic for sores and lice. The rind is carminative and stomachic.

Facts and Features

Native to the East Indies, the lime was first spread by the Arabs, who gave us the name *limah*, and brought to Europe by the Crusaders, eventually reaching the New World. Israel, Mexico, Egypt and America are leading producers. The lime is the least hardy and most tropically inclined member of the citrus family, and is unusual in that it can grow easily from seed. The well-known nickname 'limeys' for the British refers to their historic practice of carrying plenty of lime juice aboard sailing ships to prevent scurvy; the juice was given to the sailors with its edge taken off by a liberal admixture of grog. Lime oil, extracted from the skins, is a commercial by-product. Main types are the sweet lime (West Indies and Central America), key lime or Mexican lime (Florida), Bearss or Persian, an especially fragrant variety (Tahiti), and the tangerine-like Rangpur from India.

LONGAN
India

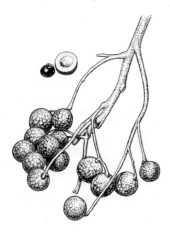

Nephelium longana
syn *Dimocarpus longan*,
Euphoria longan, *Scytalia
longan*

Fam Sapindaceae

Dragon's Eye, Lungan

China: *longan, loong gnahn,
lungan, lung ngan, lung yen*; India:
anshphal, ashphul

Nutritional Values
*Except for being very poor in
vitamin C, longan has a similar
biochemical mixture to lychee.*

cal	61	Ca	10	A	—
pro	1	P	42	B_1	—
fat	0.1	Fe	1.2	B_2	—
car	15.8	Na	—	B_5	—
fib	0.4	K	—	C	(6)

These oriental fruits are from the same group as lychees and rambutans. They are round, some 2.5cm (1in) across, with a brown or sometimes yellow or reddish skin; there are many tiny 'goosebumps' making it rough to the touch. This thin, brittle shell easily splits to disclose the semitranslucent flesh, grey-white, sweet and apparently dry but which is quite juicy when broken. Grape-like in flavour though drier in texture, it embraces a sizeable, shiny dark-brown stone.

Selecting the Best
Longans are available during the summer from oriental stores. They are often sold on the branch. They ought to be firm and should not be split.

Storage and Preparation
They are ready to eat when the skin is near the splitting stage. Try to store without the fruits touching one another.

Culinary Uses
Longan is said to be an acquired taste for those unused to tropical fruit; some consider it superior to the lychee, if more aromatic. The fruit can be used like the lychee, and is available canned in syrup, and dried. The longan may be one of the few fruits to improve on canning—the processed product is widely praised. Frankly, it is a waste to use fruit like this in elaborate recipes. Either enjoy it on its own or perhaps in a salad with other fruit of equally delicate flavour. Dried longans are used in Chinese slow-cooked soups and poultry dishes.

Herbal Properties
In China, the longan's flesh (aril) is used to treat nervous breakdown and insomnia; the seed kernel is styptic.

Facts and Features
Native to India, the longan is widely cultivated in China and some parts of the tropics, but is not so common in Europe. Called in China 'lychee's little brother' it is indeed a relative, like the rambutan, but far sweeter. Also hardier, it is capable of cultivation over a larger climatic area.

LOQUAT
China

Eriobotrya japonica

Fam Rosaceae

*Japanese Medlar, Japanese Plum,
Lurquart, Nispero*

*China: lu kwyit, pei pa, pi pa;
France: bibasse, nèfle du Japon;
Italy: nespola giapponese; Japan:
biwa; West Indies: nespola
giapponese (Cuba)*

Nutritional Values
*Though pleasant to eat, the loquat
has little nutritional value.*

cal	87	Ca	20	A	670
pro	0.4	P	36	B_1	—
fat	0.2	Fe	0.4	B_2	—
car	12.4	Na	—	B_5	—
fib	0.5	K	350	C	1

Recipe:
*Pigeon with Almond Loquats, page
189*

The delicious loquat or Japanese medlar is a
relative newcomer to British markets and shops.
The apricot is the nearest familiar fruit in shape,
colour and size. Loquats are round or slightly
egg-shaped, yellow to orange and about 5cm
(2in) in diameter. They have a downy coat, a lot
of which gets rubbed off in transport. Their
yellow to apricot flesh is firm, juicy, lightly acid
and sweet smelling. The flavour varies from
mildly sweet to quite sweet and aromatic,
depending on quality, cultivar and ripeness—the
riper the fruit the sweeter it is. Embedded in the
flesh are one to five large, smooth, shiny-brown
seeds which are inedible.

Selecting the Best
Look for robustly-coloured fruit and try to avoid
blemished specimens which, unfortunately, are
quite common. Loquats come to market in spring
and throughout the summer.

Storage and Preparation
Once ripe eat immediately. The thin skin is
somewhat tough and is easily peeled if desired.
Cut along the fruit to remove the stones and their
papery jacket, the latter being fairly fibrous. For
stewed or poached loquats it is better to peel
them after cooking.

Culinary Uses
Perhaps at their best when eaten raw on their
own or in fruit salads, loquats are also delicious
lightly poached in syrup with lemon or lime
juice, particularly if a few stones are added to the
pan. These will give a subtle almondy
flavour—remove them before serving. Jams,
tarts, candies and jellies are among the
commonest recipes, and you can happily
submerge loquats for several months in a sweet
spice pickling mixture, treating them like
apricots, for use with meats and savouries. .
Loquats may be mixed with lychees and jellied
bean curd for a refreshing dessert. They go
surprisingly well with chicken, hot or cold,
where ginger is a curious catalyst. Most exotic of
all is a recipe from the Sichuan region of China
where minced breasts of pigeon in a hot, spicy
sauce are scattered with fried pine nuts and
garnished with loquats filled with almond cream.

Herbal Properties
The fruit itself is not used in folk medicine but

the leaves are used as an expectorant and in cough remedies. The seeds are mildly poisonous.

Facts and Features
Indigenous to China, from where it spread to Japan, the loquat is happy at high altitudes in the tropics or in the low sub-tropics. The name comes from the Chinese *lu-kwyit*, and the botanic name *Eriobotrya* from the Greek 'wool cluster', deriving from the appearance of the downy fruit. A garden tree, the loquat however thrives best under plantation conditions, and is being cultivated in India, Africa, America, Australia and the Mediterranean. Like many exotica the loquat reached Europe in the late eighteenth century.

LOTUS ROOT
Asia

Nelumbo nucifera
syn *Nelumbian nelumbo*,
Nelumbian speciosum

Fam Nymphaeaceae

Chinese Water Lily, Hindu Lotus, Indian Lotus, Jamaica Water Lily, Lotos, Pink Water Lily, Sacred Lotus

China: leen ngow, lien ngo, lin ngau; France: lotos, lotus; Germany: Agyptische bohne, Lotos, Nilli Lili;

The underwater roots of the lotus have been likened to a link of long fat sausages. They are also recognisable by the cavities that run their length. These are usually visible in the market as the roots are often cut off revealing holes like a mincing machine cutter—typical of the pieces obtainable canned, dried or in Chinese restaurants. The root segments vary considerably in size from 13–30cm (5–12in) in length, and 5–8cm (2–3in) in diameter. Some are cleaned, others are covered in dried mud. The thin skin is quite tough, buff to pink; the flesh varies from white to pink to orangey depending on age and growing conditions. It is mucilaginous but fibrous in old roots. The constrictions between the roots often bear remnants of leaf shoots. Young tender roots are delicate, sweet and bland with crunchy white flesh, and a sweet aroma. Older ones, tinged pink or darker, are less tender.

Selecting the Best
Lotus roots are available from Chinese stores in the summer. It is difficult to tell young roots from old without cutting them open—young flesh is white, old pinkish—so it is wise to ask the shopkeeper. Choose unblemished roots carefully as if the skin is broken it is difficult to clean out the dirt. Dried slices are also available in Chinese shops.

Storage and Preparation
They will keep for up to 3 weeks in the salad crisper. Scrub very dirty roots before peeling off the skin with a knife or potato peeler and cutting off the ends. Have ready a bowl of acidulated

India: ambuj, bh(i)en, kakadi, kamal, kanwal, kaval, kumala, padam, padma, pamposh, pankaja, suriyakamal; Indonesia: ambal (Tamil), t(a)rate, thamarai (Tamil); Iran: nilufu; Italy: giglio de Nilo, loto, ninfea d'Egetto; Japan: hasu-n-ne, renkon; Malaysia: patma, senthama, tarate, thamara; Philippines: baino; Spain: loto, ninfea; Thailand: bua luang, dok bua, hua bua, rarg bua

Nutritional Values

Lotus root is rich in starch—in China a flour called nagau fan *is made from it. It is a useful source of vitamin C; Indian varieties are rich in vitamin B₅, but are correspondingly poorer in the former.*

cal 42–82	Ca 19–27	A 0–33
pro 1–1.7	P 55	B₁ 0.09–0.22
fat 0.1	Fe 0.5	B₂ 0.04–0.11
car 10–20	Na	B₅ 0.4–2.1
fib 0.8	K	C 15–31

Recipe:

Tempura, page 182

water in which to put the prepared root as it rapidly discolours. It is sometimes sliced across thinly into 1.5–3mm (1/16–1/8in) rounds or ovals; often halved lengthways and cut into slivers; cut into chunks; or more rarely, left whole. Cooking times vary enormously depending on the age of the vegetable. A minute's blanching is sufficient for some, others may take more than 2 hours, but the lotus root's characteristic crunchiness is always retained. Tough roots are usually pre-cooked. Dried slices should be soaked for at least 30 minutes in hot water with a squeeze of lemon juice before cooking.

Culinary Uses

No less exotic than its legendary flower, lotus root variously appears in Chinese, Japanese, Korean, Vietnamese, Nyonyan and Indian cookery. In the Chinese style it is stir-fried with beef, slowly braised with pork or made into sustaining soups, as it will readily absorb more resolute flavours. On special occasions the whole root is steamed, stuffed with rice or seasoned mung beans. Slices first sautéed in oil then briefly simmered in lemon juice and water make a Japanese delicacy. As an ingredient of *tempura*, lotus root slices add a touch of glamour. Indian mixed pickles often contain them, and slices are pickled on their own in mustard oil with turmeric, mustard seeds and chillies. In the Punjab and Kashmir regions lotus root is first cooked, then mashed and formed into spicy meatless balls. However, as its appearance is surely lotus root's most attractive feature it seems a pity not to display it to advantage. Cooked simply like potato crisps and sprinkled with salt it will prove a puzzle to the uninitiated as well as a decorative snack.

Herbal Properties

Being a sacred plant and symbolic of birth, life and death, every part of the lotus is used in folk medicine. In India the root is used as a remedy for piles, indigestion and diarrhoea, as a diuretic and bile promoter, and to cure ringworm and other skin problems. In China it is used to stop bleeding and excess mucous secretions, to cure colic and similar troubles in children, and as a blood tonic.

Facts and Features

Indigenous to Asia, the Indian lotus has been cultivated since antiquity. The plant was sacred to the Egyptians and is still holy and mystical in India, Japan and China. All its features of growth and shape are important symbols in these cultures. The flower represents the sun, much as our sunflower does, and its growth through water to reach light and air is symbolic in Buddhist tales of the soul's search for *nirvana*. The lotus position is an important pose in yoga and meditation. On a less ethereal plane, in China the bud represents the male organ and the blossom the female one. In India the sexual act is symbolised by the rising and opening of the flower. Unlike the common water-lily, lotus flowers do not float on the surface of water but grow above it. Lotus seeds are viable for long periods, some of a recorded age of 200 years successfully germinated when planted. The rhizome is also utilised in brewing and as a dyeing and tanning mordant.

LYCHEE
China

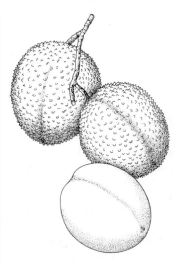

Litchi chinensis
syn *Nephelium litchi*,
Scytalia chinensis
Fam Sapindaceae

*Chinese Cherry, Lichee, Lichi,
Litchee, Litchi*

White succulent lychees are so familiar that it comes as somewhat of a surprise to learn that the fresh fruit is actually a bright red, warty affair quite different from the processed version. It has a thin, oval, brittle shell, rough in texture, about 4cm (1½in) in diameter. Inside is the supple, white, translucent flesh embracing a single, shiny-brown seed. Highly sugary and fragrant, the pulp becomes juicy on eating but starts off pleasantly dry. Sweet-sour varieties exist.

Selecting the Best
Fruits should be a good, bright rosy colour, full and firm, unbroken and not 'weeping'. Lychees are available all year but are likely to be scarce in late summer and autumn. The fruit is also available canned.

Storage and Preparation
Keep under refrigeration. If the fruit is properly ripe, breaking the skin with a fingernail will cause the flesh to pop out. Ripe fruit will freeze well for 3 months. Just put the whole unshelled fruit complete with stalks in a polythene bag in the freezer.

Culinary Uses
This fruit is most often used as a dessert—either fresh or canned, or with cream, fruit salads, sorbets or ice-cream. However, like most exotic and fine-flavoured fruit, the lychee can well be

China: la ee tzee, lai chi, li tze; Thailand: leenchee; West Indies: leechee (Cuba)

Nutritional Values
The lychee is a very good source of vitamin C.

Raw fruit:

cal	60	Ca	6	A	—
pro	0.8	P	40	B_1	—
fat	0.3	Fe	0.4	B_2	0.05
car	16	Na	3	B_5	—
fib	0.2	K	170	C	60

used as a breakfast fruit with cereals, or in Chinese sweet and sour dishes, and with hot meats. Chicken or duck salad improves wonderfully upon its introduction, dressed with soy sauce and Chinese sesame oil. It can go into, or indeed be stuffed with, a savoury salad based on cottage cheese, ginger and mayonnaise. As a sweet afterthought, you can marinade lychees overnight in brandy, and serve with ice-cream, whipped cream and pistachio nuts. Lychees also pickle and freeze well, tasting similar to the fresh fruit.

Herbal Properties
Lychee fruit is used in China as a cough relief, to stop diarrhoea and as a general tonic. Crushed seeds are prescribed to relieve stomach and intestinal pains and swollen testicles.

Facts and Features
Native to China, with a long history of oriental cultivation—especially in Thailand and the Philippines—the lychee now also thrives in India, Australia, New Zealand, Japan, South Africa and the US. The fruit grows on an attractive evergreen 10–12m (35–40ft) tall, with small greenish flowers descending in great panicles. It is closely related to the rambutan (see page 146) and the longan (see page 101).

MANGO
Indo-Burma

The luscious mango is justifiably called the 'King of Fruits'. Commonly round, oval or kidney-shaped, sometimes with a little beak at one end, mangoes can weigh up to 1kg (2lb) although they are usually lighter. All mangoes start life dark green, but ripen to yellow, orange, red, pink, purple or even black, often with a two-tone sunspot or blush. The different colours and shapes of the many varieties have given rise to a series of names whose main use appears to be to confuse your greengrocer: apple mango, banana mango, peach mango, strawberry mango etc. In all varieties the thin, strong skin is smooth but inedible. The flesh is naturally fibrous, but modern crossbreeds are increasingly smooth-textured and extremely juicy. Usually it is pale orange, sweet and flavoursome, somewhere along the 'peach-pineapple' axis. Inferior varieties are likely to be woody, turpentiny and disappointing. There is a large, flat, uneven stone tightly embedded in the flesh.

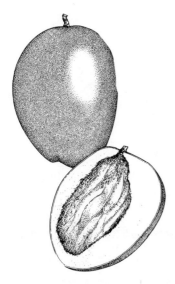

Mangifera indica
Fam Anacardiaceae

Indian Mango

China: *mon go;* France: *mangue;*
Germany: *Mango;* India: *a(a)m,*
amb, amra; Indonesia: *manggah,*
pao, pelem, poh; Italy: *mango;*
Malaysia: *mangga;* Spain: *mango,*
manguey; Thailand: *mamuang*

Nutritional Values
Mangoes are rich in vitamin A and
have significant amounts of vitamins
B and C. There is 10–20 per cent
sugar. Green mangoes are
particularly high in vitamin C, up to
130mg per 100g.

Ripe fruit:

cal	60	Ca	10	A	2–6,000
pro	0.6	P	13	B$_1$	0.05
fat	0.3	Fe	0.4	B$_2$	0.05
car	15	Na	7	B$_5$	1
fib	0.8	K	190	C	30–50

Recipes:
Hawaiian Nectar, page 212; Mango
Snow, page 200; Sticky Rice, page
201

These days you will find tiny—less than 5cm
(2in) in length—green mangoes in Indian shops.
These are used in pickling and curries.

Selecting the Best
Different varieties of mango are available all year
round. Choose those with shiny and unblemished
skins; they should be only slightly yielding.
Pickling mangoes, available from Asian shops
should be generally healthy looking.

Storage and Preparation
Mangoes will store in the cool, if firm, for several
weeks and the puréed flesh freezes well. Mangoes
are notoriously juicy, stoning is an art. To stone:
cut a thick slice lengthways down each side of the
stone, leaving a thin central slice containing the
stone. The flesh can be scooped out of the two
halves with a spoon and the central part peeled
and the flesh cut or bitten off the stone. In the
days of 'White Mischief' in 'Happy Valley',
Kenyan settlers believed the only way to eat
mangoes was in the bath. To purée: blend the
flesh in a liquidiser or processor until smooth. If
the flesh is fibrous, pass it through a sieve. For a
novel presentation: take a mango half and make
criss-cross cuts down to the skin but not cutting
through it. Now with both thumbs press the skin
upwards from underneath to produce a chequered
hillock.

Culinary Uses
Refrain from ruining this delicacy by
over-elaborate treatment. Since mangoes are
expensive, it is permissible to eke them further by
modest and discreet catering. They will go with
ice-cream, cream, cottage cheese and other dairy
produce. They can be made into ice-cream,
mousse and fruit drinks. Being very juicy, they
are ripe for fruit salads when mixed with other
fruits that might be of a drier texture. The fruit
can be candied or crystallised, and unripe ones are
dried and sliced or powdered (*amchur*) for use in
Indian cookery. In the West Indies they are used
like apples in baking, especially in tarts and
tartlets or even large pies. A favourite dish in
Thailand is sliced mango served with glutinous
rice cooked in coconut milk and perfumed with
pandanus leaves. Small green mangoes are made
into chutneys and spicy side dishes. They are
curried with mutton or on their own and are an
ingredient of *avial*, the vegetable curry from

Malabar. Grated green mango is used in Indian salads instead of lemon juice. In the West, ripe mangoes also have savoury uses such as being teamed with Parma ham as an appetiser or prepared in the chequered effect (see above) topped with crabmeat or prawns with a lemony dressing.

Herbal Properties
In India all parts of the mango tree are used in local medicine. The ripe fruit is antiscorbutic, astringent, diuretic, laxative and tonic.

Facts and Features
The fifteen species of mango have been under cultivation for some 4,000 years, hence their origin is indefinite, agreed to be somewhere in the India-Burma-Malaya area. Husbanded in India since 2000BC, the fruit was taken first to Africa and South America, then the West Indies and virtually everywhere else in the tropics and sub-tropics. India is the largest commercial producer and claims to grow the best ones—unsurprisingly, since the mango features in Hindu legend and mythology. Among the many parks and retreats presented to Buddhist monks during their founder's lifetime was a magnificent mango grove in Northern India. Possibly the largest tropical food crop in the world, the mango is comparable to the apple of the temperate West, growing wild everywhere as well as in cultivation, and is a summer staple in many parts. Early windfalls go to make chutney and the leaves are used as salad. Harvesters have to be careful of the burning sap in the stalks.

MANGOSTEEN
Malaysia

Unattractive on the outside, this fruit contains an inner bonanza of unsurpassed flavour. The mangosteen is spherical, up to 8cm (3in) in diameter. The outer skin is thick and leathery, but brittle and crusty, a rich dirty purple colour with spots and blemishes, and a generally rugged appearance. The knobbly top is formed by four pronounced persistent sepals, which are light green, and a thick green stalk. Within is a thick matted layer of pink pith, enclosing the beautiful flesh, translucent and waxy white, divided into five to seven glossy segments, some containing a large flat seed or the beginnings of one. This soft, creamy-textured, mouthwatering flesh is shot through with pale pink veins. It is juicy and sweet, with a refreshing acidic undertone and a

Garcinia mangostana
Fam Guttiferae

Mangistan

*France: mangouste; Malaysia:
manggis; Thailand: mang-khut,
mungkut; West Indies: mangostain,
mangostan, mangosteen*

Nutritional Values
*A nutritional mirage; only about 30
per cent of the whole fruit is edible
and that, apart from sugar, has
insignificant nutritional values.*

Raw fruit:

cal	76	Ca	18	A	—
pro	0.7	P		B_1	0.06
fat	0.8	Fe	0.3	B_2	0.01
car	18.6	Na		B_5	0.4
fib	1.3	K		C	2

complex flavour reminiscent of strawberry, peach and grape. Many who have tasted superior specimens judge it to be the world's best fruit and have become eternally addicted. Unfortunately away from local areas it can take quite a bit of hunting down.

Selecting the Best
Mangosteens appear intermittently from March to October in oriental and specialist greengrocers. Choose relatively large ones as they contain more flesh. They must yield enough to be opened by hand.

Storage and Preparation
Eat soon after buying. To open, hold firmly in the cup of a hand and with the other hand deftly twist off half the shell. The soft segments are easy to separate. Alternatively, use a blade but beware of cutting too deep into the skin—there is a messy tannic juice which may affect the flesh. Mangosteens will store for a few weeks, but treat delicately for fear of the tannins. If kept too long mangosteens go rock hard and ferment inside, the flesh decomposing into a brown evil-smelling mush.

Culinary Uses
Most exotic tropical fruits only suffer from culinary interference—this is especially true of the mangosteen. We forbid you to abuse it in any way. The fruit is occasionally available canned or otherwise preserved. In such cases, the flavour, originally delicate, is further diminished. In Indonesia where the fruit is common enough to be taken for granted, it is made into pickles and vinegars. An intriguing Chinese application is for the whole crushed fruit to be used as a *bouquet garni* in yam and watercress soup.

Herbal Properties
Mangosteen bark yields an extract used in India to treat amoebic dysentery and enteritis. The fruit used to be recommended for reducing fever, which perhaps led to the famous Malaysian belief that it does not mix with brandy.

Facts and Features
Native to Malaysia, the mangosteen grows on a small scale throughout Southeast Asia, especially Java, and there is some production in the West Indies and experimental development in Florida.

This fruit is uncommon in that it is still largely confined to its home, not having reached other tropical countries very successfully. Nor is it exported on any great scale—its economic viability is questionable, which is unfortunate as it has been praised as the finest of all fruits by many admirers of all nationalities. The tree, which contains a tacky latex like other Guttiferae, takes fifteen years to mature, a lengthy time for a fruit crop. A black dye and tannin are also obtained from the tree. The twigs provide chewing sticks.

MELON
Africa

Cucumis melo
Fam Cucurbitaceae

Cantaloupe, Casaba, Musk Melon

China: doan gwa, dung gwa, har mut guai, heung kwa, tim kwa; France: melon; Germany: Melone; India: kharbooza, k(h)arbuja, kharbuz(a), khurbooj, sakkar; Indonesia: bhaloongka(k), blewah, blewek, garbis, krai (bali), semangka landa; Italy: melone; Middle East: shumman; Spain: melón; West Indies: cantaloupe, musk, sweet melon

A multitude of melons nowadays defies exact classification, but there are three main groups. Winter melons, including the famous 'Honeydew', and the superior pale-skinned 'Lavan', form the series known as 'Cassaba' (*C.m. inodorus*). These are green or yellow, with a hard, ribbed skin and a pale green or white flesh, crisp, sweet and inodorous. They are oval, often elongated. Netted (musk or nutmeg) melons (*C.m. reticulata*), appear as if inside a net bag, but this is a relief feature of the skin. They are yellow-green, oval or round, with juicy aromatic flesh, green, orange or pink. They are greenhouse grown, and known as 'cantaloups' in the US. A common variety is the brownish or honey-coloured 'Galia'. Finally, there are the cantaloupes or rock melons (*C.m. cantaloupensis*), with rough, pitted, grooved skins, usually green, and juicy, slightly granular flesh of a pink, orange or green colour, and peachy flavour. The 'Ogen' probably belongs in this group. It is small and green-fleshed with green stripes down its speckly orange skin. The 'Charentais' seems a variety on its own. It is a fine French specimen, green with orange flesh, but now commercially superseded by the Galia type. A newcomer from Turkey is the 'Tiger' melon which has a yellow-orange-black striped appearance; its flesh is soft and has an apple-like flavour. 'Musk melon' is a general US term for non-water melons.

Selecting the Best
Melons should feel dense and heavy. Avoid those that seem light for their size. Some varieties yield at the ends. If you can detect the perfume by smelling the top end, the melon is ready to eat. Don't hesitate to ask your greengrocer for advice.

All melons are basically similar and are useful sources of vitamins A, B and C.

Fresh fruit:

cal	30	Ca	14	A	3–4,000
pro	1	P	16	B$_1$	0.04
fat	0.1	Fe	0.4	B$_2$	0.03
car	7	Na	12	B$_5$	0.6
fib	0.5	K	250	C	30

Recipe:
Melon Alaska, page 200

Storage and Preparation

Honeydews keep for a month or longer. With other varieties eat soon after purchase. You can eat the seeds, although most people do not. Keep melons at room temperature until they are ripe. Serve from the refrigerator, but do not freeze. Wrap cut or whole fruit carefully in plastic film as their smell is all-pervading. Large melons are cut into wedges, small round ones are halved and the seeds and fibres discarded. Melon balls are scooped out with a special implement. To prepare melon wedges for serving: cut the flesh from the rind and divide it across into 2.5cm (1in) pieces and push out alternate pieces to the left and right like oars.

Culinary Uses

Always serve chilled; this intensifies the flavour. Like much tropical fruit, melon is good for breakfast—with cereal instead of sugar. As an appetiser, it goes well with Parma ham or smoked meats or fish. It can be cubed with seafood—for example, in a prawn cocktail. A welcome addition to savoury salads, it is excellent with cucumber, yoghurt, curd or cottage cheese with nuts and herbs. Ginger has long complemented melon; it is best to use fresh or preserved stem ginger. Melon filled with port is another long-time favourite but we do not recommend it. As a cold soup, melon flesh can be puréed with orange and lemon juice and sweet spices, or wine. Serve from the shell. Use the shell to hold a fruit salad or water ice or ice-cream for an alaska. Make preserves or marmalade adding lemon, orange or lime. The inner rind makes jam, using lemon juice and sugar, or an interesting pickle—make with an ordinary sweet pickling syrup, appropriately spiced. The seeds are best dried and roasted.

Herbal Properties

In China the seeds and stalks of young melons are used medicinally; the former as a digestive and cough relief and the latter, which contains a dangerously powerful purgative called elaterin, as an expectorant and emetic.

Facts and Features

A fat cucumber at heart, the melon comes from the squash family. It was cultivated in ancient Egypt, but did not reach Europe until the Renaissance, when it was adopted with enthusiasm, as reflected in many old culinary paintings, and is still grown intensively in parts of France. Now the melon is cultivated worldwide, Israel and Spain being major developers and exporters. The netted melon is best for hothouse production in cold climates while the Honeydew thrives in Spain. The cantaloupe is named from Cantalupo Castle in Italy, where it was first developed, the Ogen from the Israeli *kibbutz* where it was commercially grown, although originally a Dutch breed, and the Charentais from French Charentes. Industrially, melons yield a semi-drying oil used in soap and in oil lamps. The water melon is a different species and is described on page 171.

MONGRI (RAT-TAILED RADISH)
India

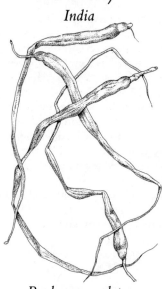

Raphanus caudatus
syn *R. sativus* var *caudatus*
Fam Cruciferae

Aerial Radish, Java (Tree) Radish, Madras Radish, Rat's Tail Radish, Serpent-tailed Radish, Tree Radish

France: radis serpent; India: mogri, mongri, mungra, sengri; Indonesia: mougri

Although called rat-tailed radish, the mongri is not a radish as we know it but the seed pod of a related species grown for its pods rather than its root. The pods are unmistakable, being purple or violet with tinges of green, long, thin and sinuous as the English name suggests. They are plumpish at the stalk end, narrowing to a tail, faintly ribbed and slightly bulging like most seed pods. They vary enormously in length, anything from 10–40cm (4–15in), and in their country of origin they have been seen as long as a metre (3ft). The pods contain small light-green 'beans'. The flavour of the whole is sharp, very much like a good English radish.

Selecting the Best
These curious-looking pods are available from Indian shops in the summer and should show no sign of dryness, toughness, shrivelling or mildew.

Storage and Preparation
Store in the salad drawer and use as soon as possible, as they do not keep well. Wash the pods and cut off the stalk. Mongri is left whole, or chopped or ground to a paste—the latter is a lengthy procedure without a processor.

Culinary Uses
This intriguing vegetable is pickled in vinegar or eaten raw in salads, contributing a pleasing purple colour and a good radishy flavour. In India, it is finely chopped and added to yoghurt with fresh coriander and spices as a dip to accompany savoury snacks. A fresh chutney is made by

112

Recipe:
Mongri Baji, page 195

grinding mongri together with coriander leaves, green ginger, salt, chilli powder and lemon juice to form a coarse paste. The pods are also cooked whole with onions and spices and served as a side dish for curries.

Herbal Properties
The young seeds may contain raphanin which has anti-bacterial properties. In India, mongri is considered a healthy and tonic vegetable.

Facts and Features
Little has been written about this vegetable but it was recorded as coming to Britain in 1816 from Java. It is popular in India, whence its recent appearance in this country. It is easy to grow, however, so if seed can be obtained sow in May in a sunny position and within 3 months pods will be yielded. Pods from the common radish can be treated like mongri provided they are tender.

MOOLI (DAIKON, WHITE RADISH)
China, Japan

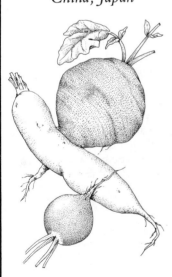

Raphanus sativus
var *longipinnatus*

Fam Cruciferae

Oriental white radishes commonly seen in British shops are very much larger than our own white 'icicles'. They are long and conical, up to 30cm (12in) in length and 8cm (3in) in diameter at the widest part. Large as these may be they are mere dwarfs compared to the 23-kg (50-lb) monsters of Japan that we fear will never reach our markets. Usually the thin skin is white with few rootlets; a long rat-tail-like tap root extends below. Most white radishes are regular in shape but some are crooked and distorted. The aroma of the cut radish is pungent and the flavour strong and biting but milder than conventional radishes. The pungency reduces in cooking.

Selecting the Best
Whether large or small, look for firm, smooth and unblemished radishes. Test that they are not spongy or flabby; any leaves attached should appear fresh.

Storage and Preparation
Moolis will keep in the salad drawer for about 2 weeks. They are prepared in a variety of ways, raw or cooked. Peel and cut them into dice, matchsticks, slivers, thin or thick rounds or rectangles; or shred or grate coarsely. For Japanese-style presentation, shred and stand in cold water for 30 minutes. Diced, they cook in

Chinese Radish, Japanese Radish, Oriental Radish

Burma: monla; China: loh bak, loh paak, lu fu; India: mooli, mula, muli, mulla(ngi), mullanki, mullong; Indonesia: lobak, mullangi (Tamil); Japan: (hatsuka-) daikon; Malaysia: lobak; Middle East: figal; Philippines: labaños; Sri Lanka: ripani; West Indies: mourai, radish

Nutritional Values
Radish root is less nutritious than its leaves but is a minor source of vitamin C. It is low in calories. The pungent principle is allyl isothiocyanate.

Raw:

cal	19	Ca	35	A	10
pro	0.9	P	26	B₁	0.03
fat	0.1	Fe	0.6	B₂	0.02
car	4.2	Na	—	B₅	0.4
fib	0.7	K	180	C	15–40

Recipes:
Tempura, page 182

about 10 minutes. Smaller varieties of radish may be prepared in the same way and tired-looking ones will revive remarkably if steeped in iced water for 30 minutes or so.

Culinary Uses
Beloved by the Japanese and Koreans, mooli (daikon) is an essential accompaniment to *sashimi* (raw fish); it is also cut into decorative shapes to adorn *miso* soups, and made into pickle to be consumed at the end of a traditional Japanese meal. It often partners carrot in salads. It is equally popular in Indian cookery when, often retaining its leaves, it is curried, pickled, mixed with yoghurt or stuffed in *parathas*. Try chilled, finely-sliced radish with cheese to end a meal—a welcome change from celery—or thinly sliced in sandwiches. If white radish is unobtainable it is still hard to beat a little Scarlet Globe or French Breakfast variety eaten with fresh butter and sea salt as an appetiser.

Herbal Properties
In China, white radish is accorded digestive and diuretic properties. In India, it has additional uses in respiratory complaints. Both leaves and root are used to dissolve calculi.

Facts and Features
Radishes are as ancient as man's need for food and have been mentioned in the literature of all northern hemisphere countries. There are hundreds of different kinds, every country producing its own varieties and cultivars. Unusual radishes of interest include the black-skinned ones, or Spanish Black, which should have crisp white flesh (sometimes it is grey and grained), and the large globular reds, much larger than our own reds, almost as big as a tennis ball.

OKRA (LADY'S FINGERS)

Tropical Africa

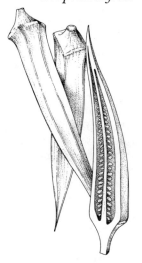

Hibiscus esculentus
syn *Abelmoschus esculentus*
Fam Malvaceae

*Bamies, Bamya, Bendee, Gobo,
Gombo, Gumbo, Ochro, Ocra,
Okro*

*Africa: nk(u)ruma (Ghana, origin of
name); Burma: you-padi; China:
chaan ke, tsau kwai; France: bamie;
India: bendi-kai, b(h)indi,
chatushkhand, dheras, dheros, mesta,
ramturai, vendakai; Indonesia:
kechang liohin; Japan: okura;
Malaysia: kachang bendi, kachang
lender, kopi arab, sayur bendi;
Middle East: bamyah; Portugal:
quin-gombo; Thailand: grajee-ap
morn, kachieb, krajieb si kheow;
West Indies: bamie, gombo, ladies'
finger, lady fingers, molondron,
ochra(s), ochro, okra, okro,
quimbombo, quingombo, salian, six
week*

Okra or lady's fingers are now a common vegetable in greengrocers and supermarkets. As the latter name implies they are like long pointed fingers. However, the resemblance to most ladies' fingers ends there because they are green, five- to six-sided and ridged. They vary in length from 2.5–23cm (1–9in) and are 1–2cm (½–¾in) in width for most of their length until they taper rapidly to a bluntish tip. The skin is slightly fuzzy and the stalk end has a broad 'cap'. Within the thin flesh a hollow interior contains rows of creamy edible seeds attached to a membrane—one row to each outside ridge. The raw flavour is reminiscent of runner beans with a pleasant sticky texture. When cooked this texture becomes more glutinous and tends to obscure the flavour.

Selecting the Best
Okra is now widely available all the year round. Small to medium-sized tender pods are a good green, unblemished and crisp. They should snap like young beans. It is not worth buying discoloured ones—they will be stringy and disappointing. Okra is also available canned, frozen and dried, whole or cut into pieces. The dried version is popular in the Middle East as a winter vegetable and can also be seen in London shops catering for the Nigerian community.

Storage and Preparation
Okra keeps for several days wrapped in a plastic bag in the salad drawer. Opinion is divided on how okra should be prepared before cooking but this very much depends on various regional traditions. For soups and stews of African origin, whose mucilaginous quality is the outstanding feature, just wash, top, tail and chop into rounds or grate if desired. This rather slimy characteristic can be counteracted or cut by adding a little lemon or lime juice to the pan. Fuzziness can be removed by scrubbing the okra gently under running water before cutting. For eating whole, wash and dry, trim off both ends, paring round the conical stem end and taking care not to cut into the pod. To reduce stickiness and prevent splitting, soak prepared okra in acidulated water for 30 minutes or so, then rinse and dry. For stuffing, trim as above and make a lengthways slit, being careful not to puncture through to the other side. Avoid overcooking and do not use pans made of copper, brass or iron. Okra also freezes well.

Nutritional Values

American and Caribbean varieties appear to be the best nutritionally, although okra is not outstanding in this respect. Indian varieties have less vitamins than the others.

cal	25–42	Ca	66–92	A	88–520
pro	1.8–2.4	P	51–62	B_1	0.07–0.17
fat	0.2–0.3	Fe	0.6–1.2	B_2	0.07–0.21
car	7.6–9.7	Na	3–6.9	B_5	0.6–1.1
fib	1–1.2	K	103–249	C	13–31

Recipes:

Callaloo Soup, page 179; Okra with Tomatoes, page 196

Culinary Uses

Creole *gumbo* and West Indian *callaloo* are perhaps the best known dishes of African origin associated with okra, but there are also *coo-coos*—starchy Caribbean side dishes—chowders, pepperpots and 'Limping Susan', a cunningly-named counterpart to 'Hopping John'. In India, okra, known as *bhindi*, is served as a vegetable or curry accompaniment and is often stuffed with spices and braised in oil. In the Balkans and the Middle East, *bamia*, as it is named, is much prized and after careful preparation is cooked with meat and poultry and, really delicious, stewed with tomatoes—a happy combination contrasting flavour, colour and texture. Try okra gently fried in olive oil and served with lemon wedges, or deep-fried in batter, as an appetiser. Very fresh tender okra can be eaten raw in salads or as a *crudité*.

Herbal Properties

The mucilage contained in all parts of the plant, but especially in the fresh pods, is valuable as a thickener and binder. In India, decoctions of okra pods are considered of much value in treating problems of the genito-urinary tract. They are also beneficial in chest infections and the mucilage itself is demulcent and emollient, an application also appreciated by the Turks. Among modern uses for the mucilage is its inclusion in a preparation which is a blood plasma substitute and a blood-volume increaser.

Facts and Features

Okra is indigenous to West Africa and was taken to the Americas by slaves. In fact the name 'okra' has evolved from *nkuruman*, its name in the Twi language of Ghana; similarly, 'gumbo' evolved from Angolan *ngombo*. Okra has spread throughout the tropics and sub-tropics. It was recorded in the United States in the mid-eighteenth century, but five centuries earlier in Egypt. There are several varieties of okra including quick-growing dwarfs, long-podded and round-podded. The seeds of the ripe pod are alleged to be the best coffee substitute in existence.

ORIENTAL LEAF VEGETABLES

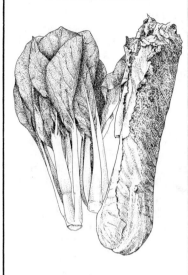

AMARANTH
Tropics

Amaranthus spp
Fam Amaranthaceae

Chinese Spinach, Edible Amaranth, Jacob's Coat, Tricolor

China: hon toi moi, in choi, in tsoi, yin choi; India: badi chaulai, (bari) ch(a)ulai, bhaji, data sak, lal sag, lal sak, marsa, nate sak, ranga sak; Indonesia: bayem, senggang, tarnak; Japan: hiyu; Malaysia: bayam merah, bayam puteh; Philippines: urai; Thailand: p(h)ak khom; West Indies: agonment, bhagi, bhaji, bush spinach, cal(l)aloo, caterpillar, kallaloo, spinach, z'herbage, zipina

Recipes:
Bhaji and Lentil Side Dish, page 191; Callaloo Soup, page 179

The following nine oriental leaf vegetables are now quite common in Asian shops and markets, particularly Chinese stores. Many of their names reflect the preferences of shopkeepers as much as anything, and may vary considerably according to locality. Pak choi can sometimes be observed in the more enterprising supermarkets, but petsai or Chinese leaves are now as common as lettuce. Like any greens, all these should be fresh, unblemished and well-coloured. Storage is as for any salad—keep spinach and cabbage types in a plastic bag in the salad drawer—most will stay crisp for a week. Those with stalks can be kept in a glass of water, as we treat cress. It is more authentic, and kinder to the vegetable, to fry or steam these leaves rather than to boil them in the Western manner. Though they may be used in cold salads, the Chinese never eat them raw. In fact they never eat anything raw, even to the extent of always boiling their drinking water.

There are over fifty species of edible amaranth growing worldwide. We have come across three, one each in a Chinese, Indian and West Indian store. The Chinese version, known as *in choi*, has a largish green leaf, 9×9cm (3½×3½in), with an unmistakable purple patch in its centre; a completely green variety is common in China. *Bhaji* or *chaulai*, the Indian type, has several smaller, rounded leaves, 3×4cm (1¼×1½in), on stalks, and the West Indian *callaloo* (also the term used for *arvi*, see page 9), has a large, 8×15cm (3×6in), deep-green, soft and more pointed ace-of-spades type leaf. This latter variety is actually grown in Leicestershire. The cooked flavour of all varieties is similar to spinach.

Selecting the Best
Amaranth is available throughout the summer; the usual rules for choosing leaf vegetables apply.

Storage and Preparation
Pull the leaves from the stalks and discard coarse stems. The leaves can be chopped or kept whole. Coarser leaves can be softened by rubbing whilst washing.

Culinary Uses
Amaranth is eaten throughout Asia, the West Indies and parts of southern Europe. In Chinese cookery, *in choi* is generally used in soups and the

whole leaves are excellent stir-fried with garlic and a pinch each of salt and sugar. In India, *bhaji* is also known as *sag*—a general term for spinach-type leaves. It appears as a side dish for curries, in *pakoras*, cooked with potatoes and curried with beef. It is an ingredient of the famed West Indian *callaloo* soup, whence its Caribbean name. Use amaranth as a substitute for spinach—a little mint is a happy addition.

GAI LAN (CHINESE KALE)
Southeast Asia

Brassica alboglabra
syn *B. oleracea* var *albiflora*

Fam Cruciferae

China: gai lan tsoi, kai lan tsoi;
United States: Chinese broccoli

Recipe:
Red-cooked Pork with Gai Lan Stalk, page 187

Gai lan or Chinese kale is the oriental leaf vegetable most like a failed cabbage or spring greens. Its branching white flower and succulent stalk make it easily distinguishable. The main stalk is light green, round, tapering, 8–20mm (⅓–¾in) in diameter, bloomed and ribbed. The leaf stalk, round and grooved, 5–6mm (⅕–¼in) in diameter, is nearly as long as the leaf. Mature leaves are oval, about 9×14cm (3½×5½in), younger ones more oblong. They are dark green, lighter on the underside, bloomed, with a cabbagy texture. The raw flavour is slightly bitter, like cabbage; when cooked, gai lan is mild and pleasant, quite like calabrese.

Selecting the Best
Choose those in flower if possible.

Storage and Preparation
If necessary, pull away the fibrous part of the stalk before cutting off the leaves. Alternatively, cook the whole thing together.

Culinary Uses
Gai lan adapts well to recipes for broccoli, as one of its other names implies. It is more delicate in flavour and should be steamed or stir-fried rather than boiled so as not to destroy its subtle taste. It goes particularly well with red-cooked pork.

PAK CHOI (CHINESE WHITE CABBAGE)
China

Brassica chinensis var *chinensis*
syn *B.c.* var *communis*

Fam Cruciferae

Despite their name, these small leafy bunches are quite unlike cabbage. The crisp, tightly-bunched white stalks are unmistakable although at some times of the year they are more pale green than white; they are moderately cusped or grooved and about half the overall length of the plant. The soft, oval leaves are about 9×12cm (3½×4¾in), mid-green, paler on the underside. A small, yellow, branched flower is sometimes carried.

Chinese Cabbage, Chinese (White) Mustard (Cabbage), Mustard Greens

China: bak choi, bok choi, pak choi, pak tsoi (and various other spellings); India: pechai; United States: spoon cabbage; West Indies: pakchoi

Recipes:
Chinese 'Seaweed' or Green Floss, page 204; Pak Choi Salad, page 196

The raw flavour is similar to gai lan; cooked, it is mild, sympathetic and broccoli-like.

Selecting the Best
Choose flowering specimens if possible.

Storage and Preparation
Detach the stalks from the leaves. Trim and slice stalks diagonally and chop or shred leaves. The stalks take somewhat longer to cook.

Culinary Uses
Pak choi leaves, which cook to a marvellous green brilliance, may be treated in the same way as spinach although, of course, they are dissimilar in flavour. They may also be eaten raw, and provide the ideal green for making Chinese 'seaweed', a favourite restaurant hors-d'oeuvre.

CHOI SUM (CHINESE FLOWERING CABBAGE)
China

Brassica chinensis var
parachinensis
syn *B. parachinensis*
Fam Cruciferae

Flowering Pak Choi, Flowering White Cabbage

China: choi sum, (pak) tsoi sum, tsai shim

There are several varieties of spinach-like choi sum. The curved, juicy stalks vary from white to light green, and are faintly bloomed. The plant reaches an overall length of 38cm (15in). The spinach-shaped leaves are mid to dark green, soft and smooth. A small, bright yellow flower is carried. The raw flavour is strong in the stalk and rather bitter in the leaf, but is improved by cooking, when the stalks taste rather like asparagus.

Selecting the Best
Insist on flowering specimens.

Storage and Preparation
Trim the stalks and prepare like broccoli.

Culinary Uses
Considered the most delicious of the brassica types, choi sum is universally popular in China, appearing most often in soups and noodle dishes. Its stalks are excellent served with butter in the same way as asparagus. This vegetable is best steamed.

GAI CHOI (MUSTARD CABBAGE)
Asia

Brassica juncea var *rugosa*
syn *B. rugosa*

Fam Cruciferae

Bamboo Mustard (variety),
Broad-leaf Mustard, Leaf-mustard
Cabbage, Swatow Mustard (variety)

China: (chuk) gai choi, kai tsoi

Recipe:
Gai Choi Soup, page 179

There are many varieties of mustard cabbage; the one described here is the most commonly seen in the UK. Gai choi is about 30–36cm (12–14in) in overall length. The pale-green leaf stalks are smooth, crisp and stout, half-rounded and deeply cusped; some have a twisted look. The oval, pointed leaves grow in loose bunches; fairly large, 13 × 20cm (5 × 8in), light to mid-green, duller and prominently veined on the undersides, they have wavy edges and are wrinkled towards the base. The flavour is hot, pungent and mustardy when raw, becoming milder after cooking.

Storage and Preparation
Chop both stalks and leaves. Blanch for 2 minutes.

Culinary Uses
Gai choi's mustardy flavour may be too determined for some to eat raw although in small quantities it is a spicy addition to green salads. In China it is stir-fried after blanching and makes an exceptionally good soup.

PETSAI (CHINESE LEAVES)
China

Brassica pekinensis
syn *B. chinensis* var
pekinensis, B. petsai

Fam Cruciferae

Celery Cabbage, Chefoo Cabbage,
Chihli Cabbage, Chinese Cabbage,
Nappa Cabbage, Pekin(g) Cabbage,
Shantung Cabbage, Shantung
Petsai, Tientsin Cabbage

China: chik tung, shu tsoi, wong nga
pak, wong nga tsoi; India: China
badhakapi; Japan: hakusai

There are two types of this vegetable, both with tightly-packed, wrap-around leaves with jagged edges. The cylindrical type is pale green, 20–30cm (8–12in) long and 8–12cm (3–5in) in diameter; the barrel-shaped version is white to pale green, 10–20cm (4–8in) long and 10–15cm (4–6in) in diameter. The texture is crisp and crunchy when raw and the flavour is midway between lettuce and cabbage. When cooked, petsai takes up surrounding flavours.

Selecting the Best
Choose tightly-formed heads. The longer variety is considered superior.

Storage and Preparation
Cut as required, returning the remainder to the refrigerator to keep for a week or so. Remove any tough outer leaves and cut off hard stem base. Separate leaves, or slice or shred from the top end as desired.

Culinary Uses
Chinese leaves are now a firm favourite as a salad vegetable but are even nicer cooked. The outer stalks can be cooked like celery or cabbage and

the whole, finely shredded, is excellent stir-fried or cooked in boiling salted water for a couple of minutes then tossed in butter.

TONG HO (CHOPSUEY GREENS)
Mediterranean
Chrysanthemum coronarium var spatiosum
Fam Compositae

Chopsuey Chrysanthemum, Crown Daisy, Garland Chrysanthemum, Shungiku, Sicilian Chrysanthemum

China: tong ho; Japan: shun giku

Similar in appearance to the dandelion, chopsuey greens can easily be identified by their strong chrysanthemum-like aroma. The main stalk, round, finely-ribbed and grass-green is succulent and snaps cleanly. The leaves, slightly darker green, are narrow at the base, then broaden, usually to two divisions; they are indented, wavy, thickish, soft and succulent. The overall length of the plant is 20–30cm (8–12in). The flavour is herby and slightly pungent when raw, becoming milder on cooking.

Selecting the Best
Available in the summer. Select fresh-looking and good-coloured leaves.

Storage and Preparation
A bad keeper—use within a day or so. Wash carefully as grit collects at the leaf base. Pull off the leaves, discarding the stalk, and chop into 5cm (2in) lengths or leave whole. If they are to invigorate a salad, scald them and refresh in cold water to tone down their somewhat overpowering flavour.

Culinary Uses
A most interesting vegetable, its decorative and pungently aromatic leaves are employed in Chinese, Vietnamese and Japanese cookery. In China it is used in soups, or stir-fried on its own, and is an ingredient of Mongolian Firepot, a type of *fondue* where meat, fish and vegetables are simmered in stock at the table. Similarly, in Japan it is an ingredient of *yudofu*, this time with beancurd instead of meat and a stock flavoured with seaweed and dried tuna—an acquired taste.

GAU GEI (CHINESE BOXTHORN)
China, Japan
Lycium chinense
Fam Solanaceae

Gau gei is now more readily available than a few years ago. It has a tough, woody, inedible main stalk, which is buff and brown, slightly twisted and ribbed. The short, soft leaf stalks carry pointed, oval leaves, 4–5cm (1½–2in) long; these are mid-green with paler veins and are duller in colour on the underside. The plant is quite long, 45–60cm (18–24in), and bears its numerous leaves

Lord Macartney's Tea, Tea Tree

China: gau gei (choi), kau kei;
Indonesia: daun koki

close to the stem. Bitter, sharp and pungent when raw, gau gei becomes milder and more flavoursome when cooked.

Selecting the Best
Available during the summer. Look for fresh, green leaves.

Storage and Preparation
Bruise stem bottoms and keep in water like flowers. To strip the leaves, grasp the top of the stem in one hand and pull firmly downwards with the other. Discard the stems. We recommend one stem of leaves per person.

Culinary Uses
Gau gei is used almost exclusively in soups, either plain or with pork liver or duck eggs. Try adding a handful of leaves to chicken stock for an extra bite.

UNG CHOI (WATER SPINACH)
Tropical Africa, Asia and Australia

Ipomoea aquatica
syn *I. repens, I. reptans*
Fam Convolvulaceae

Swamp Cabbage

China: tung tsoi, ung, ung choi, ung tsoi; India: kalmi sak; Indonesia: kangkung, vallai-kirai (Tamil); Malaysia: kangkong; Philippines: cancong

There are several cultivars of this plant with different leaves and leaf arrangements. The main stalk, generally up to 38cm (15in) long, is pale green, hollow, round, faintly ribbed, succulent and bears several very tiny black spikes or bumps. The spear-shaped leaves, which can be either broad or narrow according to type, are mid-green, paler on the underside, soft and smooth. The raw vegetable, though slightly bitter, has little flavour, but takes up ambient flavours in cooking.

Selecting the Best
Watch for short stalks and large upper leaves.

Storage and Preparation
Use within 2 days. Cut off the stems 5cm (2in) from the bottom and separate the leaves. Cook the stems for 1 minute before adding the leaves.

Culinary Uses
Water spinach may be treated like ordinary spinach but in the Chinese style it is much liked cooked with fermented beancurd or shrimp sauce. In spicy Nyonya cookery it is fried with chillies and dried prawns, sometimes with added coconut milk.

Herbal Properties (all species)

Oddly enough, few special properties for these leaf vegetables have been recorded by the ancient Chinese herbalists, renowned though they were for finding a 'virtue' or twenty in every plant, and a 'correspondence' or 'signature' to match. However, the bitter varieties may have some uses in folk remedies and the seeds of gau gei (boxthorn) are used in Chinese medicine.

Nutritional Values (all species)

The oriental leaf vegetables are generally very nutritious and good sources of all vitamins. Indian amaranth (chaulai), and mustard cabbage (gau choi), appear to be the best 'all-rounders'. The former is also an exceptional source of iron but has the disadvantage of being top of the league in oxalic acid content. No data are available for gau gei (Chinese boxthorn).

All raw (averages):

	IN CHOI (1)	CHAULAI (2)	GAI LAN (3)	PAK CHOI (4)	CHOI SUM (1)	GAI CHOI (4)	PETSAI (4)	TONG HO (5)	UNG CHOI (4)
cal	32	42	29	15	25	21	12	12	25
pro	2.5	3.7	3.3	1.6	2.2	2	1.6	2.3	2.7
fat	0.4	0.6	0.2	0.2	0.5	0.3	0.3	0.2	0.5
car	5	6.7	5.5	2.4	3	3.7	2.2	2	4.2
fib		1.2		0.6		0.8	0.5	1	1.2
Ca	200	326		103	130	174	38	102	86
P	46	83		33	53	32	42	28	43
Fe	4.8	4–25		1.4	0.2	1.8	0.6	1.7	2.1
Na				26				23	
K				306				253	150
A		9,025	3,500	3,560	3,050	6,300	220	5,900	5,350
B_1		0.04	0.1	0.04	0.05	0.06	0.05	0.05	0.08
B_2		0.12	0.21	0.1	0.06	0.2	0.07	0.1	0.12
B_5		1.15	1.1	0.65	0.06	0.75	0.45	0.5	0.5
C	35	93	118	35	49	112	30	21	28

(1) Hong Kong
(2) India and Caribbean
(3) USA
(4) Hong Kong, Caribbean, Taiwan and USA
(5) Hong Kong and Taiwan

OYSTER MUSHROOM
Northern Temperate Zone

Pleurotus spp

Fam Fungi

*Abalone Mushroom, Bracket
Mushroom, Pleurotte Mushroom*

China: kwan; France: pleurote

Nutritional Values
*Authorities differ on the nutritional
value of mushrooms, some saying
any value they have is locked in
digestion-resistant cellulose, while
others claim they are good in protein,
iron and vitamin B$_5$ (niacin). No
composition data are available for the
oyster mushroom.*

Recipe:
Baked Oyster Mushrooms, page 190

We are all familiar with the 'ear-like' fungi found
on dying or dead garden and woodland trees.
These are oyster mushrooms which are now
grown commercially in Europe and the UK and
can be found in some supermarkets. These
mushrooms are quite different from conventional
ones; shaped like a flattened 'cornucopia', they
epitomise succulence. Soft, pliable and
rich-looking, they come in a variety of
colours—pink, buff, grey, fawn, brown, cream.
The upper surface is smooth and the underside
gilled as usual; the edges of older ones are slightly
tattered. They vary in size from 2.5–10cm (1–4in)
in height and diameter. Younger oyster
mushrooms are mostly fat stalk with a small top.
All oysters are open on one side owing to their
horizontal growth pattern out of tree trunks,
posts, etc. The flavour is pronounced and
good—stronger than ordinary mushrooms.

Selecting the Best
They are usually sold in transparent packs and
should look plump, smooth and velvety.

Storage and Preparation
Store unopened packs in the salad drawer for up
to 5 days. They should not need any cleaning.
The 'stalk' end can be a little tough so cut off a
slice if you wish.

Culinary Uses
These fleshy and tasty mushrooms, highly prized
in China, may be adapted to a wide variety of
dishes and it is well worth experimenting with
them. Obviously perfect candidates for
stir-frying, their firmness and pronounced flavour
also make them ideal for fillings and stuffings.

Herbal Properties
None known.

Facts and Features
Oyster mushrooms were once only found in
colonies growing on dead trees, especially beech,
and rotting stumps and posts, but are now
commercially cultivated on artificial support
systems. In Singapore, they and many other
types of edible mushroom are grown on a large
scale and a thriving cottage industry has
responded to government encouragement. There
are thousands of species of fungi, many being
highly toxic, so if you go mushroom gathering
be sure you know what you are looking for.

PAN
Malaysia

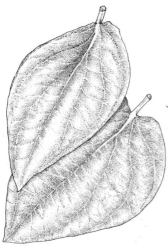

Piper betle
syn *Chavica betle*

Fam Piperaceae

Betel Pepper

India: paan, pan

Nutritional Values
Pan leaves are rich in vitamin B complex and vitamin C. Their pungency depends on contained essential oils which vary according to the origin of the leaves.

Recipe:
Supari, page 209

Pan or betel leaves are now common in the Indian shopping areas of Britain. Pan is a must in Indian life—thus its ubiquity. You will ordinarily see two types of leaf: a larger, darker green one and a smaller, paler variety. They are used independently, the larger ('male') for savoury pan and the smaller ('female') for sweet pan. Shaped like the ace of spades they are quite veined and the larger ones sport tiny reddish dots—their oil glands. These are the spicier ones. The larger average 15×10cm (6×4in) and the smaller 14×9cm (5½×3½in). The flavour varies considerably depending on their origin and breeding, but is basically slightly pungent with sweetish undertones. The paler pan leaf is hot and spicy with floral and coriander leaf notes.

Selecting the Best
Always available from Indian greengrocers, pan leaves should look fresh and pliable.

Storage and Preparation
Keep them flat in a polythene bag in the salad drawer where they should remain fresh for a few days. Wash them carefully and pat thoroughly dry prior to use.

Culinary Uses
Strictly for the *aficionados*, pan, considered by some to be the ultimate digestive, is easy to make at home but not so easy to acquire a taste for. The leaf is in fact an edible envelope for an infinite combination of spices, seeds and flavourings with betel nut, red-staining catechu and lime paste. It is this latter which proves a bitter pill to swallow for the uninitiated. The small triangular parcels can be sweet or savoury and are chewed whole after a meal as an aid to digestion or as a go-anywhere snack. A small quantity of lime paste, available in various forms from Indian shops, is spread on the centre of the leaf and a mixture of such spices as aniseed, cardamom, cloves or fennel seed, together with the shredded betel nut, pumpkin or melon seeds and tiny sugar balls, is added. These mixtures, known as *supari*, are also available from Indian shops. The leaf is then folded into a triangle and sealed with a whole clove. These mouthfuls may be further adorned with *vark*: edible gold or silver leaf. Special decorative boxes for storing leaves and fillings and a cutter called a *sarota* for slicing whole betel nuts complete the almost ritualistic aura of the process.

Herbal Properties

In India, pan leaves are used in a multitude of remedies ranging from aphrodisiac and antiseptic to rubefacient and vermifuge. They are best known as breath purifiers and mild stimulants. The *Ananga Ranga* allows the inclusion of the pods of betel in a formulation 'for hastening the paroxysms of woman'.

Facts and Features

Pan is probably the only leaf vegetable that is endemic in India. To high and low alike, pan is almost as much a necessity of life as water. Its only comparable equivalent in the West is the chewing gum of the United States. There is an astonishing range of quality available, from the fifty-guinea gold *vark*-encrusted pan to the lowly two-pence version that barely conceals a single fennel seed in its meagre envelope—however, a delight to all. Of interest is the lime paste that appears in all descriptions. It is fine powdered mineral lime slaked from sea shells and mixed with water into a paste. It gives a sour and astringent note to the concoction as well as preserving other ingredients from bacterial ravages.

PANDANUS
Malaya

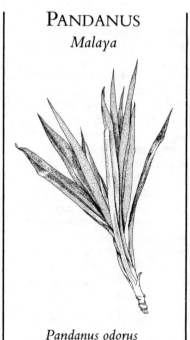

Pandanus odorus
Fam Pandanaceae

Bunches of pandanus look very much like the leaves of a narcissus. They are long, flat and a healthy green. They terminate in a clump which appears to have been snatched from a main plant. Crushed or split the leaves emit a sweet bouquet reminiscent of newly-mown grass and the flavour is agreeably fragrant.

Selecting the Best

Select pandanus leaves as fresh as you would a bunch of flowers. Dried leaf pieces are also available in vacuum packs. A powdered form exists too.

Storage and Preparation

Stand them in a little water and use before they lose their pliability. However, should they dry out their aroma is not lost and they can be revived in water. They are used either in leaf form or as juice. To prepare the leaves—recipes demand from two to as many as twenty—either cut them into 5cm (2in) lengths or, as is more usual, tear them down the middle and tie them into knots. To extract the juice, wash, cut into

*Indonesia: daun pandan(g);
Malaysia: daun pandan; Thailand:
bai toey*

Nutritional Values
*As a flavouring, pandanus has no
nutritional value and is in fact purely
digestive. The hay-like fragrance and
flavour suggest the presence of
coumarin.*

Recipe:
Sticky Rice, page 201

pieces and pound them strenuously until they are finely crushed. Add a tablespoon of water for every six leaves and squeeze out the green juice.

Culinary Uses
Dubbed the vanilla of the East, pandanus lends its special fragrance to a multitude of sweet and savoury dishes from Southeast Asia. Concoctions of glutinous or 'sticky' rice, sago or tapioca, flavoured with coconut, palm sugar and pandanus are particularly popular in Indonesia and Thailand. Multi-hued jellies refreshed with pandanus' cool lime-green colour are sold in the streets where, fittingly, cones and baskets made from the leaves form aromatic receptacles for all kinds of sweets and snacks. A new tourist attraction on Thailand menus is deep-fried pandanus parcels of soy-marinated chicken morsels. Pandanus scents spicy soups, coconut-filled, green-tinged pancakes and rice to accompany *satays*. In Sri Lanka the leaves together with coconut milk traditionally assist in a hot duck curry.

Herbal Properties
Pandanus is utilised in folk medicine but there is little literature, if any, describing such uses.

Facts and Features
Native to Malaya, pandanus has not spread beyond Indo-China, Indonesia and a few islands of the Indian Ocean. Its leaves, for culinary use, are flown into London fairly regularly from Malaysia and Thailand. In the Philippines, half-dome-shaped moulds of hardened brown sugar are sold wrapped in pandanus leaves. Pandanus also participates in ritual in handsome bouquets offered to the spirits, its sweetness symbolising the better aspects of human nature. In this respect it is like its larger relative, also known as screwpine, *Pandanus odoratissimus*, the source of Indian *kewra*, undeniably the sweetest and most fragrant of all natural scents. In mundane contrast this tree's leaves are woven into baskets, hats and umbrellas (it is called the 'umbrella tree'), its fruit is edible (in times of famine) and fibre is obtained from its roots and leaves. To confuse matters further it has 599 relatives.

PAPAYA
Central America

Carica papaya
syn *Papaya carica*
Fam Caricaceae

Apaeya, Mamaeiro, Medicine Tree, Papai(a), Papaja, Papaw, Papaye, Pawpaw, Pawpoi, Popoy, Tree Melon

China: fan mo kwai (foreign wood melon), muk gwa, shu kwa; East Africa: papai; France: papaye; Germany: Papai(j)a; India: papaya, papeeta, papeya, papita; Indonesia: gandool, g(h)edang, kates, malakor, tela; Italy: papaia; Malaysia: betik, papaya; Mexico: melon zapote; South America: mamao (Brazilian); Thailand: malakor; West Indies: fruita de bomba, lechosa, papaya, papaye, pawpoi, popoy

Papayas are tropical fruit now common in our shops. They can vary enormously from small pear shapes to long melons. The former are easily the most common. These are 12–20cm (5–8in) long and weigh about 455g (1lb), with a thin, inedible skin, mottled yellowy-orange, sometimes green. The ripe flesh is firm, juicy and easier to spoon out than a ripe melon; sweet and lightly scented it varies in colour and flavour from yellow (mild) through orange to strawberry (strongest). If the fruit is cut crossways a star-shaped cavity is revealed containing hundreds of black seeds covered in a bittersweet gelatinous coating with a flavour akin to mustard and cress.

Selecting the Best
Papayas are continuously available. Larger fruit can be bought in Asian shops. Buy when firm, green through orange to yellow, and unblemished. Freckles are natural, but soft spots indicate bruising. Price varies with the country of production.

Storage and Preparation
Papayas may be ripened by maturing in a kitchen drawer for several days. The fruit is ready when it gives against a gentle squeeze. To prepare: halve the fruit lengthways and scoop out the slippery seeds and connective tissue, then cut as desired. As it does not discolour, it may be prepared in advance. If papaya pulp is required, liquidise the peeled and seeded fruit with a little lemon or lime juice. The raw fruit is unsuitable for freezing.

Culinary Uses
Highly versatile, papayas may be eaten as either a fruit or a vegetable, although the high market price they fetch in temperate zones may restrict their uses, making them something of a luxury. Serve them halved or quartered, seeded, sprinkled with sugar and lemon or lime juice as an exotic start to a James Bond style breakfast. Alternatively, try them with a little salt. A refreshing summer salad is made by peeling the fruit, cutting it across into rings, seeding and stuffing these with herbed cottage cheese and serving on a bed of crispy lettuce. Papayas, diced or sliced, are a delicious addition to tropical fruit salad and a perfect base for mousses, fools, ice-creams or sorbets. The unripe fruit may be

Nutritional Values

Papaya is a fair source of vitamin A but has more vitamin C than oranges.

cal	39	Ca	20	A	1,750
pro	0.6	P	16	B_1	0.04
fat	0.1	Fe	0.3	B_2	0.04
car	10	Na	3	B_5	0.3
fib	0.9	K	234	C	56

Recipes:

Indian Papaya Pickle, page 207
Parma Ham with Papaya, page 204;
Papaya Cheese Salad, page 196

stuffed with savoury meat fillings, added to soups for texture, stewed, or treated in other similar ways to marrow. If you suspect tough meat, stewing it with diced green papaya has a marked tenderising effect. Similarly, the flesh and seeds make a fine marinade for chops and steaks. Papayas make excellent jam and chutney and the seeds, with their mustard and cress flavour, can be incorporated into a refreshingly tangy salad dressing: just liquidise a teaspoon of the seeds with the dressing into a coarse grind. The flesh may be liquidised with other fruit for cool summer drinks. Where abundant, unripe papayas are spiced with cloves and cooked like apples in pies and flans. However, they take longer to cook.

Herbal Properties

The papaya certainly earns its nickname 'medicine tree'—all parts of the plant are used in India: in remedies for beri-beri, constipation, open wounds, dysentery, worms, indigestion, piles and to remove warts and freckles. In Queensland, the Aborigines use the seeds as an aphrodisiac. The raw fruit is famed for its excellent digestive properties; it contains the enzymes papain and chymopapain. The protein-splitting properties of chymopapain are used in 'slipped' discs, a technique recently approved in the US but commonly used in Great Britain and Canada for some time. About a third of a teaspoon of purified chymopapain is injected into the herniated disc. Within a few seconds the spongy tissue dissolves, relieving the pressure on the nerves. This revolutionary method is quicker, cheaper, more comfortable than lumbar disc surgery and just as safe. Papain extracted from papaya is a universal meat tenderiser and beer clearer and is used to clot milk in place of rennet. Pectin occurs in unripe fruit.

Facts and Features

Originating in South and Central America, papayas are now widespread throughout the tropics and sub-tropics. In parts of Africa the papaya is considered a free food to which one helps oneself with impunity, though certain planters may hardly agree. In the tropics, tough meat is wrapped in papaya leaves for a day to exploit the remarkable tenderising effect. Papaya thrives in these regions but cannot stand frost. It is essential that at least one male plant exists for anything from ten to a hundred female plants. In Kenya they say if you stand next to a female tree you must be able to see a male tree, otherwise the female will be barren. Gerard (1597), describing what he calls the Dug trees or Mamoeras, remarks: '. . . they are so loving, and of such nature, that if they be set asunder, and the female have not got a male neere her, shee becomes barren and beares no fruit . . .'

PASSION FRUIT

You are likely to come across three varieties of this glorious fruit.

PURPLE PASSION FRUIT
Southern Brazil
Passiflora edulis f edulis
Fam Passifloraceae

Bell Apple, Purple Granadilla

France: fruit de la passion, grenadille, pomme liane; Italy: granadiglia; Spain: granadilla; West Indies: ceibey, cocktail fruit, egg fruit, granadilla, mountain sweet cup, pomme de liane

This is the well-known purple, smooth or wrinkled passion fruit now in every food market and shop. Its often wizened, egg-size, pith-lined shell contains juicy, darkly-seeded pulp that is light orange with tinges of red, and is truly delectable. A tantalising perfume and a sweet nippy flavour make it a favourite everywhere. The seeds, small and black, are crunchy when bitten but usually miss the teeth.

YELLOW PASSION FRUIT
Tropics
Passiflora edulis f flavicarpa
Fam Passifloraceae

Yellow Granadilla

Malaysia: buah susu; Other names as for purple passion fruit

Slightly larger than its purple sisters, of which it is a mutation, this canary-yellow passion fruit also wrinkles as it ripens. It is more acidic in flavour, is pithier, and does not have that subtle refinement.

SWEET GRANADILLA
Tropical America
Passiflora ligularis
Fam Passifloraceae

Orange Passion Fruit

Found in Asian shops, this smooth-skinned orange passion fruit also seems inferior to the universally available purple variety. It is about the same size but less sweet and aromatic. Curiously, the yellow pulp with its complement of black seeds rattles in the skin when shaken. However, it is reckoned by some to be the finest.

Hawaii: watermelon
Other names as for purple passion
fruit

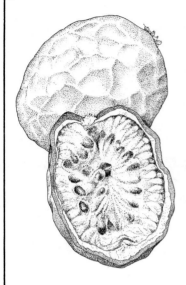

Nutritional Values (all varieties)
Passion fruits are a healthy source of
vitamins B₂, B₅ and C.

Fruit pulp:

cal	90	Ca	13	A	700
pro	2.2	P	64	B₁	trace
fat	0.7	Fe	1.6	B₂	0.13
car	21.2	Na	28	B₅	1.5
fib	—	K	348	C	30

Recipes:
Passion Fruit Juice, page 212;
Passion Fruit Mousse, page 200

Selecting the Best (all varieties)
Passion fruits appear regularly throughout the
year. Don't be put off by the wrinkled look, this
usually means the fruit is perfectly ripe. If there
are soft spots it will be going off. Orange fruit
should be smooth and full looking.

Storage and Preparation
Ripe passion fruits will keep for a couple of days
in the salad drawer. Leave unripe fruit to mature
on a sunny windowsill. To extract the pulp: cut
in half and scoop it out with a teaspoon. Rub
through a sieve to remove the seeds. To make
juice for drinks or fruit salads: heat the pulp in a
saucepan with a very little water, orange or
lemon juice; sieve and, if desired, reheat with
sugar until it dissolves.

Culinary Uses
This delectable fruit is perfect on its own. Just
slice off the top and eat straight out of the skin
with a spoon—add cream and sugar if you must.
However, there are other delicious ways to enjoy
passion fruit: ice-cream, fruit salad, sorbet,
mousse and pavlova are all ideal to show off its
exotic fragrance. The juice is made into jelly,
punch, sherbet and cocktails. A jam is made from
the whole fruit and the sweetened pulp thickened
with cornflour makes a lovely hot sauce for
ice-cream.

Herbal Properties
Unsurprisingly it is the passion flower (*Passiflora
incarnata*) that is used in folk medicine. The leaves
and flowers are antispasmodic and sedative,
owing to their alkaloid principles. Various tisanes
and extracts figure in remedies for certain
nervous heart troubles, and insomnia.

Facts and Features
Native to South America, passion fruits come
from a family of tropical climbers of 350
members. Nowadays they are grown
commercially in Australia, Africa and
southeastern United States. The name derives
from the Jesuit missionaries habit of illustrating
the Passion to South American natives by
analogy with the passion flower: petals and
stamens represent the apostles; style, the nails;
stamens, Christ's wounds; filaments, the crown
of thorns.

PEPPER
India

Piper nigrum
Fam Piperaceae

Green Pepper, Green Peppercorns

India: hara mirch, sava mirch; Indonesia: lada, merica, milagu (Tamil), mreetje, mreeyos, pedes, saang, sakang; Malaysia: lada, maluku, mereetja; Middle East: filfil; Thailand: prik thai

Nutritional Values
Pepper is used in small quantities so has little nutritional value. No data exist for green pepper; the following are for black pepper, which is the whole green peppercorn dried.

cal	347	Ca	130	A	—
pro	12	P		B_1	0.04
fat	7	Fe	10	B_2	0.02
car	59	Na		B_5	1
fib	4.9	K		C	—

Real, fresh, raw pepper grows in long clusters close to a central stem, resembling plump jade-green currants. Each round peppercorn is slightly larger than its common dried black counterpart, being about 4–6mm (⅙–¼in) in diameter. The best specimens are bright green but by the time they reach Europe from the tropics they have lost a little of this dazzle. Split, they emit a unique 'peppery' bouquet delicately anticipating that of the pepper we know so well. The flavour is similarly milder, fresher and subtler, appealing to nouveaux and traditionalists alike.

Selecting the Best
Green peppercorns are available spasmodically from specialist shops and some supermarkets. Usually sold in punnets they are at their best when green throughout, plump and shiny. Reject them if they are turning black—a sure sign of a brief future.

Storage and Preparation
Use green peppers as soon as possible since they deteriorate swiftly, but if absolutely necessary keep in the refrigerator. On no account freeze them. Remove the fruits from the stem and either leave them whole or mash them with a fork or the flat of a knife.

Culinary Uses
Although dried peppercorns have been used in the West since Grecian times, the recent importation of fresh green corns is a very welcome development for cookery buffs. Less biting than black pepper their piquancy and strikingly fresh aroma go wonderfully well with fish and grilled meat and poultry. Simply crush the peppers with a little salt and add to warmed fresh cream for a sauce for fish, or mash with butter, garlic and a squeeze of lemon—excellent when chilled for grills. Use them whole in terrines and pâtés or lightly mashed onto steaks instead of crushed black pepper. New devotees will sprinkle them whole over their food. In India, green peppercorns are pickled alone in brine, or in oil together with green mangoes, chillies and ginger. They enjoy a special place in Thai recipes for game where, with basil and a lavish larding of chillies, they grace wild boar as well as other perhaps more curiously intriguing dishes of creatures such as bat, snake, crocodile and iguana.

Herbal Properties

Pepper's pungent principles, mainly chavicine and piperine, stimulate the digestive system. For this reason, and for its carminative and febrifuge properties, it was once popular in Western medicine, but is used hardly at all today in such capacities. In the East it still has a fairly important role in folk medicine, with many more properties attributed to it than those above, mainly for complaints of the respiratory, genito-urinary and digestive systems. Modern Western folk medicine believes a mixture of butter and ground white pepper licked at regular intervals is an authentic cure for sore throats.

Facts and Features

If black pepper is the 'King of Spices' then its green original could be called 'Princeling Pepper'. Pepper may be a 'king' but as with so many monarchs, 'villain' would be an apter expression. The quest for the once-legendary spice by European kingdoms, merchants and adventurers was a central purpose in the activities of imperialism and exploitation, only now, if at all, being lived down by the world's self-styled 'civilised' nations. Green peppers are harvested immature, the rest ripening to red and treated to create black and white peppers.

PERSIMMON (KAKI, SHARON)
China, Japan

Persimmons are the sort of fruit most people view with some circumspection before they decide to try one. They resemble brown-orange or rich red-orange tomatoes with bulges capped by a dry-looking calyx, and commonly measure up to 6cm (2½in) in diameter. Oriental varieties, called kakis, have large almond-like seeds in a slippery jacket embedded in their juicy pulp, whilst the latest Israeli products, sharon fruit, are seedless. With a shiny thin skin, the flesh of all varieties is soft and watery and does have a tomato-like texture. The fruits have to be very ripe before they can be eaten otherwise they are unpleasantly sour and astringent. Softness and an over-ripe look indicate maturity, when the flavour becomes very attractive, sweet and thirst quenching. The skins of the cultivar types, like sharon, are edible, although leaving a dryish aftertaste; when cut in half equatorially the flesh is a brilliant glistening orange with an eight-pointed translucent star—where the seeds used to be.

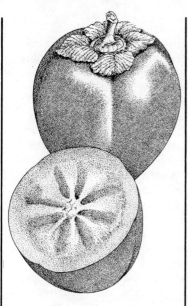

Diospyros kaki
syn *Embryopteris kaki*

Fam Ebenaceae

*Chinese Date Plum, Chinese
Persimmon, Date Plum, Japanese
Persimmon, Kakee, Keg-fig, Sharon
Fruit, Virginian Date*

*China: chee; India: halwa tendu;
Japan: kaki*

Nutritional Values
*Nothing is known of sharons'
nutritional qualities but the
composition of American persimmons
is given below:*

cal	77	Ca	6	A	2,710
pro	0.7	P	26	B_1	0.03
fat	0.4	Fe	0.3	B_2	0.02
car	19.7	Na	6	B_5	0.1
fib	1.6	K	174	C	11+

Recipe:
Sharon Ginger Cream, page 201

Selecting the Best
Persimmons are now offered for sale by
greengrocers and supermarkets, and are usually
available between the end of October and
February. They must be soft to be eatable.
Bruised or split ones are obviously undesirable
but old-looking fruit are, strangely enough, the
best buy, having lost their bitterness and callow
stiffness.

Storage and Preparation
If you buy firm specimens they can be ripened at
home stored at room temperature—just monitor
the ageing process, looking out for some
incandescence.

Culinary Uses
Freeze the pulp for a natural sorbet, or whip up
with a tot of liqueur for a frothy fool.
Persimmons are used in a variety of traditional
early American dishes such as cakes, pies and
puddings. These fruits are enhanced by sweet
spices such as nutmeg, cinnamon and mace.
Sharon fruit, at home in savoury dishes, can be
treated like melon or avocado, served with
vinaigrette, salad or Parma ham. In Iran,
persimmons are pickled with dates, dried limes
and aromatic spices.

Herbal Properties
In China, the ripe fruit is used as a remedy for
stomach complaints and piles, the stalk for
respiratory ailments and hiccups, and the juice
from green fruit for high blood pressure.
Persimmon is said to have a high iodine content.

Facts and Features
Persimmons, of which there are hundreds, can
basically be divided into two groups: American
and oriental. The American persimmon,
Diospyros virginiana, was a godsend to the early
settlers who learned from the American Indians
how to use and enjoy it. Oriental persimmons
(kakis) are grown commercially in the
sub-tropics, while sharon fruit, a refined cultivar,
belongs to Israel. Modern varieties on sale,
originally only from China, are now grown in
Europe and the Mediterranean lands. In America,
the oriental version has replaced the native stock
commercially. The persimmon has always been
loved in the orient, especially Japan where it
enters into mythological history.

134

PETAI
Malaysia

Parkia speciosa
syn *P. roxburghii*
Fam Leguminosae

Stinkbean

India: khorial, supota; Indonesia:
pete(j), petteh, sindootan; Malaysia:
pete

Nutritional Values
*Petai is an extremely nutritious food
in the tradition of legumes. It is a
good source of protein and is rich in
vitamin B complex. Some related but
less common types are quite useful in
vitamin A.*

Dry beans (no moisture):

cal	443	Ca	259	A
pro	27.3	P	283	B_1 0.38
fat	27.6	Fe	2.4	B_2 0.04
car	40.5	Na		B_5 3.41
fib	1.7	K		C 20

Petai, pronounced 'pet-ay', are weird-looking pods, long and twisted like sticks of barley sugar. They come from the Far East. Hanging in clusters, they measure up to 45cm (18in) long and are about 3cm (1–2in) wide with distinct seed swellings lying across the pods rather than downwards like broad or runner beans. Usually green, they tend to collect some blemishes by the time they reach UK shops. The edible portion, the seeds or beans, are enclosed in a slightly sticky beige coat that sometimes has to be removed. The beans themselves resemble broad beans in shape and size but are of a much brighter green. The raw flavour is pungent and rather garlicky. Cooked, they have a bitter-sweet nutty savour and a meaty texture which goes down famously in Southeast Asia.

Selecting the Best
In theory, petai is an all-year crop but as yet is seen only sporadically in specialist Indonesian and Thai shops. A few bunches or 'strings' are considered sufficient due to their pungency. Discoloured pods are not necessarily 'off' and the shopkeeper's word will have to be relied upon.

Storage and Preparation
Keep in the cool and use as soon as possible. The stalks and pods are discarded, and regrettably petai are not as simple to prepare as broad beans. In older ones the tough leathery bean pod has to be removed with a certain amount of vigour to extract the actual beans. If they are young use the complete bean otherwise remove the outer beige coat.

Culinary Uses
Petai beans are relished in Indonesia and Thailand for their pungent flavour which it would seem is quite addictive. They are especially good included in *sambal udang*, a spicy side dish of prawns, onions and chillies. They are also liked with pork and with beancurd, dried shrimps and bean sprouts and of course chilli. The Thais bathe them in chilli sauce alone and they are a prized addition to the *rijsttafel*.

Herbal Properties
In Thailand, petai is believed to be a urinary system tonic and purifier. In India, the leaves and bark go into lotions for skin diseases. In Malaysia the seeds and pods are used to relieve stomach complaints.

In Southeast Asia there are several members of this group of plants whose pods and seeds are eaten for both flavour and nutrition. In fact Indonesian market sellers are never left with *pete* on their hands. The tree is regarded as very attractive—it is quite tall and bears millions of finely-feathered leaves—but like others of this family the pods that remain on the tree ferment and give off an unpleasant smell. The genus *Parkia* is named for Mungo Park, the great African explorer who perished in the Niger river at Bussa, Nigeria in 1806.

PHYSALIS
Peru

Physalis peruviana
syn *P. edulis*

Fam Solanaceae

Alkekengi, Barbados Gooseberry, Cape Gooseberry, Cherry Tomato, Chinese Lantern, Golden Berry, Ground Cherry, Winter Cherry

India: tepuriya, tipari; Polynesia: poha

The plump calyx that embraces this berry gives us its exotic oriental name—Chinese lantern. The spherical fruit, 1–2cm (½–¾in) in diameter, is originally green, ripening to orange, or occasionally brown, tan or purple. It contains many small edible seeds. The calyx turns from green to beige as it dries. The flavour is sharp and sweetish, rather like unripe blackberries.

Selecting the Best
Physalis are available from specialist shops during the winter months. Open a sample if you can and look for unblemished, tight, shiny orange skin. Green berries are unripe.

Storage and Preparation
In storage, leave the berries in the husks and consume as soon as possible once ripe. Peel back the papery husks to reach the fruit and remove stalk and husk if required. To prepare the fruit for eating alone or for *petits-fours*: retain the stalk for handling and peel back the natural divisions of the husk to form a halo of 'petals' behind the berry. Use scissors if necessary.

Culinary Uses
These fruits can be used raw or cooked. They are said to produce excellent jam, but in areas where they are less well known, it is well to serve them fresh so that the lantern can be displayed for decorative effect (see above). The berry can be dipped in rum-flavoured fondant (popular since Victorian times as part of the *petits-fours*) or glazed, or eaten straight, with Kirsch, or sometimes dipped in honey. These are all popular after-dinner treats served with coffee. Among cooked uses are purées, compôtes and cakes.

Nutritional Values
Physalis is rich in vitamin B_5 and has useful amounts of vitamin B_1.

cal	53	Ca	9	A	720
pro	1.9	P	40	B_1	0.11
fat	0.7	Fe	1	B_2	0.04
car	11.2	Na	—	B_5	2.8
fib	2.8	K	—	C	11

Herbal Properties
The berries of *Physalis alkekengi*, the ornamental relative, are diuretic and laxative. The whole plant is used medicinally in China.

Facts and Features
A member of the tomato family, physalis is native to the regions of Mexico, South America and the southern US. It has been under cultivation for some two hundred years in southern Africa, and the special interest shown it in the Cape of Good Hope supplies its best-known name, Cape gooseberry. Following its introduction to France it became a gastronomic rage in the Paris of the late eighteenth century, where they dreamed up all manner of elaborate ways to serve it. In cultivation similar to the tomato, physalis not only has an ornamental variety, the winter cherry (*P. alkekengi*), but edible cousins, the Mexican tomatillo or jamberry (*P. ixocarpa*) and the American ground cherry or strawberry tomato (*P. pruinosa*).

PLANTAIN
Southeast Asia

Musa paradisiaca
Fam Musaceae

East Africa: ndizi; India: kadally, kela, ram kulla, wali-kulla;

Plantains or 'macho bananas' are, strictly speaking, unripe bananas but the term is used as the name for those large, usually green or yellow, bananas that are cooked before eating. They are characterised by hard green skins and dryish, starchy, fibrous flesh. Ripe plantains turn from green through yellow to black and sweet. At 20–30cm (8–12in) they are larger than the average banana. They are easy to spot in that they look hardier and wilder than their effete dessert cousin.

Selecting the Best
Available from Asian and West Indian outlets, plantains are selected according to the ripeness suitable for a particular recipe. Unripe ones are plump and bright green. These will ripen in a matter of days to yellow, half ripe, and then to black when they are fully ripe and soft to the touch when gently squeezed.

Storage and Preparation
Plantains are always eaten cooked. Ripen them on a window sill. Do not refrigerate. They may be cooked in their skins whole or topped and tailed, or peeled. Ripe ones are easily peeled but green ones are cut along the ridges and the skin pared off with a knife. Peel under water to prevent

Indonesia: g(h)ed(d)ang, keesang, peesang, pisang hijau, tjao; Malaysia: pisang; West Indies: plantain

Nutritional Values
Although a staple in some parts of the world the plantain is not a complete food, being poor in protein and calcium.

cal	119	Ca	7	A	11,000
pro	1.1	P	30	B_1	0.06
fat	0.4	Fe	0.7	B_2	0.04
car	31.2	Na	5	B_5	0.6
fib	0.4	K	385	C	14

staining of the hands. For roasting or barbecuing, slit the plantain skin from end to end and turn frequently during cooking. It will be tender in 15–20 minutes. Boiling green fruit in their skins takes about 30 minutes. For crisps, cut wafer-thin slices of green or half-ripe plantain and soak in cold water for 30 minutes before drying and frying.

Culinary Uses
South and Central America, the Caribbean, India, Southeast Asia and tropical Africa are the regions where plantain is eaten as a staple. Its changing characteristics as it ripens make it quite versatile; it has a yam-like starchiness when green, is potato-like when half ripe and soft and fruity when ripe. In South America it commonly goes into soups, stews and *tostones*, Venezuelan fritters: 25mm (1in) slices are fried for 10 minutes, pressed flat between two boards or stones and then fried again. Similar fritters are enjoyed in India, flavoured with turmeric. Plantain chips, sprinkled with chilli powder are a common Ghanaian wayside snack. In Africa and the Caribbean *foo foo* is made from plantain, alone or with other starchy vegetables. *Tum tum* is a Trinidadian favourite, when butter, seasoning and milk are added to *foo foo*, which is then shaped into dumplings for serving with *callaloo* (see page 179) or stews. Spicy dumplings, or *koftas*, in a curry sauce are popular in India. Many sweet dishes can be made from plantains. They are delicious baked in their skins, slit open and sprinkled with brown sugar and rum. Flavoured with cinnamon and vanilla in the West Indies, or cardamom in India, cooked ripe plantains are mashed with egg and flour and fried in spoonfuls until crisp. They are made into steamed desserts, *halva* and a sweet dish of yoghurt, mango, pineapple and honey scented with rose water. An interesting wine can be made from the fruit.

Herbal Properties
In India, all parts of the plant are used. The fruit is given to relieve diarrhoea, as well as being a laxative. It helps respiratory troubles, and the ash of the peel is used as a dressing on broken skin. Ripe plantains with ghee are given to restore sexual virility.

Facts and Features
As the banana (see page 15) is one of the world's most important tropical plants in commerce, so is

the plantain important in local terms. Hardier and more widespread than the refined sweet banana, it is a major fruit, even a staple, in many parts of the tropics, growing happily in moist conditions. The tree provides roofing and packaging materials, a sap from which toddy is made, and plenty of much-needed shade. The flowers are eaten in Southeast Asia. Plantain plants grow in large clumps, continuously spreading.

POMEGRANATE

Iran

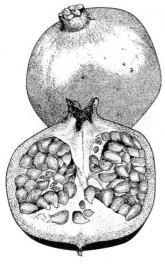

Punica granatum

Fam Punicaceae

Grenadier

China: (on) shek lau; France: grenade; Germany: Granatapfel; India: a(r)nar, dalim, darim, darimba; Indonesia: mathulam param (Tamil); Iran: anar; Italy: melagrana; Japan: zakuro; Malaysia: delima; Middle East: rana, roman, ruman; Spain: granada; West Indies: granada, grenade, grinard, pomegranate

The pomegranate looks like an apple with a small tufted crown. It is spherical, often 6–9cm (2½–3½in) in diameter, yellow or red-brown, sometimes with a light blush or sunspot. There is a hard tough hide, quite inedible, and a rubbery yellow inner skin which penetrates through the fruit dividing the seed-strewn flesh into many small compartments. This yellow pith is extremely bitter, and not to be eaten. The flesh is a swarm of crisp and pulpy seed covers of a beautiful translucent deep pink resembling so many small jewels. It is refreshingly acid-sweet, and the crunchy seeds it encloses are also edible, but bitter. These seeds are sometimes available dried, as a spice, well known in India as *anardana*.

Selecting the Best
This is an autumn fruit. Buy clean and unblemished pomegranates with a firm skin and a deep blush.

Storage and Preparation
Keep refrigerated until required—at least a week. To extract the seeds: cut a slice off the top and then cut downwards into sections. Carefully pull away sections of the seeds from the skin. Now press the seeds through a sieve to obtain juice and try not to crush the bitter black seeds.

Culinary Uses
Pomegranates are most usually eaten raw; you can add sugar or salt. In cookery, the juice is mostly used but the seeds are edible and also make a beautiful jewel-like garnish. The fruit goes favourably into most kinds of salad, and pomegranate can make ice-cream, water-ice, jelly, or a syrup to go with other fruits, also a sweet-sour piquant sauce for meats and stews. This latter use is typically Middle Eastern where pomegranate seeds are combined with walnut in a sauce for duck or chicken, in a stuffing for fish

Nutritional Values
Pomegranate has little to offer nutritionally.

cal	65	Ca	3	A	trace
pro	0.65	P	8	B_1	0.05
fat	0.5	Fe	0.45	B_2	0.03
car	16.3	Na	3	B_5	0.6
fib	0.2	K	259	C	6

and a topping for cooked wheat. Cinnamon is nearly always used to complement pomegranate. The juice laces a dish of spinach and lentils and is made into a cold fruit soup, or cold drinks and sherbets. The pomegranates used in Middle Eastern dishes are more sour than those imported into the UK so add a little extra lemon juice or *sumac* to the recipe. The French syrup *grenadine*, originally made from pomegranates, lends its rich colour to numerous cocktails.

Herbal Properties
Pomegranate has powerful properties—dangerous in high dosages. Rind, fruit and flowers are astringent and demulcent, and are used in gargles and douches, combating diarrhoea and fever. In India, the juice is a styptic. The seeds and bark were formerly purgative of tapeworm, famed in British India but now considered too dangerous!

Facts and Features
Native to the region from the Mediterranean to India, limited by some botanists to Iran, the pomegranate comes from a two-member group. Popular with the Moors who cultivated it in what is now the eponymous Granada, it presently grows all over the tropics and sub-tropics, especially South America. There are a few poor-fruited garden forms. It was early known to man, and is a candidate for the apple of the tree of life in Eden, amongst many exotic fruits. Known to the ancient Egyptians and Romans, who named it *punicum* after Carthage, the fruit has widespread religious connotations, being mentioned in the Bible and the *Quran*, and featuring in Chinese art. The persistent calyx is explained in a Greek myth as a cruel jest of Bacchus after he promised one of his nymphish conquests that she would wear a crown—she was metamorphosed into the first pomegranate. The seeds were Persephone's only food in the underworld, and they determined that she would stay down there for half the year, while we upstairs had winter. The rind produces a red dye for morocco leather.

POMELO
Malaysia

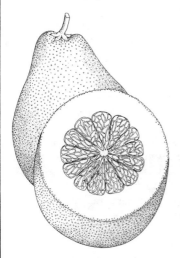

Citrus grandis
syn *C. decumana, C. maxima*
Fam Rutaceae

Pummelo, Shaddock

China: lok yaw, yao; India: batavi-neboo; Indonesia: djerook bali; Malaysia: limau betawi; Thailand: som or; West Indies: forbidden fruit, fruit defendu, pomelo, shaddock, shadette

Nutritional Values
Like all citrus fruits, the pomelo is a useful source of vitamin C and modest in calories.

Raw fruit:

cal	34	Ca	26	A	0
pro	0.6	P		B$_1$	0.04
fat	0.2	Fe	0.5	B$_2$	0.02
car	8.5	Na		B$_5$	0.2
fib	0.8	K		C	35

Recipe:
Forbidden Candy, page 210

The pomelo is the largest citrus fruit and probably grandsire of the grapefruit. It can measure 10–30cm (4–12in) across, is usually round with flattened ends and has extremely thick green to yellow rind. The firm flesh, pale yellow, cream or pink, is divided into the usual segments. Pomelo lacks the bitterness of grapefruit, although the pleasant-tasting juicy flesh is coarser. Some varieties are seedless.

Selecting the Best
Choose well-rounded fruit; avoid ones with soft patches.

Storage and Preparation
Store pomelos in the cool, they will keep for several weeks. To peel the fruit and obtain even-sized pieces of peel for candying: wash the fruit, cut off the top and make twelve or more downward incisions. Pull away the strips of peel, deepening the cuts if necessary. To obtain skinless segments of fruit: with a sharp knife pare away membrane and remnants of pith and carefully separate the segments from the skin.

Culinary Uses
Use like grapefruit. Serve it as a dessert fruit or steep it in rum and sprinkle it with coconut; make marmalade and preserve the rind. Pomelo does especially well in salads—with shellfish, avocado or salad leaves.

Herbal Properties
No special properties are known for the pomelo.

Facts and Features
Native to Malaysia and Thailand, this fruit grows in tropical lowlands, while other citrus fruits do best in the sub-tropics. In a poor form it has escaped to thrive wild in parts of the Mediterranean, and reached Britain in the seventeenth century. The alternative name 'shaddock' is owed to the East India captain, Shaddock, who transported seeds to Barbados. The best fruit is from Perak and Thailand. In the orient it replaces the grapefruit, which may be a hybrid between pomelo and orange. Cultivation is on various scales, and commercial production is on the increase in Israel.

PRICKLY PEAR
possibly South America

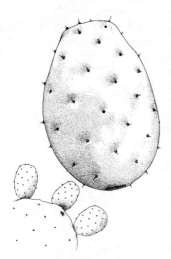

Opuntia spp

Fam Cactaceae

Arridari, Barbary Fig, Barbary Pear, Bastard Fig, Cactus Berry, Cactus Pear, Indian Fig, Indian Pear, Tuna

France: figuier de Barbarie, raquette; Germany: Feigendistel, Kactusfeige, Opuntie; India: chappal, naphana; Italy: fico d'India; Spain: chumbera, higo chumbo

Nutritional Values
Prickly pears have some vitamin C.

cal 40	Ca 20–110	A 55
pro 0.8	P 28	B$_1$ 0.03
fat 0.2	Fe 0.4	B$_2$ 0.04
car 9.8	Na 0.2	B$_5$ 0.3
fib 2.1	K 166	C 20

Prickly pear, as the name suggests, is the fruit of cactus plants. There are several varieties but the ones you are most likely to come across are about 8cm (3in) long, 5cm (2in) wide, grenade-shaped, plum red or greeny-orange with pink blushes and—their most characteristic feature—spotted over their skins with tiny tufts of bristles. These 2 mm (⅛ in) wide clumps of spines occur about 1cm (½in) apart and actually form a discernible pattern of diagonal lines. They are very sharp, barbed and painful. The skin, thin and quite soft, encloses a dense deep orange or red pulp swarming with small crunchy brown seeds, edible but swallowed whole. The aroma of the juicy flesh is fresh and floral, like marigold, and its flavour is sweet and melony, needing an addition of some sharp contrast such as lemon or lime to be really appreciated.

Selecting the Best
Prickly pears are available during the late summer. Do not buy soft ones—avoid prickle nests when testing for firmness. A good pinky-orange or plum colour is indicative of ripeness.

Storage and Preparation
They keep well under refrigeration—up to 2 weeks. They are difficult to handle without getting pricked. Hold with a fork and peel with a knife—two implements are essential. Top and tail, peel and slice or halve lengthways and scoop out the flesh with a spoon. If you want to discard the seeds rub through a sieve.

Culinary Uses
Oddities like these should be treated as naturally as possible. Eat them fresh with some citrus juice—lemon, orange or lime. Have them with cream, or in a fruit salad. Prickly pears make a good jelly with the added tang of passion fruit and orange. The fruits can also be made into jam, candied or preserved. The 'leaves' (or 'pads') and shoots are sometimes cooked as a vegetable.

Herbal Properties
In India, prickly pears are considered cooling, demulcent and expectorant. The fruit or its syrup is applied in several chest complaints and venereal disease. The fleshy branches and leaves provide poultices and their juice is purgative.

Facts and Features

Native to the Americas, these cacti have spread throughout the world, escaping to become wild in areas like Greece and Italy. They are widely used in the southern Mediterranean as well as the Americas, and are a staple in hard times among poor rural communities in Mexico. The prickly pear may have been brought back from the New World by Columbus, and was introduced to California by the Franciscan monks. In India and the Mediterranean it is cultivated as a garden plant, for food, and in Africa for *bomas* and *kraal* fences.

PURSLANE

Eastern Europe and Western Asia

Portulaca oleracea

Fam Portulacaceae

Garden Purslane, Green Purslane, Pigweed, Porcelane, Portulaca

China: kwa tze tsoi; France: pourpier; Germany: Portulak; Greece: glistrida; Holland: postelain; India: (bade) lunia, dholica, kulfa, nuniya sag; Indonesia: gelang, kerayapan, kradjep, krokot, poslen, rek-serekan, re-sere(y)an; Malaysia: gelang, krokot; Middle East: bagli, ba'le, khurfa, turuk; Spain: verdolaga; United States: pussl(e)y

Purslane is a small succulent herb. It has fattish red-tinged stalks with soft, rounded mid-green leaves, whose undersides are silvery. The leaves vary in size, 3–6cm (1¼–2½in) long by 2–3cm (¾–1¼in) broad. They are thick and juicy with no aroma. The raw flavour, which is reduced on cooking, is mild, refreshing and slightly tart.

Selecting the Best

Purslane can be found in Indian, Greek and Middle Eastern food stores during the summer. Sold in bunches, both stalks and leaves should be plump and well rounded. Perhaps to facilitate identification, Herklots informs us that the Malawi name signifies 'the buttocks of the wife of a chief'.

Storage and Preparation

It is best to use purslane as fresh as possible but it will keep in the salad drawer for a day or so. The leaves and stalks can be used separately or together.

Culinary Uses

With its increasing availability in the UK it is hoped that purslane will recover its reputation as a succulent and flavoursome vegetable. It is served as a salad with vinaigrette dressing, often with other leaves, and may also be cooked like spinach. The stalks are pickled in vinegar. Purslane is also delicious in soups, especially with potatoes or peas, giving them a particularly smooth texture. As well as in southern Europe it is grown and relished in India, China, Southeast Asia, East and Central Africa and the Middle East. In these areas it is eaten raw or cooked in

Nutritional Values
Purslane is a good source of iron and a minor one of vitamins A, B₅ and C. These benefits are, however, offset by its high oxalic acid content, a substance that inhibits the absorption of calcium and magnesium.

Nutritional Values
Purslane is a good source of iron and a minor one of vitamins A, B$_5$ and C. These benefits are, however, offset by its high oxalic acid content, a substance that inhibits the absorption of calcium and magnesium.

Raw/Cooked:

cal 21/15	Ca 103/86	A	2,500/2,100
pro 1.7/1.2	P 39/24	B$_1$	0.03/0.02
fat 0.4/0.3	Fe 3.5/1.2	B$_2$	0.1/0.06
car 3.8/2.8	Na —/—	B$_5$	0.5/0.4
fib 0.9/0.8	K —/—	C	25/12

Recipe:
Fattoush, page 192

the appropriate regional style. One of the best known recipes including purslane is from Syria—a bread salad called *fattoush*.

Herbal Properties
Purslane has had worldwide uses in traditional medicine. In China, the leaves are employed in cases of dysentery, diarrhoea and inflamed piles. In India, it is used to relieve a multitude of ailments, including scurvy, skin diseases, renal and lung problems, fevers, prickly heat (with the stem juice) and intestinal troubles. In English folk medicine purslane is considered a vermifuge; it is also believed to remove warts, allay fevers, assuage thirst, ease inflammations, dysentery and toothache, and to be 'good for teeth that are set on edge with eating of sharpe or soure things' (Gerard, 1597).

Facts and Features
Purslane's origin is obscure but can be narrowed down to eastern Europe and western Asia. It now occurs throughout the world and is a pest in North America. It was used in Pharaonic times and by the Persians over two thousand years ago. There are two types, green (described here) and golden-leaved (*Portulaca sativa*), but opinions differ as to which is considered best for cooking. In ancient times it was regarded as an anti-magic plant, and Grieve quotes this engaging belief: it was a sure cure for 'blastings by lightening or planets and burning of gunpowder'. In India, the plant is nicknamed 'civil servant' because its flowers open at nine o'clock and close at four. Purslane, in common with other succulents, dislikes the wet and proves this by surviving in the hottest climates, often outlasting other green vegetables.

QUINCE
Western Asia

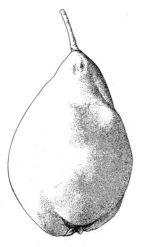

Cydonia oblonga
syn *C. vulgaris, Pyrus cydonia*

Fam Rosaceae

Coin(e), Cuoyne, Cydon Apple, Quin

China: mu kua; France: coing; Germany: Quitte; Greece: melon kydonion; Italy: (melo) cotogno; Japan: kuwinsu, marumeru; Spain: marmelo, membrillo

Quinces, the fruit of love, are similar in shape to a pear and in structure to an apple but with many more seeds in tough-sided pockets. They are hard and only eaten cooked. The skin is bright yellow with patches of down. Size varies from 6–10cm (2½–4in) long. Many modern cultivars are almost perfectly spherical. The hard, gritty, yellow flesh is acid and the whole fruit highly aromatic.

Selecting the Best
Imported quinces are available from February to May, and home or European-grown ones, though scarce, in October and November.

Storage and Preparation
Quinces should be stored like apples in a cool airy place; do not let them touch each other. They will ripen on a window sill and are ready when yellow all over. Always rub off the down with a cloth before cutting or peeling. Some recipes do not require the fruit to be peeled or cored; if necessary you will need a good peeler and a sharp knife as the flesh is hard. Quinces discolour when cut but turn a lovely deep pink when cooked. Blanch and freeze some slices to be added to apple pies and crumbles during the winter.

Culinary Uses
Enjoyed in both sweet and savoury dishes in the south and east Mediterranean, Central and South America, quinces nowadays are something of a rarity in England although once much prized. The fruit contains plenty of pectin so is ideal for jams, jellies and sweetmeats. It is cooked to advantage with apples or pears—one quince will well set off an apple pie, for instance. Quinces can make a fine soufflé with any other fruit; again, a small quantity brings out other flavours. Poach them in syrup, add them to bread puddings or bake them like apples and serve them with cream. *Contignac* is a French confection of quince paste and this sweetmeat appears under various names in the Middle East, Morocco, Spain, Italy, Portugal and Greece (where it is packed in layers interspersed with bay leaves), as well as in Mexico, Brazil, Uruguay and Venezuela. In North Africa, the Levant and Persia quinces are stuffed with cinnamon and spiced lentils and stewed with beef, chicken, lamb or game. Make a fruit spirit by steeping slices in brandy, rum or vodka with a few sweet spices or make a sherbet or sorbet from the juice left over from the quince paste.

Nutritional Values
Quinces are bereft of any useful nutritional values.

cal	57	Ca	11	A	40
pro	0.4	P	17	B₁	0.02
fat	0.1	Fe	0.7	B₂	0.03
car	15.3	Na	4	B₅	0.2
fib	1.7	K	197	C	15

Recipe:
Quince Sweetmeats, page 211

Herbal Properties
Quince is beneficial in constipation, coughs and mouth and throat inflammation. The cores are aperient. A Chinese relative, *Cydonia sinensis*, is used as an astringent and analgesic in herbal medicine.

Facts and Features
Possibly native to Iran, quinces are grown throughout the Mediterranean and in Turkey, Syria and South America; Uruguay exports annually 3,000 tonnes. The tree is a member of the rose family. The fruit was popular in classical times (Cydonia being the Greek name for Crete, a major source in those times), and was connected with marriage and fertility. It is Aphrodite's fruit, the apple of Venus, given her as a beauty prize by the hero Paris. The delicate aroma will refresh any room. Formerly grown in Cydonia were japonicas or Japanese quinces (*Chaenomeles* spp). The fruits are smaller and harder and only good for jellies, the plants being common ornamentals.

RAMBUTAN
Malaysia

Nephelium lappaceum
syn *Nephelium cappacum,*
Scytalia ramboutan

Fam Sapindaceae

'Hairy lychee' sums up the rambutan. About the same size and colour as a lychee, its leathery skin bristles with myriad soft spine-like hairs. This egg-shaped fruit is up to 6cm (2½in) long and 4cm (1½in) wide, and the hairs are about 15mm (⅗in) long. The skin encloses a firm translucent-white pulp which surrounds a large, fibrous, almond-shaped, inedible seed. The flesh is firm and juicy, grape-like in texture, melony in flavour, very like a lychee, though less aromatic.

Selecting the Best
Rambutans can be found in certain greengrocers and oriental food stores in the summer. The flesh should separate cleanly from the stone in the better varieties.

Storage and Preparation
Ripe fruit should be eaten as soon as possible. On cutting the skin a small volume of clear sweet juice exudes from the fruit, so cut over a bowl to save it.

Culinary Uses
Rambutans are sometimes sold canned together with pineapple, and can go with this or any other tropical fruits in a salad. Otherwise use like

Hairy Lychee, Rambo(e)tan,
Ramboostan, Rambustan,
Rampostan

*Indonesia: rambootan; Malaysia:
rambosteen, ramb(o)utan; Thailand:
ngo, ngor*

Nutritional Values
*Somewhat similar to the lychee in
nutritional content, the rambutan has
only half that fruit's vitamin C.*

cal		Ca	11	A	
pro	0.46	P	13	B_1	
fat		Fe		B_2	
car	16.02	Na		B_5	
fib	0.24	K		C	30

lychees (see page 105). Rambutans are
particularly delicious steeped in brandy and
topped with cream.

Herbal Properties
The fruit is believed to be astringent,
anthelmintic and stomachic. The nuts are bitter,
possibly narcotic. The leaves go into poultices for
headache, in India, and shampoos, in Indonesia.
The pericarp contains tannin and a toxic saponin.

Facts and Features
Native to Malaysia, the rambutan has been
grown for ages in the low tropics of Southeast
Asia, and is currently under some little
development in Australia. Strictly a tropical fruit,
its cultivation has not been successful elsewhere,
nor has the fruit commercially in spite of the
worldwide development of Southeast Asian
communities and vast increase in tropical
tourism. 'Rambutan' means 'hairy', from Malay
'*rambut*', 'hair'. It is pronounced ram' butan. The
Latin *lappaceum* means 'burr-like'.

SALSIFY AND
SCORZONERA
Southern Europe

Tragopogon porrifolius
Fam Compositae

Scorzonera hispanica
Fam Compositae

Salsify looks like a long thinnish carrot. The skin
is smooth, dirty-white or yellowish, with a few
hairs. The roots average 15–20cm (6–8in) in
length and are about 2.5cm (1in) at the widest
part. The flesh is white and crisp. The flavour is
'delicate' with tones of globe artichoke and
asparagus. It has also been likened to that of
oysters. In contrast, scorzonera has a brown to
black skin and is more cylindrical and sometimes
thinner, although usually the same length. The
flesh is white and similar in flavour to salsify.

Selecting the Best
Both vegetables are available from autumn to late
spring. The black scorzonera is more likely to be
offered than salsify. Select them smooth and
firm, not damaged or wizened, and handle
carefully or they will bleed and deteriorate.

Storage and Preparation
Keep, like carrots, in the salad drawer or in a
cool, dark airy place. Once cut, salsify and
scorzonera rapidly discolour so it is simpler to
cook or parboil them in their skins in salted,
acidulated water, and rub off the skins under the
tap when slightly cooled. If you do peel them
first, immediately drop them into acidulated
water and then boil them in salted water to which

Salsify: Nap-at-Noon, Oyster Plant, Purple Goat's Beard, Salsafy, Star of Jerusalem, Vegetable Oyster; Scorzonera: Black Oyster Plant, Black Radish, Black Salsify, Serpent's Root, Spanish Salsify, Viper's Grass

France: salsifis; scorsonere; Germany: Bocksbart, Haferwurzel; Schwartzwurzel, Scorsoner; Iran: sersifim; Italy: barba di becco, sassefrica; scorzonera; Spain: salsifi (blanco); escorzonera

Nutritional Values
The calorific value of both vegetables varies during storage as the contained inulin is converted into sugar. Whilst the inulin content is high (in fresh vegetables), salsify and scorzonera are safe in diabetic diets.

Raw (there is a slight reduction in values when cooked):

cal	13–82	Ca	47	A	10
pro	2.9	P	66	B$_1$	0.04
fat	0.6	Fe	1.5	B$_2$	0.04
car	18	Na	—	B$_5$	0.3
fib	1.8	K	380	C	11

Recipes:
Chicken Pie with Salsify, page 188

a tablespoon of flour has been added. Cut them before or after initial cooking into 5–13cm (2–5in) lengths according to the recipe. They will cook in 20–30 minutes depending on thickness and the texture should have a certain bite to it.

Culinary Uses
On the whole, salsify and scorzonera's popularity is confined to continental Europe—which is a pity, as they are winter vegetables of particular delicacy. Perhaps it is this very delicacy which, if masked by more determined flavours, is lost on us. Both vegetables make lovely cream soups, can be cooked and served cold with oil and lemon juice or eaten like asparagus. They are sautéed in butter and made into croquettes and fritters. They are delicious served *au gratin* with a light mornay sauce or simply boiled with *beurre noisette* added at the table. They are agreeable partners to chicken in a pie to be eaten hot or cold. If you are interested in Japanese cookery and cannot get hold of burdock or *gobo*, a salsify relative and much used in Japan, substitute either salsify or scorzonera.

Herbal Properties
Salsify is reckoned to have an anti-bilious effect and to be a febrifuge. In Mexico, scorzonera was considered by the Indians to be good for a chill. Two of scorzonera's popular names derive from an old Spanish belief in its efficacy against snake bite: '. . . and especially to cure the bitings of vipers (of which there be very many in Spaine and other hot countries, . . .) . . .' (Gerard, 1597).

Facts and Features
Salsify and scorzonera, lettuce relatives, are native to southern Europe. Salsify has purple flowers whilst scorzonera's dandelion-like flowers are yellow. Both are recorded by Gerard (1597) and were reported in America in 1806. There are two explanations of the origin of the name 'salsify': one is that it is taken from the Latin *saxa-frica*, 'stonebreaker'—presumably the root is strong enough to grow in stony ground, although all gardening authorities recommend a light soil—and the other is that it comes from the Latin *solsequium*, 'sun-following'. 'Scorzonera' is simply Spanish 'black bark'. A similar European plant is Spanish oyster plant or golden thistle, *Scolymus hispanicus*, and in Japan there is another, burdock or *gobo*, *Arctium lappa*. Both these are used like salsify and scorzonera.

SAMPHIRE
Europe

ROCK SAMPHIRE
Crithmum maritimum
Fam Umbelliferae

Crest Marine, Herbe de St Pierre, Paspar (Scotland), Pierce-stone, St Peter's Cress, Sea Fennel, Sea Samphire

France: bacile, fenouil de mer; Germany: Meerfenchel; Italy: critmo, finocchio marino; Spain: hinojo marino

MARSH SAMPHIRE
Salicornia spp
Fam *Chenopodiaceae*

Chicken Claws, Crab Grass, Frog Grass, Glasswort, Pickle Plant, Poor Man's Asparagus, Saltwort, Sea-grape, Swy

Nutritional Values (both species)
There are no data on the composition of samphires but several authorities state that rock samphire has a high iron content and, like other marine plants, contains iodine.

Two types of these seashore plants are of interest:

Rock samphire which, as its name implies, grows on the rocks and cliffs of European seashores, looks like a very fat and succulent dill. The leaves grow as fleshy, tapering spikes and are grey-green, 1–2cm (½–¾in) in length and 3–4mm (¹/₁₀–³/₂₀in) at their widest part. The smell and flavour are salty, strongly pungent and aromatic.

Marsh samphire grows on salty mud-flats below the high tide mark. Knotted and jointed like a chicken's claw, the fleshy spikes are sea-green and the whole plant is only 30cm (12in) in length. It has a crisp texture, is tangy and reminiscent of the sea, and possibly carries a hint of asparagus.

Selecting the Best (both species)
Available from spring to early summer and at their prime in May, both species are found, albeit spasmodically, on the fishmonger's slab or in some supermarkets.

Storage and Preparation
Eat them as soon as possible for they do not keep. Rinse most thoroughly and steam or boil briefly—about 5 minutes— in unsalted water. Trim the roots if not eating them like asparagus. For pickling, discard the roots and cut the rest into 2.5cm (1in) lengths. The tender young shoots are prepared in the same way.

Culinary Uses
These singular vegetables are usually pickled, whether they are our own coastal species or the Spanish, East or West Indian breeds. However, the marsh samphire is delicious eaten as a vegetable like young beans or like asparagus, the sprigs being dipped into melted butter and drawn between the teeth. Because of its seaside habitat, samphire often precedes or accompanies a fish course but the pickle is delicious too with bread and cheese. Pickled samphires have long been used as a condiment and caper substitute. Very tender little shoots or stems are added raw to salads or dressed with oil and lemon juice as an hors-d'oeuvre.

Herbal Properties
Gerard states that rock samphire is mildly diuretic and linthontriptic. He also says that marsh samphire is strongly diuretic and 'a great quantitie taken is

Recipe:
Samphire Pickle, page 208

mischievous and deadly'. He adds that the smoke and smell of this herb drives away 'serpents'.

Facts and Features

Rock samphire can actually be grown at home, close to a wall with cracks and crevices. It has long been harvested from its wild state: 'Half way down/Hangs one that gathers samphire, dreadful trade.' (King Lear, at the Dover cliffs.) Marsh samphire is related to spinach and is also commonly harvested wild. It is well known on the East Anglian mud-flats. It was formerly used in the manufacture of glass. The Arabic name for its ashes, *al-qili*, is the origin of the word 'alkali'.

SAPODILLA
Central America

Manilkara achras
syn *Achras sapota, A. zapota, M. zapota, M. zapotilla, Sapota achras*

Fam Sapotaceae

Chico, Chiku, Ciku, Dilly, Marmalade Plum, Naseberry, Nispero, Santa Domingo Apricot, Sapodilla Plum, Sapota, Sapote, Tree Potato

Round or egg-sized, sapodillas have a rather unappetising, rough brown look but if you have found good-quality ones they are quite an interesting addition to the list of exotic fruit, and are praised as one of the best South American fruits. Having a sweet pulp, soft and granular, yellow to brown, fragrant and melting, they are likened to pears or to ripe bananas, or even to brown sugar. There are up to a dozen (but more usually two) large, black, hooked seeds.

Selecting the Best

Available all the year from Asian and West Indian shops, they vary greatly in quality, and are also called naseberries or nispberries according to the intonation. Hard fruits are unripe and when scratched the skin shows green. Ripe ones are quite soft to the touch.

Storage and Preparation

If hard, store at room temperature until soft. Do not use until ripe as there is an astringent juice or latex in the immature fruit. Warning: discard the seeds with their little throat-catching hooks—they can be dangerous. Chill before peeling and slicing.

Culinary Uses

The sapodilla is eaten as a dessert fruit—you can slice and eat it with lime juice, or with coconut, a dash of rum or even mayonnaise. One tropical recipe asks you to cube the fruit (seeding them first) and heat with cooked rice, lemon peel and ginger in a little water. Another suggests a purée with cream, lemon and sugar for a fool or a combination with milk and eggs for a custard to

China: yum sum go; France: zapotier; India: chiku, sapota; Indonesia: cheko, sawo landa, sawo maneela; Malaysia: chiku, ciku, sawo maneela; Thailand: lamut (farang); West Indies: chapotee, chicle, dilly, Martinique apricot, naseberry, nesple, nispero, sapidilla, sapodilla, sapotie, zapota

Nutritional Values
For such a sugar-rich fruit sapodilla is poor in its other nutritional aspects.

cal	90	Ca	22	A	50
pro	0.5	P	16	B$_1$	trace
fat	1.1	Fe	1	B$_2$	0.02
car	22	Na	12	B$_5$	0.2
fib	1.5	K	190	C	14

make ice-cream. The pulp can be made into sweetmeats like quince (see recipe page 211) but using a third less sugar. It is a good candidate for fruit snow with the addition of a little lime juice. Sapodilla ice-cream is a favourite in the West Indies, where the pulp is also strained into dough for cakes, muffins, etc and made into sherbets.

Herbal Properties
No particular properties are known.

Facts and Features
Sapodillas are native to tropical South America, and are one of its more important fruits, especially in southern Mexico, Central America, the West Indies and Hawaii. The seeds have a long viability. The tree is a frequent fruiter and so it became popular and established in worldwide tropics. It was known to the Aztecs, and the strong red wood was carved by the Mayans—examples still remain. The milky latex sap, chicle, in the tree wood is the base of chewing gum, and is used in dental surgery as a gutta-percha substitute. Similar fruits from other families are also often called 'sapote'.

SORREL (ROSELLE)
West Africa

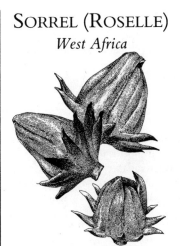

Hibiscus sabdariffa var *sabdariffa*
Fam Malvaceae

Indian Sorrel, Jamaica Flower, Jamaican Sorrel, Red Sorrel, Rosella, Thorny Mallow

At first sight on the market stall, sorrel or roselle looks like heaps of brilliant crimson flowerheads. However, sorrel, used for its juice, is actually the remnant (fruiting calyx) of a tropical flower. The attractive fleshy calyxes that remain after flowering are crimson, crisp and crunchy with a velvety sheen. Rose-bud shaped, they measure about 2.5cm (1in) high, although you will see larger and smaller ones in any batch for sale. Inside is a seed pod. Raw they are acidic and astringent but when cooked with sugar give a delightful mix of tart and sweet.

Selecting the Best
You will find sorrel in West Indian stores and market stalls around Christmas time, its bright red colour a fitting contribution to the festive air. Fruits should be succulent and unblemished; 455g (1lb) of sorrel will yield 225g (½lb) of fleshy pieces for making into juice.

Storage and Preparation
Use as soon as possible, though sorrel will keep in a polythene bag in the salad drawer for a few

Indonesia: gamet (walanda), ki soodjen; West Indies: flor de Jamaica, l'oseille, l'ozeille, rosella, roselle, rozelle, sorrel, sour-sour

Nutritional Values
Some vitamin C is available and there is sufficient pectin to make jelly.

cal	55	Ca	110	A	50
pro	1.7	P		B_1	0.04
fat	1	Fe	2.2	B_2	0.06
car	12	Na		B_5	0.4
fib	1	K		C	18

Recipes:
Rosella Jelly, page 211; Sorrel, page 212

days. It is not essential to separate the calyxes from the seed pods but it is general practice. Either cut the stem off with a sharp knife and pare round the end, removing fleshy parts in one operation, or strip them off by hand. For juice or pulp boil three measures of calyxes in two measures of water. For jelly, strain the cooked pulp overnight and add to the juice half to three-quarters its weight in sugar. The jelly will set after 5 minutes of rapid boiling.

Culinary Uses
In the West Indies, refreshing drinks and punches are made from sorrel, especially during the Christmas celebrations, whether innocuous or highly spirited. Jellies, jams and sauces—plain, spiced, sweet and savoury—are made, all of them tangy and ruby red. Sorrel is a good substitute for cranberry and is popular in American-style moulded savoury jellies.

Herbal Properties
None known.

Facts and Features
Indigenous to West Africa, sorrel, so named because of its sourness, has been taken to all parts of the tropics both for its flowers as a flavouring, and as an ornamental. Its leaves and young shoots are eaten in Indonesia; in Nigeria the dried flowers are made into soups, cakes and sweetmeat balls. Another variety (*H.s.* var *altissima*) is grown for fibre in India and the Far East.

SPROUTED SEEDS

The three types of sprouted seeds described below—alfalfa (lucerne), mung bean and soybean—are commonly available in the shops. However, for home sprouting, you can buy packets of seed mixes containing several other varieties such as adzuki, cress, fenugreek, mustard and rice.

Alfalfa (Lucerne) Sprouts
Southwest Asia
Medicago sativa

Fam Leguminosae

Other names for the full-grown plant are: Alfa-alfa, Berseem, Buffalo Herb, Cultivated Lucerne, Purple Medic(k), Purple Medicle, Sainfoin

China: kam fa tsoi, muk suk, mu-su; Middle East: fasfasah

Alfalfa sprouts are grown from the seeds of a most nutritious Mediterranean plant normally cultivated as a valuable fodder crop. They are threadlike, white, 2.5–5cm (1–2in) in length, tipped with a tiny green leaf. They should be crisp in texture and are delicate in flavour with a pleasant bitterness.

Mung Bean Sprouts
India
Vigna radiata
syn *Phaseolus aureus, P. mungo, P. radiatus*

Fam *Leguminosae*

Bean Shoots, Beansprouts, Chinese Bean Sprouts, Peasprouts, Salad Shoots, Silver Sprouts (headless and tailless). Seed names: Black Gram, Golden Gram, Green Gram, Moong Bean, Oregon Pea, Tienstin Green Bean

China: lo do ya, nga(h) choi (jai), ngun nga choi (silver sprouts), sai dau nga choi, sai tau nga tsoi, tou ya tsoi; India: titori; Japan: moyashi; Malaysia: taugeh; Thailand: tua ngork

Bean sprouts, once a rarity, are now a common sight in shops and supermarkets. Good sprouts should be shiny, white with cream tinges, firm and have two clearly-developed, yellow, embryonic leaves. Their green husk should have been removed before marketing. Sprouts average 5–15cm (2–6in) in length and their diameter varies between that of a matchstick and a drinking straw. Raw sprouts (see below) taste of a cross between pea and cabbage and cooked they are milder with a crisp, crunchy texture. In Indian shops you will find day-old bean sprouts that are mostly bean with a short shoot protruding.

Soybean Sprouts
Eastern Asia
Glycine max
syn *G. hispida, G. soja, Soja max*

Fam Leguminosae

Soybean sprouts are much larger than other sprouts. Usually about 15cm (6in) long and the thickness of a knitting needle, the stalks are ivory-white surmounted by two greeny-yellow halves of the original seed. The stalk tapers to a fine straggly root. Some stalks have a few tiny hairy roots growing out about midway up the

Big Sprouts. Long Sprouts
Seed names: Coffee Bean, Soja
Bean, Soya Bean, White Gram

China: daai dau nga choi, huang do
ya, taai nga tsoi, wong dow gna;
Indonesia: dangsool, demekan,
(katjang) kadele, (ke)dele(h); Japan:
daizu

Nutritional Values (all species)
There are no data available for
alfalfa sprouts, but it can be assumed
that their nutritional qualities are
largely similar to other sprouted
seeds. In most seeds sprouting activity
generates vitamin C absent in the
original seed, and reduces some
vitamin B complex, but cooking
drastically reduces the former. It
becomes necessary however to cook
bean sprouts in order to reduce the
contained trypsin inhibitors if the
sprouts are to accompany protein-rich
foods.

	MUNG		SOYBEAN	
	RAW	COOKED	RAW	COOKED
cal	35	28	46	38
pro	3.8	3.2	6.2	5.3
fat	0.2	0.2	1.4	1.4
car	6.6	5.2	5.3	3.7
fib	0.7	0.7	0.8	0.8
Ca	19	17	48	43
P	64	48	67	50
Fe	1.3	0.9	1	0.7
Na	5	4	—	—
K	223	156	—	—
A	20	20	80	80
B₁	0.13	0.09	0.23	0.16
B₂	0.13	0.1	0.2	0.15
B₅	0.8	0.7	0.8	0.7
C	19	6	13	4

Recipes:
Bean Sprouts with Tofu, page 190;
Chat Masala, page 209; Gado
Gado, page 193; Golden Hooks
with Jade Plates, page 180; Pickled
Bean Sprouts, page 207

stalk. The flavour is of raw pea becoming blander on cooking. The texture is firm and crunchy.

Selecting the Best (all species)
It is essential to buy alfalfa and bean sprouts when absolutely fresh. They are available loose or in plastic packs. Reject any packs which have limp-looking sprouts or have a brown moisture content. Sprouts should be clean and white. The larger soybean sprouts, available from Chinese shops, are sometimes tied in neat bundles.

Storage and Preparation
Best eaten straight away, but if bought really fresh alfalfa and bean sprouts may be kept for a day or two in the salad drawer of the refrigerator. Rinse in plenty of fresh cold water from time to time before cooking or eating raw. It is not necessary to remove any lingering bean husks. Nip off the straggly root of soybean sprouts. Indian bean sprouts are first washed and then cooked for 10–15 minutes. To sprout alfalfa and beans at home, soak a tablespoon of seeds in a jam jar full of water for 12 hours. Empty out water and rinse in fresh water twice daily. Keep in the light and they will be ready in about a week. Alfalfa may also be grown on a wet cloth like mustard and cress and is considered more digestible if blanched for a few seconds in boiling water. For Indian-method bean sprouts: soak in water for 24 hours, drain and hang up in a cloth for a further 24 hours until the sprouts appear.

Culinary Uses
Now quite a popular salad sprout, alfalfa may be mixed with green salad leaves, tomatoes or cucumbers, etc. Used thus it makes a crisp and delicate garnish and may also be used in sandwich fillings in the same way as mustard and cress. Mix sprouts into cottage cheese or add them to a mushroom and ham filling for an omelette. No doubt Chinese restaurants and take-aways have largely contributed to the now widespread popularity and availability of mung bean sprouts, which are also a favourite of the health conscious. In the Far East bean sprouts figure in soups, salads and particularly in stir-fried dishes. They are an ingredient in such well-known dishes as Chinese spring roll, Japanese *sukiyaki* and *gado gado*, cooked salad from Indonesia. They go well with beancurd or *tofu*, whose bland softness highlights their fresh crispness. This latter use

applies particularly to soybean sprouts. Indian bean sprouts, popular when fresh vegetables are scarce, are cooked in various ways such as with onions and spices in coconut milk, and in *pakoras*, or served with diced potatoes, dates, chillies and spices, soured with tamarind and lime juice—an elaborate snack accompanied by *puries*, deep-fried little Indian breads. They are ideal for vegetable soups such as *minestrone*.

Herbal Properties
Bean sprouts are little known in folk medicine, unlike their seeds which have many ascribed properties.

Facts and Features
All the above seeds used for sprouting come from plants with many interesting features. Alfalfa is one of the world's richest fodder crops, being known to the Arabs for centuries. The plant is so rich in nutrients that it is actually unpalatable to humans, but recent processing efforts are overcoming this drawback. The roots are extraordinarily prolific and sink to great depths in the soil absorbing all the nutrients available. Pollination is effected by insects releasing the stamens which are held in tension naturally like the seed pods, which are coiled spirally as the lower edge grows more rapidly than the upper. There are over 2,000 recognised types of mung bean, with many different coloured beans, hence the different names. The Chinese have sprouted mung beans for three millennia and today Japan imports over 40,000 tonnes a year purely for sprouting. Researchers at Heriot-Watt University in Edinburgh have successfully used mung beans to screen anti-epilepsy drugs, thus reducing the number of animal tests. The soybean is the richest vegetable protein source known to man and in many guises is central to Chinese and Japanese cuisine. It is now widely grown in the US corn belt for animal and human food, especially as a meat substitute for the latter.

SQUASH
Americas

Of all the tribes of fruit and vegetables that of squashes and pumpkins must surely be the most confusing. Not only are there hundreds of varieties in the tribe but single members go by a multitude of names. Here we give a basic framework for some of the types that are appearing in British shops.

WINTER SQUASHES AND PUMPKINS

Cucurbita maxima
C. mixta
C. moschata

Fam Cucurbitaceae

There are too many cultivar names to list.

China: fan kwa, nam kwa; India: (halwa) kaddu, mistikumra, mitha kumra, vilayati kaddu; Indonesia: labooh, walooh; Japan: kabocha; Malaysia: laboo; West Indies: calabaza, courba, giraumon, jarmou, pumpkin, squash

This group of squashes includes 'Hubbard', 'Delicious', 'Turban', 'Banana', 'Warty', 'Mammoth', 'Cushaw', 'Cheese', 'Crookneck', 'Butternut', 'West Indian Pumpkin' etc. Some of these names are self-descriptive. Except for the last two, the shells are hard; all shells vary in thickness, colour and texture. Similarly the shapes are extraordinarily diverse: globular, pear-shaped, banana-shaped, constricted, cylindrical, curve-necked, protuberant and many others. The flesh is usually yellow to orange, fine grained with good flavour and sweetness. To give a few examples:

'Turban' or 'Turk's Cap': Round, smooth, 'capped' (as though another squash was about to protrude); cap: orange, green and cream stripes; main body: orange; flesh: yellow–orange, firm, sweetish; 1–1.5kg (2–3lb).

'Little Gem': Spherical; very dark green; flesh: pale yellow, soft, delicious; 225–455g (½–1lb).

'Apple' or 'Little Dumpling': Spherical, gently to strongly ribbed; green and cream stripes; flesh: dull yellow, watery, sweet potato flavour; 455g–1kg (1–2lb).

'Crookneck': Smooth, swan-necked; deep yellow; flesh: orangey, soft, courgette flavour; 1kg (2lb).

'Golden Delicious': Onion shaped, faintly grooved; bright orange; flesh: orange, sweet, creamy; 1kg (2lb).

Summer Squashes, Pumpkins and Marrows
Cucurbita pepo
Fam Cucurbitaceae

Too many cultivar names to list.

India: chappan kaddu, kumra, mistikumra, mitha kumra; Nigeria: ponky; West Indies: gourd, gourge, marrow, squash

Nutritional Values (all species)
Squashes are low-calorie vegetables suitable for such diets. Summer squashes are a reasonable source of vitamin C but half is lost in cooking. Winter squashes are similarly endowed with vitamin A. The more orange the flesh, the richer it is in vitamin A precursor.

All raw:

	SUMMER SQUASH	WINTER SQUASH	PUMPKIN
cal	19	50	26
pro	1.1	1.4	1
fat	0.1	0.3	0.1
car	4.2	12.4	6.5
fib	0.6	1.4	1.1
Ca	28	22	21
P	29	38	44
Fe	0.4	0.6	0.8
Na	1	1	1
K	202	369	340
A	410	3,700	1,600
B_1	0.05	0.05	0.05
B_2	0.09	0.11	0.11
B_5	1	0.6	0.6
C	22	13	9

Recipe:
Pumpkin Succotash, page 187

This set includes 'Acorn' or 'Table Queen', vegetable marrow (English), courgette and cocozelle (Italian), pie pumpkins ('Thanksgiving'), 'Scallop' or 'Custard' or 'Patty Pan', 'Summer Crookneck' and 'Straight-neck', spaghetti marrow and 'Fordhook'. They are characterised by having paler flesh in many cases, from greenish-white through cream to yellow or pale orange, since they are usually immature fruits. The pie pumpkins have orange flesh. Again the shapes and skins vary enormously and the names are generally self-descriptive. Examples:

Pumpkin: Spherical, slightly flattened; orange, stalk heavily ribbed; flesh: orange, sweet; size variable.

'Acorn': Pointed, smooth; dark bottle-green, shiny; flesh: firm, yellowish, flavour mild; 1kg (2lb).

'Patty Pan' or 'Custard': Flattened, fluted edge; white, smooth; flesh: white, translucent, watery, sweetish; 455g (1lb).

'Scopolini': Like 'Patty Pan'; very dark green, tough shell; flesh: greeny-yellow, crunchy, sweetish; 455g (1lb).

'Golden Nugget': Spherical, faintly fluted; bright orange; flesh: pale orange, flavoursome; 455g (1lb).

Spaghetti Marrow: Cylindrical, bristly stalk; very pale greeny-yellow, smooth; flesh: pale yellow, stringy, flavour good; 455g (1lb).

Selecting the Best (all species)
Thin-skinned squashes such as custard squash and spaghetti marrow should, like courgettes, be well filled out, smooth and firm—not flabby. These types are mostly available in the summer. Hard-skinned squashes like 'Acorn', 'Hubbard' and pumpkin, usually autumn and winter vegetables, have a thick rind which resounds when sharply tapped. Large squashes are often sold in wedges when the flesh should look firm and non-fibrous. Look out for signs of mildew at the stalk end.

Storage and Preparation
Thin-skinned varieties keep for several days wrapped in polythene in the salad drawer, as do wedges of hard-skinned squashes. To store these latter types whole, they must be in perfect peak. In a cool, airy place they will keep for several months. Thin-skinned squashes are not peeled, but washed, trimmed if necessary, left whole or

sliced like courgettes. The exception is spaghetti marrow which enjoys special treatment. Cut off the stalk, insert a skewer towards the other end and boil for about 30 minutes. Halve lengthways, remove the seeds if large and eat the spaghetti-like strands of flesh out of the shell topped with a pasta sauce or just with butter and cheese. Tough-skinned squashes can be peeled before cooking, according to the recipe, are halved if small or cut into wedges or cubes. Carefully remove the seeds and fibres. If the shell is to be used for serving stews or soups, cook the whole squash in the oven at 190°C (375°F), gas mark 5, for an hour and cool. Slice off the top for a lid, making a notch to line up lid and bottom exactly. Scoop out the cooked flesh with a sharp spoon, discarding seeds and fibres.

Culinary Uses
The types of squashes described here are used in cookery typical mainly of the Americas. Other kinds of squash are discussed under gourds (page 75) and chayote (page 34). Thin-skinned ones are cooked like courgettes or vegetable marrows. Others may be peeled, cubed, steamed and then mashed with butter. Alternatively they are baked in the oven in their half shells, unfilled or stuffed with a meat or rice filling. Any way they are delicious. Yellow pumpkin is made into pie, puddings, soups, candies and succotash, an American Indian dish of pumpkin, beans and sweetcorn. Calabaza or West Indian pumpkin is cooked in various ways as a vegetable, made into soups, often with nutmeg, and into desserts, buns, breads and jam.

Herbal Properties
Only the pumpkin appears to have properties ascribed to it and these are restricted to its seeds and seed oil. Pumpkin seeds have been prescribed as a vermifuge for centuries, originally in America which was soon followed by Europe, Africa and China. Oil from the seeds is also used to soothe burns and chapped skin, and for healing wounds.

Facts and Features
There are over 750 species in the Cucurbitaceae family which includes gourds, melons, cucumbers, luffas, chayotes, gherkins, squashes, pumpkins and marrows amongst others. In the squash group (Cucurbita) there are over 25

species all originating in antiquity in the Americas. This diversity of form defies neat classification and the multitude of names becomes a nightmare. Apart from this, the species can be crossed (although not across genera) and many freaks can appear naturally in any squash-growing situation, adding to the already huge multifariousness of form.

SUGAR CANE
Asia

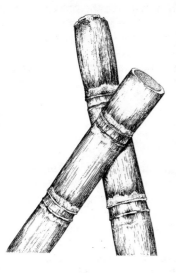

Saccharum spp
Fam Gramineae

China: kum jay; East Africa: miwa; India: ak, ik, kajooli (red), kooshiar, kulloa, ook, poorid (white); Indonesia: toorooboos; Malaysia: telor; Middle East: sukkar (sugar); South America: panela; West Indies: cane, canne

Like a solid bamboo stem, sugar cane is now seen in UK ethnic markets. Bamboo is probably familiar to you as a thin noduled stalk, but real bamboo is fat—about or over 5cm (2in) in diameter—and so is sugar cane. Whole stalks, browny-orange or purple, are on sale, cut into long poles or shorter lengths. There are also peeled and chunked pieces, a few centimetres long, fresh or chilled. Very sweet and very fibrous, sugar cane has a novel appeal, especially to children.

Selecting the Best
Stout firm sticks are best, the heavier and more solid-looking the better; light ones are fibrous and less juicy. If you prefer to skip the ritual of paring the outside buy the ready-prepared pieces.

Storage and Preparation
Wrap sugar cane pieces in cling film and keep in the refrigerator. Sugar cane consists of juicy fibrous sections separated by very hard nodes. Cut the nodes off the end of each section and peel, or use one node for control as you pare off the hard skin from the inner core. Peeled, the pithy, juicy centres can then be cut into small pieces for chewing. It is not worth trying to extract the juice at home; canned juice is available from specialist shops.

Culinary Uses
In countries where it grows, fresh raw sugar cane is a popular street or wayside snack and is mostly chewed to suck out the juice and the spent fibres are spat out, discreetly or otherwise. Slices are used to sweeten the stock for a Chinese pork and noodle soup but we suggest that, at sugar cane's current cost, this takes the quest for authenticity a shade too far. The juice makes popular drinks in India and the Caribbean and is also made into vinegar, syrup and *gur* or *jaggery*.

159

Nutritional Values
In its natural state sugar cane is mostly water, inedible fibre and sugars. It has some iron but little else.

Raw cane:

cal		Ca	8	A
pro	0.2	P	4	B_1
fat	0.5	Fe	1.3	B_2
car	12	Na		B_5
fib		K		C

Herbal Properties
Sugar cane has no special attributes apart from the energy-giving properties of its sugar content.

Facts and Features
Native to Asia and the Pacific, sugar cane belongs to a vast tribe of grasses covering much of the world's grassland. A major export crop in the tropics, it has become internationally important only in the last century, replacing the past various *ad hoc* products being used for sweetness, such as honey, beets and palms. Sugar production began in India about 3000BC, and refining spread to Venice and Antwerp in the Renaissance. It was Columbus who introduced it to the New World. Earlier, Marco Polo had been staggered by the amount he came across in the orient. Cane supplies two-thirds of the world's sugar, the rest deriving mainly from the temperate sugar-beet. A small supply comes from the date palm and the maple tree.

SWEET POTATO
Tropical America

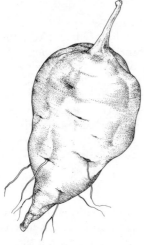

Ipomoea batatas
syn *Batatas edulis,*
Convolvulus batatas
Fam Convolvulaceae

Like our common potato, the sweet potato is a tuber, that is, a swollen starchy root. There are hundreds of varieties spread throughout the world, falling into three groups: dry, mealy-fleshed; soft, moist-fleshed; and very coarse-fleshed (used as animal feed). The tuber may be ovoid or elongated—shape is highly variable, as is size, 15cm (6in) and 455g (1lb) being a useful average. The skin may be smooth or ribbed, pink, yellow, red, purple or brown, and may show patches or mottles. The flesh is white, yellow, orange or purple. The paler the colour the drier the flesh is and the darker the colour the moister and sweeter it becomes when cooked. White or pale-coloured varieties have a caramel-cum-chestnut flavour and are quite floury. Yellow and orange ones are sweeter and more watery.

Selecting the Best
Select as you would common potatoes. Damaged or mouldy parts could be harmful. The dark red-skinned, pale-fleshed variety is suitable for both sweet and savoury applications. The brown-skinned, yellow or orange-fleshed sweet potato is better for sweet cookery. Pick those of uniform and medium size.

Long Potato, Louisiana Yam, Spanish Potato, Yam, Ycam, Yeti

Burma: myonk-ni; China: fa(a)n shue; Cyprus: glycopata; India: mistialo, sakarkand; Indonesia: bodin, boled, gumbili, katela, ketala rambet, ketela, longgha, mantang, mita-alu, sabbhrang, skurar-kanda, tela, tingalan, tunda wulung, ubi-djalar, ubi-djawa; Japan: kara-imo, satsuma imo; Malaysia: keladi, keledek, ketela, ubi djalar; Philippines: kamote; Polynesia: cumar, kumala, uala, uara, umala, umara; Sabah: ubi china; South America: camote, kumar(a), kumal; West Indies: batate douche, mabi(y), patate, (sweet) potato

Nutritional Values
Sweet potatoes have one and a half times as much calorific value and vitamin C content as ordinary potatoes. The yellow and orange varieties are rich in vitamin A; the pale ones have virtually none.

Average, raw:

cal	115	Ca	25	A	10–10,000
pro	1.5	P	50	B_1	0.1
fat	0.3	Fe	1	B_2	0.05
car	27	Na	10	B_5	0.7
fib	1	K	300	C	30

Recipe:
Southern Pudding, page 201

Storage and Preparation
Store them in a cool dark place for up to a week. Before cooking wash them carefully as the skin can break. Boil them for about 25 minutes until easily pressed with a fork or bake them for about 45 minutes at 200°C (400°F), gas mark 6. If huge and have to be cut up, wrap in kitchen foil. For chips, parboil before cutting up, drying and frying. Sometimes they are grated raw before being made into fritters, breads or cakes.

Culinary Uses
As well as being adaptable to potato recipes, this versatile vegetable also makes delicious puddings, confectionery and sweet–savoury dishes such as layers glazed with butter, brown sugar and orange juice to accompany the traditional Thanksgiving dinner. In Latin America and the Caribbean it is made into croquettes, fritters and savoury patties, is plain baked or found in spiced puddings, casseroles, soufflés, breads, cakes and sweetmeats. There are recipes for savoury pie crusts and potato cakes which are virtually identical to our recipes for potato pastry and Irish potato cakes, the flavour of the sweet potato adding a pleasant nuttiness. In Africa it is an important ingredient of *fufu* besides being universally baked on its own. Indians like it curried, particularly in a mixed vegetable curry, and in many sweet confections.

Herbal Properties
Sweet potatoes and their leaves contain antibacterial and fungicidal substances, and are used in folk medicine. Gerard (1597) considered them aphrodisiac.

Facts and Features
The sweet potato was cultivated in prehistoric Peru. It has spread round the world but how it reached Polynesia remains a mystery that is still hotly debated. On one side we have those who believe man took it there, and on the other are those who speculate that seeded vines clinging to branches or logs were swept out to sea and across the Pacific, ending up on the various islands. Columbus brought it to Europe where it predates the common or Irish potato by nearly half a century. References to potato in Elizabethan drama are directed to this now exotic tuber!

TAMARILLO (TREE TOMATO)
Peru

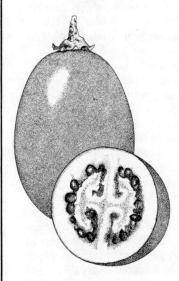

Cyphomandra betacea
syn *Solanum fragrans*

Fam Solanaceae

La Paz Tomato, New Zealand Tomato, Tamarilla, Tomarillo

Nutritional Values
Tamarillos are a useful low-calorie source of iron, vitamin B complex and vitamin C.

cal	20–50	Ca	9	A	750
pro	2.2	P		B_1	0.1
fat	0.9	Fe	0.8	B_2	0.04
car	10.3	Na		B_5	1.2
fib	1.6	K		C	30

The tamarillo or tree tomato is an egg-sized fruit originally from Peru but cultivated on a commercial scale in New Zealand and Kenya. The thin skin is red, sometimes yellow (the paler, the sweeter the fruit), tough and inedible. The flesh is firm but juicy, a mixture of brilliant red, yellow and the black of the many small edible seeds. The flavour has been likened to tomato, hence its name, and is sourish and very savoury for a fruit.

Selecting the Best
Tamarillos are available from specialist shops and supermarkets from Feb to October. They are ripe when firm but yield to gentle pressure.

Storage and Preparation
Tamarillos keep for about a week in refrigeration and will freeze well, peeled and sugared. To peel: plunge in boiling water for 2 or 3 minutes, then cool in cold water and peel from the stem end. To 'stew': slice, sprinkle with sugar and leave for several hours. The fruit becomes soft and juicy. To eat raw, scoop out pulp, sugar it and leave to stand.

Culinary Uses
Tamarillos are versatile fruits. Use them like tomato, in salads, with fruit or vegetables, or on their own with cream, ice-cream or yoghurt. Puréed tamarillos make a refreshing topping for meringues, cheesecake, pies and other desserts. They go down well with liqueurs such as Curaçao or Kirsch. On the savoury side, tamarillo slices make a tangy sandwich, with some lettuce, cottage cheese, and chicken, cold meat or fish. They are grilled or baked with meat, or added to pasta dishes, and make excellent jams and chutneys.

Herbal Properties
None known.

Facts and Features
Native to South America, probably Peru or Brazil, the tamarillo is now grown in India, Sri Lanka and many medium-altitude tropical locations, and is under development in New Zealand and Kenya as a commercial crop. In South America the fruit is often used as an alternative to tomatoes. The plant comes from the tomato-potato family and is good as a small garden fruit tree.

TAMARIND
Africa

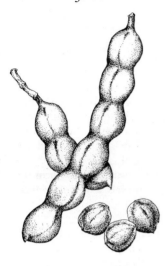

Tamarindus indica
syn *T. officinalis*
Fam Leguminosae

Indian Date, Tamarindo

India: am(b)li, amyli, chinch(a),
chinta, im(a)li, imlee, tentool, tintil,
tintiree, umli; Indonesia: asam, asem
(djawa), attjem, pulee, puli, tangkal
asem, tjelo(k), wit asem; Malaysia:
asam (djawa), kayoo asem, puli; Sri
Lanka: siyambala; Thailand:
makahm, mak kam, som ma kham;
West Indies: tamarin(d),
tambran(d), tambrun

Nutritional Values
The pods yield between 40 and 55
per cent pulp which is highly
nutritious but is not used in large
quantities owing to its sourness.
Tamarind is low in vitamins A and
C but rich in B complex. Pectin (3
per cent), plus tartaric (10 per cent),
citric, malic, oxalic and hydrocyanic
acids are also reported. The
composition of tamarind varies
greatly between Asian, African and
West Indian varieties.

Tamarind is now available in several forms: 'fresh' pods, cakes of pulp and seed, and refined extract. Resembling a fingerstall, the pods are brown with many tiny faint speckles giving them a leather-like appearance. Curved, but often irregularly shaped, they are sometimes broken revealing the darker brown flesh that surrounds the seeds. The thin and brittle pods measure 15–20cm (6–8in) in length and about 1–2cm (½–¾in) in diameter. The dense flesh is dark chocolate in colour and has a springy texture. Two or three round, stringy fibres run along its underside. The outlines of the seeds are visible. There is no aroma but the taste is sour and astringent, yet refreshing and flavoursome. Blocks of pulp and seeds similar in appearance to pressed dates are available in Indian shops. Refined and 'instant' tamarind, which looks like yeast extract, is sold in small tubs.

Selecting the Best
Fresh tamarind pods are occasionally found in Indian food shops. Avoid broken ones if possible as these may harbour insects. Blocks of pulp and tamarind extract are always obtainable. These, especially the blocks, may already be spiced, so read the label carefully.

Storage and Preparation
Tamarinds stay viable for months and need no special storage—just keep in the food cupboard. As they dry out they will take correspondingly longer to soften in water. The brittle shells are easily broken and the stringed flesh pulled out. To make tamarind juice, steep the flesh and beans in hot water for several hours—good-quality ones need only an hour—always using a glass or china bowl (tamarind juice is a traditional metal cleaner in India); then strain off the liquid. About 55g (2oz) of tamarinds to 285ml (½pt) of water should do. For paste, break up the soaked tamarind and work the pulp through a sieve, adding some of the soaking liquid as necessary. Discard the seeds and fibres. The paste can be refrigerated in a screw-top jar for several weeks, or deep frozen.

Culinary Uses
Tamarind is a souring agent like lemon juice or vinegar; it is used all over India, Southeast Asia, the Caribbean and parts of the Middle East. Lemon or lime juice can be substituted but its

Raw pulp:

cal	214–283	Ca	17–170	A	30–100
pro	2.3–3.5	P	11–113	B_1	0.2–0.4
fat	0.2–1	Fe	1–11	B_2	0.08–0.16
car	56–72	Na	3–51	B_5	0.1–1.1
fib	2–5	K	570–780	C	2–10

Recipe:
Tamarind Fish, page 182

special sweet–sour flavour cannot really be duplicated. In India, it characterises pepper water—a thin spicy soup or broth drunk as a digestive throughout a meal. It flavours *dhal* and vegetable dishes, chutneys and many curries, particularly those with fish. Tamarind is also an important feature of fish dishes in Southeast Asia, as well as in marinades for grills and *satays*, and the sauce to accompany *gado gado* (see page 193), the famous Indonesian cooked mixed vegetable salad. It makes a cool refreshing drink akin to lemonade which is popular both in the Middle East and the Caribbean. Jams and jellies include it, especially guava jelly, and tamarind sweetmeats are consumed enthusiastically in the West Indies. The pulp is mixed with sugar and a little pepper and formed round a single seed to make tamarind balls, one of many confections sold from wayside stalls in Trinidad. Tamarind is one of the 'secret' ingredients of Worcestershire sauce and essential to its flavour.

Herbal Properties
Because of its sourness, tamarind has been ascribed many properties throughout the countries of the tropics, covering almost every ailment afflicting women and men. It is also aphrodisiac but the *Ananga Ranga* finds a further use: 'applied to the linga with honey' it will 'induce venereal paroxysms in the woman and subject her to the power of man.' We merely quote.

Facts and Features
Tamarind is believed to be indigenous to Africa but it has been recorded in India since antiquity. The long-lived trees (over 120 years), growing haphazardly, need little attention, and are a common sight in villages and hamlets. Most parts of the tree are useful. The leaves and flowers go into curries. Tamarind seeds are eloquently attractive, being used in domestic adornments and providing themes for popular novels. More practically they function as a food source in times of famine and are commercially exploited to make textile sizes and a tenacious wood glue. The fruit yields pectin and tartaric acid also on an industrial scale. The flowers, leaves and bark are recorded in Ayurvedic medicine. The wood is hard, and charcoal from it is especially good for gunpowder. The leaves give a red dye and the fruit pulp cleans silver and brass.

TURMERIC

There are two turmeric-type rhizomes now available: true turmeric and mango ginger.

TURMERIC (HALDI)
Southeast Asia
Curcuma domestica
syn *C. longa*
Fam Zingiberaceae

Indian Saffron, Tumeric, Yellow Ginger

Burma: sa-nivin, ta nwin; China: wong geung fun, wong keung; India: aaldi, halad, hald(h)ar, haldi, hardra manjal, haridra, pitras; Indonesia: koneng, konje, kunir, kunjit, kunyit, manjal, munjal; Malaysia: kunjit, kunyit, manjal; Middle East: kharkoum; Polynesia: avea, cago, rerega; Sri Lanka: kaha; Thailand: kamin (leueng); West Indies: chichima, dye, tambric, turmeric

Turmeric or haldi is the root of a ginger-related plant. The roots are like ginger but smoother, smaller and not so knobbly. Their distinctive feature is the colour of the juicy, crisp flesh: bright orange like a carrot. The broken root has a minty aroma and the flavour is both attractively bitter and aromatic, but pungent.

MANGO GINGER (AM HALDI)
India
Curcuma amada
Fam Zingiberaceae

Often hard to differentiate from turmeric, mango ginger or am haldi is smaller and smoother but the flesh is quite different—it is pale yellow and has a strong distinct aroma of raw mango, hence its name in all languages. The flavour is different from turmeric, more like galangal, sharper and more aromatic.

India: a(a)m haldi, amada

Nutritional Values (turmeric)
Used as a flavouring in small quantities, turmeric has little nutritional value. The fresh rhizome yields 0.25 per cent oil and the dried version between 5 and 6 per cent. The essential oil consists mainly of borneol, cineol, phellandrene zingiberene etc. Turmeric's colour is derived from curcumin.

Turmeric:
Fresh root/Dry powder:

cal 53/390	Ca 51/200	A 0/175
pro 4.1/8.6	P —/260	B$_1$ 0.15/0.09
fat 0/8.9	Fe —/50	B$_2$ 0.21/0.18
car 10.9/63	Na —/10	B$_5$ 1.1/4.8
fib 1.2/6.9	K —/2,500	C 5/50

Selecting the Best (both species)
Haldi and am haldi are available from Asian markets and food stores and are often placed next to each other, so ask for them by name. Each should be firm, fairly smooth and clean looking. They should snap easily revealing the juicy flesh.

Storage and Preparation
Turmeric rhizomes keep for more than a month in a cool place or can be deep frozen and used as required. Peel or scrape away the thin skin and grate or pound the flesh. Use stainless utensils for turmeric as its dye is tenacious. About 2.5cm (1in) of the fresh root is equivalent to one teaspoon of turmeric powder.

Culinary Uses
Well known as a dried spice turmeric is equally effective fresh with its exhilarating and distinctively earthy flavour. Whilst fresh rhizomes are seldom used in Indian cookery, appearing only in certain curries, chutneys, pickles and sweet citrus drinks, they are essential to the Indonesian, Malaysian and Thai cuisines. The turmeric-inspired, yellow, spicy coconut sauce or *kari* for pouring onto rice typifies this style. Turmeric also colours and flavours soups, *satay* sauces, *sambals* and rice dishes—most obviously yellow rice. In seafood dishes, pounded turmeric and salt are very often rubbed inside the fish as well as into deep cuts on the outside. Mango ginger has no colouring properties but is used in much the same way as turmeric. In India it is pickled or candied.

Herbal Properties
In India the juice of the raw rhizome is used in treating skin and eye infections, and to heal smallpox sores and wounds. It is a household remedy for colds and catarrh. Stomach, liver and urinary complaints are also treated with it; and it relieves toothache and is a vermifuge. Modern research shows curcumin to be active against certain bacteria.

Facts and Features
Native to Southeast Asia, turmeric has spread round the world's moist tropical regions. Dried and ground it forms the base of curry powder to which it gives the characteristic yellow colouring. Whereas turmeric is widely cultivated, mango ginger is much less common.

UGLI
Jamaica

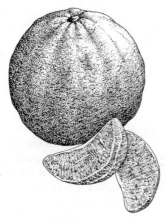

Citrus reticulata × C. paradisi

Fam Rutaceae

Tangelo

West Indies: hoogli, ugli

Nutritional Values
Like most citrus fruits, this one is quite useful in vitamin C and hesperidin (once called vitamin P) which regulates the permeability of blood capillaries.

The ugli is about the size of a grapefruit, though less shapely, having a rather knobbly green-orange skin, and is midway between orange and grapefruit in flavour. A hybrid of tangerine and grapefruit, it has all the citrus attributes—'porous' looking, rather loose skin, white pith, and juicy flesh which in reality consists of thousands of swollen hairs. The flesh is pinky-orange, sweet and often preferred to grapefruit. Seeds are few.

Selecting the Best
Avoid bruised or over-soft ones. They should feel heavy for their size.

Storage and Preparation
Keep in the cool. Uglis are easy to peel and the skin enclosing each segment should be carefully removed before serving.

Culinary Uses
Being a curiosity, this fruit is best raw, when its delicious flavour can be best appreciated. However, it mixes happily in salads and jellies, and is strangely palatable with cheese, especially soft cheeses like cream or cottage, and nuts. It makes excellent candied peel, marmalade and most things associated with citrus fruits.

Herbal Properties
Applied externally, the juice helps bruises to heal.

Facts and Features
The ugli is one of the multitude of citrus curiosities turned out by developers ever eager to extend their markets among the fruit-conscious public. Citrus fruits respond remarkably well to intermarriage, and many countries have an adoptive favourite hybrid—ugli is that of Jamaica. Tangelo is another citrus fruit of the same parents with the tangerine side dominating.

VINE LEAVES
Europe

Vitis vinifera
Fam Vitaceae

France: feuille de vigne; Germany: Rabenblatt; Italy: foglia di vite; Spain: pámpano

Nutritional Values
There are no data available on the nutritional composition of vine leaves. The tartness derives from organic acids. Tannins, mineral salts and sugars are present.

Recipe:
Stuffed Vine Leaves, page 187

The best vine leaves for stuffing are young and pliable and heart-shaped without deep indentations. They are bright green, sometimes with a fuzz on the underside, and measure 15×15cm (6×6in). There is usually a tough stalk remnant. They have a distinctive flavour—a certain tartness with a strong hint of unripe grapes. Older ones are coarse and need lengthy cooking.

Selecting the Best
Fresh vine leaves are sometimes obtainable in early summer from specialist shops; if you live in the south, try your local vineyard. They should be light to mid-green and neither dark, coarse nor wilting. Vacuum-packed or tinned leaves in brine are always available.

Storage and Preparation
They will keep quite well for a few days in the salad drawer but also they freeze very successfully after blanching. For stuffing: fresh leaves need to be washed and blanched for 3 minutes. After blanching, rinse in cold water and drain. Snip off any stalks. The stuffing process is easy, if a little fiddly, and becomes quicker with practice. Lay a leaf vein-side up and stalk end towards you. Place a spoonful of chosen filling at the stalk end and roll up like a parcel, tucking in the sides as you go. Take care not to wrap them too tightly as the filling needs to swell during cooking. Traditional Greek *dolmathes* are envelope-shaped, others are rolled up like a cigar. It is unnecessary to blanch the leaves for wrapping small fish and birds. Processed vine leaves are soaked in hot water for 30 minutes and rinsed prior to cooking.

Culinary Uses
Stuffed vine leaves are not only one of the best-known Greek delicacies but they also appear in the Middle East, Turkey and Cyprus. They are eaten as a snack with drinks or as a main course, hot or cold and with a variety of fillings. Generally those without meat are eaten cold and those with lamb or veal are served hot but, like most things in the Middle East, this is not a hard and fast rule. Greek fillings are fairly plain—rice, maybe with minced lamb flavoured with onion, mint and parsley or perhaps a little dill and cinnamon—served with a yoghurt or egg and lemon sauce. Turkish and Armenian stuffings may include pine nuts, currants and allspice and

instead of rice contain *burghul* wheat, chick peas or lentils. Whatever the combination of flavours, stuffed vine leaves are utterly delicious. Small birds such as snipe, partridge and quail are wrapped in the leaves and then covered with fat bacon before roasting to acquire a unique flavour. Red mullet and sardines are particularly good enfolded in the leaves, brushed with oil and grilled or fried until crisp. A bed of the leaves lends subtlety to braised vegetables such as courgettes, okra or mushrooms. Young fresh leaves can be used with discretion in salads and make a decorative background for the fruit bowl.

Herbal Properties
Vine leaves are astringent and stimulate liver function. They were once used to stop bleeding, diarrhoea and stomach complaints. All parts of the vine and its fruit were used and according to Gerard (1597) 'The ashes made of the stickes and dross that remaine after the pressing [of grapes], being laid upon the piles and hard swellings about the fundament, doe cure the same . . .'

Facts and Features
There are many other uses to which the grape vine and its products are put: grape seeds cover cheeses, and are pressed to make oil (10,000 tonnes a year from Provence); seeds and skins are processed to make *marc* and *grappa*; vine cuttings on an open fire impart a delicious aroma to grilled and barbecued foods. The grape vine has been cultivated since antiquity and perhaps more has been written about it than any other plant in the world. For once we shall not augment the literature, except to remark that the largest vine in the UK is at Hampton Court.

WATER CHESTNUT (CHINESE)
India, Southeast Asia, Polynesia

Chinese water chestnuts are flattened, round corms, like those of gladioli, some 5cm (2in) across, covered in peeling leaf scales. Inside this somewhat unappetising exterior lies the crisp white flesh of the kernel enclosed in a thin brown skin. It is sweetly palatable, and has been compared with coconut, crunchy and nutty.

Selecting the Best
Available in the winter from Chinese shops, they should be firm, unblemished, and unsprouted. Don't be put off by their usual dirty appearance. Water chestnuts are also available in cans.

Eleocharis dulcis
syn *E. edulis, E. tuberosa,*
Heleocharis dulcis, Scirpus
tuberosus

Fam Cyperaceae

Horse's Hoof, Matai, Spike Rush,
Spike Sedge, Waternut

China: ma(h)tai, o-yu, peci, pitsi,
po-tsai, wu-yu; Hawaii: kohekohe,
pipi-wai; Indonesia: chikai,
de(e)ke(e), dekeng, te(e)ke(e),
teki-tike; Japan: kuwai,
o-kuroguwai; Malaysia: mah tai,
peperetan, teeke; Philippines:
apulid, buslig, kalangub, nilaga,
potok, sibosibolasan; Thailand:
gajup, krachup

Nutritional Values
Water chestnuts are high in calories
(the same as the ordinary potato), in
iron, potassium and vitamin B
complex.

cal	79	Ca	4	A	0
pro	1.4	P	65	B₁	0.14
fat	0.2	Fe	0.6	B₂	0.2
car	19	Na	20	B₅	1
fib	0.8	K	500	C	4

Recipe:
Sweet and Sour Wheels, page 188

Storage and Preparation
Eat within a week, storing in salted water. Wash and peel the skin with a sharp knife. Cut into 5mm (⅕in) slices, or halve. Once opened, canned chestnuts can be refrigerated in water for at least a week. Some say change the water daily, but we do not find this absolutely necessary. Stir-fry canned chestnuts for 1 minute, fresh ones for 1–2 minutes more. Jicama or yam bean (see page 89) is a useful substitute.

Culinary Uses
Water chestnuts are much used in oriental cookery, prized for their delicate flavour and special crunchy texture undiminished by cooking. It is these contrasting qualities which make them a choice ingredient in such dishes as *dim sum* (steamed dumplings, both savoury and sweet), spring rolls, *won ton* (stuffed pastry, steamed or fried), sweet and sour sauce and myriad meat, game and vegetable recipes. *Yam krachup* is an excellent Thai salad of shellfish, pork and water chestnuts flavoured with citrus and chillies. Wrapped in bacon with a slice of chicken liver marinaded in ginger and soy sauce and grilled, water chestnuts make a tasty and unusual cocktail snack. It must be said however that eating the fresh raw water chestnut is an experience not to be missed. In China, a powder ground from the nuts, called *ma tai fan*, is used as a thickening agent.

Herbal Properties
Besides apparently having the property to dissolve metal, mentioned below, water chestnuts have recently been found to contain the antibiotic puchiin.

Facts and Features
Water chestnuts are of the sedge family, and probably native to the South China area. They grow also in India, Southeast Asia and Polynesia, and are quite popular in the US, doubtless under the influence of the sizeable oriental communities there. Martinus Martini (1665) writes that you can break and chew a copper coin if you place it in your mouth with a water chestnut. Roxburgh confirms this in relating how Indian children who have swallowed coins at play are plied with water chestnuts to relieve alarming symptoms. Do not confuse with the ordinary water chestnut, *ling gok*, a true nut, or *lut tzee*, the Chinese version of the ordinary chestnut. Several species of *Trapa*,

annual water plants grown in Europe and Asia, also go under the name water chestnut. *Trapa bicornis* is more common in India.

WATER MELON
Africa

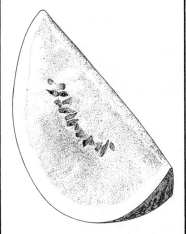

Citrullus lanatus
syn *C. vulgaris, Colocynthis citrullus*
Fam Cucurbitaceae

Burma: hpaye; China: sai kwa, sie gwai; India: kalingada, matira, tarbuz, tarmuz; Indonesia: semangka, watesan; Japan: suika; Malaysia: tembikai; Middle East: battikh; West Indies: belle apple, melon d'eau, moulon, (water) melon

Nutritional Values
Water melons are over 90 per cent water with hardly any minerals or vitamins. The seeds have 20–45 per cent oil and are abundant in the enzyme urease.

cal	24	Ca	7	A	200–600
pro	0.5	P	10	B$_1$	0.03
fat	0.2	Fe	0.4	B$_2$	0.03
car	6	Na	1	B$_5$	0.2
fib	0.3	K	100	C	52

A massive fruit, water melon is distinct from other melons. Several varieties exist, the characteristic one having smooth, hard, dark-green skin, red flesh and black seeds. It is either spherical or sausage-shaped and has no central cavity. The rind can be 4cm (1½in) thick, and the whole fruit could easily weigh 9kg (20lb). The inner rind is edible, but not the many apple-pip-like seeds embedded in the watery yet crisp flesh. There is a yellow-fleshed variety; also the striped 'Tiger' is quite common. A small variety such as 'Sugar Baby' can serve six to eight. Water melons weighing as little as 1kg (2.2lb) are now imported from Spain.

Selecting the Best
The water melon season is from May to October. Look for slightly waxy skin, deep green with a light yellow patch. They should not be soft and should make a muffled, not hollow, sound when struck.

Storage and Preparation
Water melons, whole or sliced, will keep for up to a week or two under refrigeration. Wrap the fruit, and especially the slices, in cling film. Do not freeze for long periods, though it is appropriate to leave slices in the ice-box for a quick chill just before serving. For a fancy cut, use a melon baller. Deep freeze the shell, well wrapped, for use as a fruit salad bowl.

Culinary Uses
A great thirst quencher, wedges of water melon are sold on the wayside from Honduras to Hawaii. Chill or quick-freeze for nature's ready-made sorbet. Light and crisp cubes of water melon make an unusual salad with chicken or ham on a bed of lettuce garnished with nuts and raw onion rings, marinated in a lemony dressing. Any summer fruits combined with water melon balls are lovely served in the shell, well chilled and laced with brandy. The Chinese like an elaborate mixture of chicken, shrimp and asparagus steamed in a large water melon—an impressive feast. For humbler days, steam the

inner rind and eat with butter and seasoning. The rind is crystallised in Europe and preserved in the Middle East, flavoured with cardamom seeds, and in Greece makes one of the famous *glykos*, offered to guests with a glass of iced water.

Herbal Properties

The rind of water melon is diuretic, given in cases of diabetes, alcohol poisoning and kidney inflammation.

Facts and Features

Water melons are native to Africa but have been in cultivation in diverse areas since antiquity, probably for at least 4,000 years. They figure in ancient Egyptian art and in Sanskrit literature. Growing on weak vines, they ripen sitting on the ground, and are eaten happily by wild animals as well as man, as a welcome water–source in a dry climate. The seeds are dried and eaten in Southeast Asia and yield an oil much used in African cookery.

YAM

Asiatic Yam, Greater Asiatic Yam, Ten Months Yam, White Manila Yam, White Yam, Winged Yam

China: taai shue; India: ratalu, sakourou; Indonesia: huwi, ubi, uwi; Malaysia: ubi -kelapa, -kemali, -manis; South America: name; Thailand: man (luad, taparb); West Indies: greater yam, Lisbon yam, water yam

The yams seen in shops, and in much greater profusion on market stalls, are from four species and display tremendous variations within each of those species. Below are described the three basic types that you will come across.

GREATER (WATER) YAM
Southwest Asia
Dioscorea alata
Fam Dioscoreaceae

This yam is of Asian origin but has spread round the world in its many forms and is the favourite in the islands of the eastern Caribbean, who export to Great Britain. Because it grows in such diverse forms it is impossible to give a general description. A common form, however, is the one illustrated. The skin is a grey-brown, rough, flaky and with some rootlets. The flesh is white, sticky and bland when raw. Some giants of this species have been known to weigh 60kg (132lb) but the average for market is 5–10kg (11–22lb). The cooked flavour is described as 'sweet' to differentiate it from the coarser, more bitter yams.

*Twelve Months Yam, West African
Yellow Yam*

*India: ratalu; West Indies: afou yam,
à tous temps, cut and come again,
Dominica yam, dye yam, hard yam,
yam à tous temps, yam à tout tan,
yellow yam*

Yellow Guinea Yam
West Africa
Dioscorea cayenensis
Fam Dioscoreaceae

Another West African yam that is preferred in
Jamaica, where they also export it to Great
Britain. At its best it is cylindrical with a rough
brown skin, often reddy-brown from the lateritic
soils in which it grows. Many other forms occur
but it is unmistakable for other yams because of
its sticky yellow flesh which rapidly discolours
when cut. Size is variable, from 1–3kg (2–6½lb);
the flavour is more bitter than other yams.

*Eight Months Yam, Guinea Yam,
Hard Yam, Proper Yam, White
Guinea Yam*

*India: ratalu; West Indies: Guinea
yam, negro yam, Portuguese yam,
white yam*

Common
(White) Yam
West Africa
Dioscorea rotundata
Fam Dioscoreaceae

This yam is the most important in West Africa
and is preferred to the greater yam in Jamaica.
Again there are many forms but the most
common is cylindrical with rounded or pointed
ends, and averaging 2–5kg (4½–11lb) in weight.
The skin is like thin bark, grey-brown and
roughish; the raw flesh is white and sticky,
becoming soft and quite flavoursome on cooking.

Selecting the Best (all species)
The selection of yams is no easy task as not only
is there a bewildering choice of size, shape and
colour but also quality cannot always be judged
until the vegetable is cooked. Generally, the
dark-skinned, soft white yam is suitable for most
recipes, the yellow-fleshed yam retaining a meaty
firmness even after prolonged cooking. Choose
firm and full yams, light rather than heavy for
their size, and when possible seek advice from the
vendor. They are available from some
supermarkets but a wide choice is possible in
shops and markets specialising in West Indian and
West African produce.

Storage and Preparation
White yams keep longer than yellow ones, up to
several months in a cool, dark, airy place. To
prepare: wash them and pare away the skin with
a sharp knife; cut them up like potatoes and rinse
them before cooking. Yellow yams can be

Yams are not a good staple as they are mostly starch with hardly any useful vitamin content. Diets based on yam can lead to deficiency symptoms; however, they have better results than those with cassava which, unfortunately, because it is easier to grow, is supplanting yam in many regions.

Average all types (raw):

cal 90–105	Ca 4–20	A	trace
pro 1–2.5	P 30–70	B₁	0.09–0.12
fat 0.05–0.2	Fe 0.6–1.1	B₂	0.01–0.04
car 15–25	Na —	B₅	0.4–0.5
fib 0.5–1.5	K 600	C	8–13

Recipe:
Undihu, page 198

dropped into acidulated water as you cut them to prevent a rusty discoloration, most of which disappears on boiling. For chips, cut them up and boil them for 10 minutes before drying and frying them. For roast yam, cut into chunks leaving the skin on and cook in charcoal or a moderate oven, peeling before eating.

Culinary Uses

An important starch staple, yams are eaten all over tropical Africa—West Africa especially—as well as the southern US, South America, the Caribbean, India, Southeast Asia, China and Japan. Like eddoes and sweet potatoes they are served in both sweet and savoury dishes, their bland taste ideal for absorbing or contrasting with spicier flavours. In African-style cookery, yams are best known in *fufu*, on their own or with other starchy vegetables such as plantains, cassava or sweet potatoes. They also appear in soups, substantial stews and in patties and pies. In India, yams are popular in mixed vegetable curries, and boiled, sautéed and dusted with *amchur* (dried mango powder). The Chinese like them mashed; mixed with lotus root, wrapped in lotus leaves and steamed. Otherwise use as you would potatoes.

Herbal Properties

Wild yams, many of which are deadly poisonous and require a laborious cleansing process, are used in African and Indonesian traditional medicine, as well as for poisonous hunting weapons. In China, the Chinese yam is prescribed as a tonic and cure for inflamed bowels, diarrhoea, bed wetting, nervous breakdown and nocturnal emissions. In India, extracts are used for arthritis. Modern herbalism considers yam to be antirheumatic, diuretic and expectorant. Yam is also an important source of diosgenin, which is used in oral contraceptives.

Facts and Features

There are well over 600 species in the family Dioscoreaceae (named for Dioscorides who probably never saw a yam in his life), mostly of the tropics, and many of which are highly poisonous. Each of the three main continental systems has come up with its own indigenous species of yam but the cultivable ones have spread right across the world's tropical zone. Yams are generally underground tubers of vine-like plants but some vines bear aerial tubers, e.g. *Dioscorea bulbifera*, the potato or air yam.

ZALAK
Malaysia

Salacca edulis
syn *Zalacca edulis*

Fam Palmae

Salak, Zalacca

Indonesia: salak; Malaysia: salak; Thailand: lakam

Nutritional Values
No data are available.

This amazingly unlikely-looking object is actually a fruit—perhaps something one might only consider eating with a recommendation. We recommend it. Conical or pear-shaped, the hard, red or brown, scaly, snake-like skin holds shiny white flesh rather like that of longan or lychee. Inside the flesh are two or three fair-sized stones. The flavour is sweet with acidic tones, a nice change from the sweeter lychees etc. This unusual fruit from a tropical palm is 2–4cm (¾–1½in) long.

Selecting the Best
Available in shops receiving produce from the Far East, zalaks are sometimes sold on the branch in clusters. They should be full and shiny. In Indonesia, zalak crops in December, April, May and June, peaking in December and April.

Storage and Preparation
Eat as soon as possible. Break open the shell as you would a lychee. Take the flesh off the inedible stones.

Culinary Uses
Largely eaten fresh; the young fruit are pickled where the crop is plentiful, and ripe fruit kept in a sugary brine.

Herbal Properties
No information is available.

Facts and Features
Common in Indonesia and the Malay archipelago, zalaks grow from a low spiny palm, thriving in low coastal areas. Recognised varieties include 'Condet', 'Bali' and 'Sleman'. Sholto Douglas (*Alternative Foods*, 1978) notes that the fruits are preserved in cans with salt water and eaten by Muslim pilgrims going to Mecca. It may be just a coincidence that in the Indian Khasi language *salak* is the word for pangolin, the scaly anteater. The modern spelling of zalak is salak.

FURTHER READING

Chinese Herbs, John D. Keys (Charles E. Tuttle, Vermont, 1976)

Cooking with Spices, Carolyn Heal and Michael Allsop (David & Charles, 1983)

The Cook's Encyclopaedia, Tom Stobart (Batsford, 1980)

Dictionary of Gastronomy, André L. Simon and Robin Howe (André Deutsch, 1978)

Encyclopaedia Britannica

An Encyclopaedia of Chinese Food and Cooking, Wowona W. and Irving B. Chang and Helene W. and Austin H. Kutscher (Crown, New York, 1980)

Flora Indica, W. Roxburgh (Today & Tomorrow's Printers & Publishers, New Delhi, facsimile 1832 edn)

Food, Waverly Root (Simon & Schuster, New York, 1980)

Food Legumes (Tropical Products Institute, MOD, London, 1979)

Fruits of Hawaii, Miller Bazore, Barlow (University Press of Hawaii, 1981)

Fruits for Southern Florida, David Sturrock (Horticultural Books Inc, Florida, 1980)

Handbook of Legumes of World Economic Importance, James A. Duke (Plenum Press, New York, 1983)

The Herbal or General History of Plants, John Gerard, 1597 (Dover, New York, 1975)

Hong Kong Food Plants, S. Y. Zee and L. H. Hui (Urban Council, Hong Kong, 1981)

An Introduction to the Botany of Tropical Crops, Leslie S. Cobley (Longman, 1983)

Medicinal Plants of India and Pakistan, J. F. Dastur (D. B. Tapore-Vala Sons & Co, Bombay, 1977)

A Modern Herbal, Mrs M. Grieve (Penguin, 1980)

New Larousse Gastronomique (Hamlyn, 1979)

Root Crops (Tropical Products Institute, MOD, London, 1973)

Some Common Flora and Fauna in Thailand (IPTST, Bangkok, 1982)

Sturtevant's Edible Plants of the World, ed. V. P. Hedrick (Dover, New York, 1972)

Tropical Crops, J. W. Purseglove (2 vols) (Longman, 1979)

Tropical Pulses, James Smart (Longman, 1976)

Useful Plants of India and Pakistan, J. F. Dastur (D. B. Tapore-Vala Sons & Co, Bombay, 1977)

The Vegetable Garden, M. M. Vilmorin-Andrieux (Ten Speed Press, California, facsimile 1885 edn)

Vegetable Growing in India, S. L. Katyal (Oxford & IBH Publishing, New Delhi, 1977)

Vegetables, B. Choudhury (National Book Trust, New Delhi, 1967)

Vegetables of the Dutch East Indies, J. J. Ochse (A. Asher, Amsterdam, 1980)

Vegetables in South-East Asia, G. A. C. Herklots (Allen & Unwin, 1979)

PART TWO
RECIPES

Queer Gear ingredients are shown by a star.
Some other ingredients may be unfamiliar and are
described in the Glossary of Culinary Terms on
pages 213–14.

Weights and Measures

Solid & Liquid

oz/fl oz	g/ml (to nearest 5)	g/ml	lb	oz/fl oz
1	30	5		⅕
2	55	10		¼
3	85	20		¾
4	**115**	30		1
5	140	40		1½
6	170	**50**		1¾
7	200	60		2
8	**225**	70		2½
9	255	80		2¾
10	285	90		3¼
11	310	**100**		3½
12	**340**	200		7
13	370	300		10½
14	395	400		14
15	425	**500**	1	1¾
16 = 1lb	**455**	600	1	5¼
2lb	905	700	1	8¾
3lb = 1.36kg		800	1	12¼
4lb = 1.81kg		900	1	15¾
5lb = 2.27kg		**1000**		
		= 1kg	**2.2**	3¼

Spoons

Imp	Metric	US
1tsp (⅕fl oz)	= 5ml	= 1tsp
1tbsp = 3tsp	= 15ml	= 1tbsp
		= ½ fl oz (US)

Cups

Imp 1 cup = 10fl oz = ½pt = 285ml
= 1⅕ cups (US)
= 9.6fl oz (US)

US 1 cup = 8fl oz US = ½pt US
= 235ml = ⅘ cup (Imp)
= 8.4fl oz (Imp)

Oven Temperatures

	Electric		Gas
	°C	°F	Mark
very cool	90	200	
very cool	110	225	¼
very cool	120	250	½
slow	135	275	1
slow	150	300	2
moderate	160	325	3
moderate	180	350	4
fairly hot	190	375	5
hot	200	400	6
hot	220	425	7
very hot	230	450	8
very hot	250	475	9
very hot	260	500	

SOUPS

CALLALOO SOUP
Caribbean

Judith Procope's delicious version from Trinidad.

SERVES 4
★225g (8oz) arvi leaves, stripped of tough
  stems, chopped and washed
★115g (4oz) okra, washed, trimmed and
  chopped
½ onion, chopped
4 spring onion tops, chopped
★1 clove garlic, crushed
★1 hot chilli, left whole
1 sprig thyme or ½tsp dried
★1½ cups coconut milk
2 cups water or stock
115g (4oz) crabmeat, cooked
30g (1oz) butter
salt to taste

Place all ingredients except the crabmeat,
butter and salt into a saucepan, bring to
the boil and simmer for 20–30 minutes
until tender. Remove the chilli, swizzle
or liquidise briefly. Add the crabmeat and
butter, and salt to taste. Simmer for 5
minutes before serving.

CREAM OF CHARD SOUP
England

A rich, distinctive soup.

SERVES 4–6
55g (2oz) butter or margarine
1 onion, finely chopped
★455g (1lb) chard, stems and leaves washed
  and separately chopped
1½ cups chicken stock
1 cup milk or single cream
salt and pepper to taste
nutmeg

Melt the butter in a saucepan and cook
the onion until transparent. Add the
chard stems, cover and cook for 10
minutes, stirring occasionally. Add the
leaves, cover and cook for a further 10–15
minutes or until tender. Purée the
contents of the saucepan in a blender or
food processor until smooth. Return the
mixture to the pan. Gradually add the
stock and milk or cream, reheating
gently to just below boiling point.
Season to taste and serve with a grating of
nutmeg.

GAI CHOI SOUP
China

Made with mustard cabbage, this soup is
light and delicate and best with
home-made stock.

SERVES 4–6
4 cups chicken stock
★1 slice ginger
★455g (1lb) gai choi (see Oriental Leaf
  Vegetables), stalks finely chopped and leaves
  shredded
1 carrot, grated
2tsp soy sauce
2 spring onions, finely sliced
salt and pepper to taste

Bring the stock to the boil with the
ginger and then add the gai choi, carrot
and soy sauce. Simmer for 20 minutes,
adding the spring onions after 15
minutes. Season to taste and serve in
individual bowls.

GOLDEN HOOKS WITH JADE PLATES
China

This evocatively-named Chinese summer soup is light and appetising. Mung bean sprouts may be substituted.

SERVES 4
3 cups clear chicken stock
★*1 slice ginger root*
285g (10oz) tofu, cut into squares or rectangles, 1cm (½in) thick
★*225g (8oz) soybean sprouts (see Sprouted Seeds), trimmed and washed*
salt and pepper to taste.

Bring the stock gently to the boil with the ginger and beancurd. Add the bean sprouts and simmer for 20 minutes. Remove the ginger and adjust seasoning.

PALESTINE SOUP
France

This rich and creamy version may be served with croûtons.

SERVES 4
★*455g (1lb) Jerusalem artichokes*
55g (2oz) butter
1 onion, chopped
★*1 clove garlic, minced*
3 cups chicken or veal stock
2 egg yolks
1 small carton double cream
salt and pepper to taste
1tbsp chopped chives
croûtons (optional)

Peel and slice the artichokes and set aside in acidulated water. Melt the butter in a saucepan and cook the onion and garlic gently for a few minutes. Now add the drained artichokes, cover and 'sweat' for 5 minutes. Add the stock and simmer for about 30 minutes until the vegetables are tender. Pass the contents of the pan through a sieve or use a liquidiser or processor and return the mixture to the pan. Mix the egg yolks with the cream and beat gradually into the soup. Season to taste. Do not allow to boil. Sprinkle with chives before serving with croûtons if desired.

TOM YAM SOUP
Thailand

Aromatic and hot, with a sharp flavour, this famed Thai soup is best served from a steam boat, otherwise in individual bowls.

SERVES 4
455g (1lb) raw or cooked prawns with shells OR 455g (1lb) chicken pieces
4 cups water or chicken stock
★*4 slices galangal 6mm (¼in) thick*
★*2 stalks lemon grass, bruised and chopped into 2.5cm (1in) lengths*
★*4 small green chillies, 2 coarsely sliced, 2 whole*
★*4 small red chillies, 2 coarsely sliced, 2 whole*
★*4 lime leaves*
★*6tbsp coriander leaves, chopped*
1 tbsp nam pla (fish sauce)
6tbsp lime or lemon juice

Shell the prawns or bone the chicken. Halve large prawns or thinly slice the chicken flesh and set aside. Put the shells or bones into a saucepan with the water or stock, galangal, lemon grass, chillies and lime leaves. Bring to the boil and simmer gently for 20 minutes (the bones will take longer, 30 minutes). Strain and remove the whole spices. Return the liquid, whole spices and half the coriander to the pan and re-boil. Add the prawns or chicken and simmer for about 3 minutes. Stir in the fish sauce and lime juice, pour into a steam boat or bowls, garnishing with the rest of the coriander.

FISH AND SHELLFISH

NASI GORENG

Indonesia

The most famous Indonesian rice dish,
rather like a risotto or paella, but with
the delightful addition of eggs and
banana as a garnish. Cook the rice the
day before it is required.

SERVES 6
2 eggs
salt and pepper
2tbsp oil
½ onion, minced
★1 clove garlic, crushed
1–2tsp sambal bajak (see page 208)
340g (12oz) beef or chicken, cut into 6mm
(¼in) slices
115g (4oz) peeled prawns
1kg (2lb) cooked rice 340g (12oz)
uncooked)
2tbsp soy sauce
1 tomato, sliced
2 spring onions, finely sliced
¼ cucumber, sliced
★1 banana, sliced (optional)
2 tbsp onion flakes, crisped in oil

Make a large, thin, unfolded omelette
with the eggs and seasoning, using a
teaspoon of the oil to fry with. Let it
cool, roll up and slice across into shreds
and reserve. Heat remaining oil in a
wok or a large frying pan and stir-fry
the onion, garlic and *sambal bajak*, until
the onion is soft. Add the meat and
prawns and stir-fry for about 5
minutes. Add the rice and soy sauce and
stir constantly until hot. Transfer
mixture to a serving dish and garnish
with the tomato, spring onions,
cucumber and banana. Finally arrange
the omelette strips down the centre of
the dish and top with the onion flakes.

SALADE NIÇOISE

France

Everyone has their own version of this
popular, attractive salad. This is our
favourite, served with plenty of French
bread.

SERVES 4–6
★½ endive or batavia, washed and torn into
pieces
1 round lettuce
2 tomatoes, quartered
12 French beans, cooked and cut into 2.5cm
(1in) pieces
2 hard boiled eggs, quartered
½ onion, thinly sliced
1×200g (7oz) tin tuna, drained and flaked
8 anchovies
12 black olives
1tsp capers
1tsp parsley, chopped
★1tsp basil, chopped
½ cup garlicky French dressing

Line a large salad bowl with the endive
and lettuce, and arrange the tomatoes,
beans, eggs, onion and tuna on top.
Garnish with the anchovies, olives and
capers, and sprinkle on the herbs. Toss
with the dressing just before serving.

SMOKED FISH PLATTER WITH HORSERADISH SAUCE

Scandinavia

A luxurious fish dish with horseradish
sauce—the combination of fish can be
varied according to your taste and
pocket.

SERVES 6
1tsp caster sugar
★2–3tbsp grated horseradish
1tsp lemon juice

½ cup soured cream
salt and pepper to taste
1 smoked trout or mackerel
170g (6oz) smoked salmon, thinly sliced
115g (4oz) smoked eel, sliced or divided
into portions
2 lemons, cut into wedges
1 bunch watercress

Mix the sugar, horseradish and lemon juice with the cream, and season to taste. Chill for at least an hour. Skin and fillet the trout or mackerel and divide into neat portions. Arrange all the fish on a large dish and decorate with the lemon wedges and watercress. Serve with the horseradish sauce.

TAMARIND FISH
Straits Settlements (Chinese)

SERVES 4

455g (1lb) cod fillet or other firm white fish
★4tbsp tamarind pulp (made from 30g (1oz)
pressed tamarind)
4tbsp water
1tsp sugar
½tsp salt
½tsp pepper
★1 fresh green chilli, chopped
oil for deep frying
1 cucumber, cut into wedges

Cut the fish across into 1cm (½in) slices. Mix the rest of the ingredients together except for the oil and cucumber and pour over the fish. Leave to marinade for at least an hour. Drain the fish and pat dry. Heat the oil and deep fry the fish slices, a few at a time, for about 5 minutes turning them over once. Serve with cucumber wedges.

TEMPURA
Japan
Tentsuyu (dipping sauce):
½ cup chicken stock or dashi
3tbsp sherry or mirin
3tbsp shoyu
pinch of msg (optional)

Batter:
1 egg
¾ cup plain flour
¼ cup cornflour
1 cup water, ice-cold

Tempura:
oil for frying
★4 slices lotus root, 6mm (¼in) thick
★1 aubergine, cut into 1cm (½in) rings
★1 green capsicum, seeded and cut into 4cm
(1½in) squares
12 green beans, left whole
★12 mangetout peas (see Beans and Peas),
left whole
4 mushrooms, halved if large
8 raw king prawns, shelled and deveined
Many other ingredients may be substituted
for the above, such as asparagus, onion,
carrot, ★ artichoke hearts, parsnip, ★ sweet
potato, fish fillets or sliced beef

To serve:
★10cm (4in) mooli (daikon), grated
★5cm (2in) ginger, grated

Sauce: pour the stock, sherry and shoyu into a saucepan with a pinch of msg if desired and heat to boiling point. Keep hot.
Batter: this should be made immediately prior to use. Break the egg into a bowl. Sift the flour and cornflour together and mix into the egg with chopsticks or a fork. Add the water and mix quickly—a very thorough mix is not necessary.

To cook: you will need sufficient fresh vegetable oil for deep-frying plus a tablespoon of dark sesame seed oil if you like its distinctive flavour. Heat the oil to a fairly high heat. Dry the ingredients as thoroughly as possible. Starting with the lotus root and ending with the prawns, dip into the batter a few at a time and fry until crisp for a minute or less. Drain and serve immediately together with the sauce; offer the mooli and ginger in separate bowls as an accompaniment.

MEAT

BANGKOK BEEF CURRY
Thailand

This dish is really worth trying with the authentic ingredients. However, if you cannot get Chinese keys substitute ginger; it will not be the same but still makes a memorable meal.

SERVES 4

★1 finger or 'key' of Chinese keys or ginger, chopped
★2.5cm (1in) galangal or 1tsp laos powder
★1 lemon grass stalk, chopped
½ onion, chopped
★2tsp grated lime peel
★4 dried red chillies or 1tsp chilli powder
1tsp ground black pepper
½tsp salt
2tbsp oil
455g (1lb) minced beef
1 cup water
1tbsp nam pla
3 lime leaves, torn into pieces
pinch of dried mint
★pinch of dried basil

Put the first eight ingredients in a mortar or processor and reduce to a paste, using a little oil if necessary. Put the beef in a bowl together with the paste and thoroughly blend together. Heat the oil in a large frying pan or wok over medium heat and stir-fry the beef until evenly coloured. Gradually add the water, bring to simmering point, cover and cook for about 30 minutes. Add a little more water during cooking if necessary. Stir in the sauce, lime leaves and herbs and simmer for a few more minutes. Serve with noodles or rice.

BHUNA GHOSH
India

This is basically Richard Seal's excellent recipe for a 'dry' curry, highly spiced yet containing no chilli, which he created after years of careful experimentation and adjustment. Freshly roasted and ground spices are essential to achieve a perfect result.

SERVES 6

4tbsp ghee
1tsp black mustard seeds
½tsp fenugreek seeds
★10–15 curry leaves
★4 cloves garlic, crushed
★1tbsp freshly-grated ginger
1 large onion, chopped
5tsp ground cumin
5tsp ground coriander
½tsp ground cardamom (seeds from about 12 pods)
¼tsp ground cloves
¼tsp ground fennel
1tsp ground cinnamon
1kg (2lb) beef, cubed
½ cup water
1tsp salt
71g (2½oz) tomato purée (small tin)

Melt the ghee and fry the mustard, fenugreek, and curry leaves for 5 minutes. Add the garlic, ginger and onion and fry gently until they are soft and golden. Do not allow to brown. Add the cumin, coriander, cardamom, cloves, fennel and cinnamon to the onions and stir-fry gently until the mixture is very aromatic, about 5 minutes. Now add the beef and water and stir constantly until juices run out. Add the salt, cover and simmer very gently for 30 minutes, stirring occasionally. Mix in the tomato purée and cook for another hour until the beef is tender. Check that the mixture does not brown, adding a little water if necessary. Serve with saffron rice.

BITTER MELON WITH BEEF AND SALTED BLACK BEANS
China

A piquant addition to a Cantonese-style meal. Lambs' liver makes an excellent substitute for the beef.

SERVES 4

Marinade:
1tsp cornflour
1tsp soy sauce
2tsp sherry or rice wine
¼tsp sugar
¼tsp sesame oil (optional)

225g (8oz) beef steak, thinly sliced
2tbsp peanut or corn oil
2tbsp salted black beans, rinsed and mashed
★2 cloves garlic, crushed
★1 bitter melon (see Gourds), halved, seeded, cut into slivers, blanched and dried
1tsp soy sauce
½tsp sugar
1tsp cornflour, mixed with a little stock
½ cup stock
2 spring onions, finely sliced

Mix together the marinade ingredients, add the beef and leave for 20 minutes. Heat the oil in a wok or frying pan, add the beans and garlic, and stir-fry over a brisk heat for 15 seconds. Now add the beef with marinade and stir-fry until the meat is browned. Stir in the bitter melon, fry for a minute, add the soy sauce and sugar and cook for another minute. Lower the heat and gradually add the cornflour and stock and stir until the sauce thickens. Sprinkle over the spring onions and serve.

BRAISED ARROWHEADS WITH PORK
China

Good on their own with a salad or with other Chinese dishes.

SERVES 2–4
1tbsp oil
★1 clove garlic, crushed
1tbsp salted yellow beans, mashed
170g (6oz) diced belly of pork
★455g (1lb) arrowheads, peeled and trimmed
1tbsp soy sauce
1tsp sugar
¾ cup water

Heat the oil in a saucepan, add the garlic and beans and fry for a minute. Add the pork and seal all over. Add the arrowheads, and turn them gently for a minute until lightly coloured. Stir in the soy sauce, sugar and water. Bring to the boil, cover and simmer for 20–30 minutes until tender.

GINGERED LAMB CUTLETS
Europe

A mildly spicy marinade gives these cutlets a pleasant flavour and they are excellent with new potatoes and buttered carrots.

SERVES 2–3
6 lamb cutlets
½ onion, chopped
★1tsp grated ginger
1tbsp salad oil
juice of 1 orange
1tsp brown sugar
8 allspice berries, crushed
½tsp black pepper, ground

Place the lamb cutlets in a shallow dish. Combine the rest of the ingredients and pour over the meat, ensuring that it is well coated. Marinade for at least 4 hours. Grill under medium heat until tender, turning once and basting occasionally with the strained marinade.

HAM-WRAPPED CHICORY IN CHEESE SAUCE
Belgium

Delicious as a light luncheon or supper dish.

SERVES 2
★4 heads chicory, trimmed
salt
lemon juice
4 slices ham
30g (1oz) butter
30g (1oz) flour
1/2 cup milk
1/2 cup water, reserved from cooking
115g (4oz) cheddar cheese, grated

Put the chicory into boiling salted water with a squeeze of lemon juice and simmer for 10 minutes. Drain, reserving half a cup of the liquid, and gently squeeze excess liquid from the chicory in a cloth. Wrap each chicory head in a slice of ham and lay side by side in a small, buttered ovenproof dish. Make the sauce with the butter, flour, milk and reserved cooking water, adding half the cheese at the final stage. Pour over the chicory, sprinkle on remaining cheese and bake in the oven, 180°C (350°F), gas mark 4, for 20 minutes.

KEEMA METHI
India

This is a 'dry', spicy dish, using yoghurt, and is best served with *naan* bread or *chapatis* and chutney.

SERVES 4
2tbsp oil
1/2tsp cumin seeds
1 onion, finely chopped
★2.5cm (1in) fresh ginger, grated
★1 clove garlic, crushed
★1 hot green chilli, finely chopped
1/2–1tsp chilli powder
1tsp coriander, ground
1tsp turmeric powder
455g (1lb) beef, finely minced
3tbsp plain yoghurt
1/2tsp salt
★1 bunch fenugreek, chopped, tough stalks removed

Heat the oil in a saucepan, add the cumin seeds and fry until they pop. Add the onion, ginger, garlic and green chilli, and cook until the onion is soft and golden, stirring frequently. Sprinkle on the ground spices and stir again. Now put in the beef and brown evenly, breaking up any lumps. Thoroughly mix in the yoghurt and salt before adding the chopped fenugreek. Cover and cook very slowly for about 30 minutes. Add a little water if necessary.

LAMB CUTLETS WITH CELERIAC
Turkey

Simple, substantial and blessed with the fresh tang of lemon. Accompany with brown rice.

SERVES 4
2tbsp butter
8 lamb cutlets
★1 medium celeriac, peeled, cut into 1cm (1/2in) rounds and halved
1 medium onion, sliced
1 1/2 cups chicken stock
1/2tsp chopped dill (optional)
2 eggs
2tbsp lemon juice
salt and pepper to taste

Melt the butter in a saucepan or casserole and brown the cutlets on both sides. Add the vegetables, stock, and dill if required. Bring to the boil and cook until tender, about 35 minutes. Remove the meat and vegetables from the pan, arrange in a serving dish and keep warm. Reserve the stock. In a separate bowl, beat the eggs and slowly add the lemon juice. Take a ladleful of hot stock and pour it onto the egg mixture, stirring constantly until smooth. Return this to the stock and stir until it thickens. Season to taste. Do not allow it to boil. Pour this sauce over the meat and serve at once.

MOUSSAKA
Greece

Rich and delicious—very Greek. An ideal family or party dish.

SERVES 6–8
6tbsp olive oil
★1kg (2lb) aubergine, cut into 1cm (1/2in) slices, salted for 1 hour, drained and dried
55g (2oz) butter
1 onion, finely chopped
★1 clove garlic, crushed (optional)
680g (1½lb) lamb or beef, minced
2 tomatoes, chopped
1–2tbsp tomato purée
1 glass red wine
1tbsp parsley, chopped
1/2tsp cinnamon
salt and pepper to taste
85g (3oz) grated cheese (cheddar, parmesan or, best of all, kefalotiri)

Sauce:
55g (2oz) butter
55g (2oz) flour
2 cups milk
salt and pepper to taste
1 egg
1/4 tsp nutmeg

Heat the oil and fry the aubergine slices lightly on both sides. Drain on kitchen paper. In a clean pan, heat the butter and fry the onion and garlic until golden. Then add the meat and stir around until evenly coloured. Now add the tomatoes, tomato purée and wine and bring to simmering point. Stir in the parsley, cinnamon, salt and pepper. Then cover and simmer for 30 minutes.

In a buttered oblong baking dish place a layer of aubergine slices topped by half the meat mixture and a sprinkling of a third of the cheese. Repeat the process and place a final layer of aubergine skin side up. For the sauce, melt the butter in a saucepan, stir in the flour and cook gently for a minute or two stirring constantly. Gradually add the milk stirring until the sauce is quite thick and smooth. Season to taste. Beat the egg and to it add a little of the hot sauce. Pour this back into the rest of the sauce and season with nutmeg. Spoon the sauce over the aubergines, sprinkle with the remaining cheese and bake in the oven at 190°C (375°F), gas mark 5 for about 45 minutes until golden brown. Allow the dish to rest a little before serving, cut into squares.

PORK WITH KOLOKASSI
Cyprus

A favourite Cypriot dish—satisfying and the base of a good hearty meal.

SERVES 4–6
2tbsp corn oil
1 onion, chopped
1kg (2lb) boneless pork, cubed
4 stalks celery, chopped
3tbsp tomato purée
★1kg (2lb) dasheen or eddoe, prepared in wedges
juice of one lemon
salt and pepper

Heat the oil in a heavy saucepan, and fry the onion until softened. Add the meat and fry until sealed. Add the celery, tomato purée, and sufficient water to cover. Cook for 30 minutes. Prepare the dasheen or eddoe into wedges, and add to pan with the lemon juice, salt and pepper. Cover and simmer for a further 45 minutes until all is tender. Serve with a green salad.

PUMPKIN SUCCOTASH
USA

A creamy combination of bacon, pumpkin, corn and beans; it is an American Indian dish with many regional variations.

SERVES 4
115g (4oz) fat bacon or salt pork, finely diced
★*455g (1lb) pumpkin or any hard-skinned squash, peeled and cut into 2cm (¾in) dice*
3 tomatoes, chopped
225g (8oz) broad or lima beans
225g (8oz) sweetcorn kernels, fresh, frozen or canned
salt and pepper to taste
½ cup single cream

Fry the bacon until crisp, remove from the fat and set aside. Add the pumpkin to the pan and cook, stirring occasionally for about 5 minutes. Stir in the remaining vegetables, cover and simmer for about 20 minutes until the pumpkin is tender. Season, stir in the cream and serve sprinkled with bacon.

RED-COOKED PORK WITH GAI LAN STALK
China

A marvellously aromatic dish. Knuckle ends of pork may be bought for a few pence and one will yield about 115g (4oz) meat. Noodles are a good accompaniment as part of a Chinese meal.

SERVES 2 OR MORE
1 small knuckle end of pork, very well scored
¼ cup soy sauce
1 star anise
6 anise pepper or black pepper corns
1 small piece dried tangerine peel
★*2.5cm (1in) ginger, finely sliced*
½ onion, sliced
1tbsp brown sugar
2 tbsp oil
★*1 clove garlic, crushed*
★*225g (8oz) gai lan (Chinese kale, see Oriental Leaf Vegetables) stalk, cut into 5mm (¼in) diagonal slices*

Place the pork in a saucepan, add the next seven ingredients and sufficient water to cover. Bring to the boil, cover and simmer until the pork is tender—at least 1 hour. Remove the pork and when cool enough bone and cut into 5mm (¼in) slices. Boil the cooking liquid hard until it has reduced to about ½ cup. Strain and reserve. Heat a wok, add the oil and cook the garlic for a few seconds. Add the kale stalk and stir-fry for a minute. Now add the pork and stir-fry for another minute. Finally add 1tbsp of reserved stock.

STUFFED VINE LEAVES
Middle East

SERVES 4
★*36 vine leaves (225g/8oz pack)*
2tbsp oil
1 small onion, finely chopped
115g (4oz) rice
225g (8oz) minced lamb or beef
2tsp dried mint
2tbsp parsley, finely chopped
½tsp salt
¼tsp black pepper
2 tomatoes, chopped
1tbsp lemon juice
¼ cup plain yoghurt

Prepare the vine leaves and leave to drain. Heat the oil and fry the onion gently until soft. In a large bowl mix the onion, rice, meat, herbs and seasoning together, then fold in the chopped tomatoes. Stuff the leaves with about a tablespoon of the filling each. Line a small saucepan with any broken leaves and arrange the stuffed leaves closely together in two layers. Sprinkle with lemon juice and just cover with water. Place a plate on top of the leaves and cover with a lid. Simmer for about an hour, adding more water if needed. Cool slightly before serving with yoghurt.

SWEET AND SOUR WHEELS
China

SERVES 4–6 as part of a Chinese meal.
225g (8oz) minced pork
★*4tbsp water chestnut or chayote, peeled and finely chopped*
½ egg, beaten
pinch Chinese Five Spice powder
salt and Sichuan pepper
oil for deep frying

Batter:
115g (4oz) flour
2tbsp oil
½ egg, beaten
½ cup water

Sauce:
2tsp cornflour
55g (2oz) grated jaggery or brown sugar
1tbsp soy sauce
3tbsp vinegar
½ cup pineapple juice or water
1tbsp preserved ginger, chopped
1 spring onion, chopped
1 carrot, finely sliced
★*1tbsp water chestnut or chayote, cut into matchsticks*

Mix the pork with the water chestnut or chayote, egg and seasonings and form into two 'sausages' 15cm (6in) long. Place on an oiled plate and steam, covered, for 20 minutes. Allow to cool, then refrigerate until required. Put the flour in a bowl, gradually add the oil, egg and water and beat until smooth. Rest for 20 minutes. Place cornflour, sugar, soy sauce, vinegar and pineapple juice in a liquidiser and blend thoroughly. Pour into a saucepan and cook until fairly thick, stirring continuously. Add remaining sauce ingredients and cook for a further 2 minutes. Cut the 'sausages' into 1cm (½in) slices, coat in batter and deep-fry in hot oil until golden—about 2 minutes. Pour the sauce over the pork and serve immediately.

POULTRY

CHICKEN PIE WITH SALSIFY
England

Serve this delicately-flavoured pie with rice or creamed potato.

SERVES 8
1.5kg (3lb) chicken
½ onion, sliced
1 carrot, sliced
1tsp grated lemon rind
1 bouquet garni
salt and pepper to taste
55g (2oz) butter
55g (2oz) flour
2 cups stock
1 cup milk or cream
2tbsp finely chopped parsley
★*455g (1lb) cooked salsify, cut into 5cm (2in) lengths (1kg/2lb raw salsify)*
340g (12oz) short crust pastry
a little beaten egg or milk

Put the chicken, onion, carrot, lemon rind, bouquet garni and seasoning into a large saucepan, cover with cold water, bring to the boil, skim and simmer with the lid on until tender. When cool, strain and reserve the stock. Remove the meat from the carcase and chop it into bite-sized pieces. Make a sauce with the butter, flour, stock, milk and parsley, season to taste and mix with the chicken and salsify. Cool the mixture a little and turn into a pie dish; cover with the pastry, brush with egg or milk and cook in the oven at 200°C (400°F), gas mark 6 for 25 minutes.

PIGEON WITH ALMOND LOQUATS

Sichuan, China

A rich dish with an exotic garnish. Serve as a special Chinese meal with noodles and salad.

SERVES 4–6
*12 loquats or apricot halves
4tbsp almond cream (see page 199)
2tbsp soy sauce
2tbsp vinegar
2tsp brown sugar
4tbsp water
1tbsp cornflour
2tbsp oil
4 pigeon breasts, minced—about 225g (8oz)
1 egg white
1tbsp salted black beans, mashed
*2 fresh red chillies, thinly sliced
*2 cloves garlic, crushed
6 spring onions, cut into 2.5cm (1in) slices, including green part
*4 water chestnuts, finely chopped
*2 slices ginger, finely chopped
2tbsp pine kernels, fried to a golden brown

Cut the tops off the loquats, remove the stones and fill with almond cream. Chill until required. Mix the soy sauce, vinegar, sugar, water and cornflour together and leave aside. Heat the oil in a wok or frying pan, mix the pigeon meat with the egg white and stir-fry until evenly coloured. Reserve. Stir-fry the bean paste, chillies, garlic, onions, water chestnuts and ginger for a minute, add the pigeon and stir well. Pour on the sauce mixture, and stir-fry until slightly thickened. Serve sprinkled with pine kernels and surrounded with almond loquats.

THAI CHICKEN CURRY

Thailand

Another delicious and different curry from Thailand. Serve with salad, rice and *sambals*.

SERVES 4–6
*1½ cups thin coconut milk
1.5kg (3lb) chicken, skinned, boned and cut up into bite-sized pieces
3tbsp Thai green curry paste (see page 209)
455g (1lb) small new potatoes, or cut-up larger ones, cooked
1tbsp nam pla (fish sauce)
*2 lime leaves or strips of lemon peel
*2tbsp fresh basil, chopped, or 1tbsp dried
*1 cup thick coconut milk

In a wok or saucepan bring the thin coconut milk to the boil, add the chicken and simmer uncovered until cooked (25–30 minutes), stirring occasionally. Strain and set aside both chicken and stock. Reboil half a cup of the cooking liquid, add the curry mixture and boil hard until the contents of the pan form a thick paste. Now slowly add the remaining cooking liquid and simmer until quite thick. Add the chicken, potatoes, *nam pla*, lime leaves, basil and thick coconut milk. Simmer for 5 minutes and serve. Like most curries it will keep and can be reheated and served the following day.

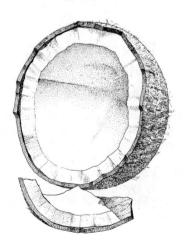

VEGETABLES AND SALADS

AUBERGINE PILAF
Armenia

Aubergine and nutty brown rice combine robustly in this honest dish which can be eaten on its own or served as an accompaniment to grills.

SERVES 4
2tbsp olive oil
1 onion, finely chopped
★*1 clove garlic*
170g (6oz) brown long-grain rice
1tbsp tomato purée
1 bay leaf
2¾ cups light stock
★*1 aubergine, cubed, salted, rinsed and dried*
★*½ green pepper, chopped*
1tsp oregano, dried
1tbsp parsley, finely chopped
1tbsp parmesan cheese (optional)

Heat the oil and fry the onion and garlic until soft. Add the rice and stir round until well coated with the oil. Carefully add the tomato purée, bay leaf and half the stock and bring to simmering point. Cover and cook gently for 20 minutes. Add the remaining stock, aubergine, green pepper and oregano. Stir, cover and cook for about 20 minutes longer, until the stock is all absorbed. Serve sprinkled with parsley and cheese.

BAKED OYSTER MUSHROOMS
England

Eat these meaty mushrooms on their own as a supper dish or with grilled meat and chicken.

SERVES 2–4
★*225g (8oz) oyster mushrooms*
55g (2oz) butter
★*1 clove garlic, crushed*
2tbsp dry white wine

2tbsp finely-chopped parsley
½tsp paprika

Cut the mushrooms into thick slices and place them in a well-buttered, shallow ovenproof dish. Melt the butter in a saucepan, add the garlic and cook gently for a minute. Add the wine, parsley and paprika, bring to the boil and simmer for another minute. Pour over the mushrooms and cook in the oven at 190°C (375°F), gas mark 5 for 15–20 minutes.

BEAN SPROUTS WITH TOFU
Japan

A highly nutritious vegetable course.

SERVES 4 as part of a Japanese meal.
170g (6oz) tofu (beancurd), cut into 2.5cm (1in) squares
1tbsp flour
2tbsp oil
★*1 clove garlic, crushed*
★*225g (8oz) bean sprouts (see Sprouted Seeds)*
1–2tbsp soy sauce
pinch shichimi-togarashi or cayenne pepper

Place the *tofu* between the folds of a clean cloth and weight down to drain for 10 minutes. Pat dry and coat lightly with flour. Heat the oil, add the garlic and fry until golden. Add *tofu* and fry on all sides until coloured. Add the bean sprouts, soy sauce and seasoning and stir-fry for a few minutes. Serve immediately.

BHAJI AND LENTIL SIDE DISH

India

Amaranth or spinach combines well with the green lentils to make a good side dish with curry.

SERVES 4
115g (4oz) whole green lentils
2tbsp oil
★*1–2 fresh chillies, thinly sliced*
★*1 clove garlic, crushed*
★*2½cm (1in) ginger, freshly grated*
★*1 bunch amaranth (see Oriental Leaf Vegetables) or 225g (8oz) spinach, washed and roughly chopped*
★*4tbsp fresh coriander, chopped*
salt to taste
2tbsp lemon juice
½tsp garam masala (optional—see page 213)

Wash the lentils, and put them in a saucepan with plenty of cold water. Bring to the boil and simmer them for about 50 minutes until just tender. Drain and set them aside. Heat the oil in a saucepan, add the chillies, garlic and ginger and fry gently for half a minute. Add the amaranth and coriander and stir around until wilted. Now mix in the lentils, salt and lemon juice. Cover and cook gently for 10 minutes. Sprinkle on the *garam masala* just before serving.

CAROLE'S BREADFRUIT CASSEROLE

Trinidad

A spicy vegetable medley, nutritious, very filling and entirely fat free.

SERVES 4
2 cups stock or water
★*½ medium breadfruit, prepared in 2.5cm (1in) pieces*
★*1 15cm (6in) piece of yam, peeled and sliced*
★*1 aubergine, cut into 2.5cm (1in) squares*

4 onions, chopped
4 tomatoes, skinned and chopped
★*3 cloves garlic, sliced*
2tbsp tomato purée
2 bay leaves
1tsp ground turmeric
★*4 hot fresh chillies, left whole*
4 cardamom pods
1 5cm (2in) stick cinnamon
4 cloves

Heat the stock to boiling point, add the breadfruit and yam and simmer for 10 minutes. Add all the remaining ingredients and cook for a further 30–40 minutes until tender.

CELERIAC SALAD

England

Refreshing and tangy—ideal for a lunchtime meal.

SERVES 4–6
★*225g (8oz) celeriac, cut into matchsticks and blanched*
225g (8oz) chicken, cooked and diced
1 medium cooking apple, cored and diced
4tbsp mayonnaise
4tbsp yoghurt
salt and freshly ground black pepper
1 lettuce heart
1tsp mint, finely chopped

Combine the first six ingredients and pile the mixture onto a bed of lettuce leaves in a serving bowl or individual dishes. Sprinkle with mint and serve.

CHAYOTE SALAD
Europe

Chayote adds crunchiness to this colourful salad.

SERVES 4–6
★2 chayotes, medium sized
115g (4oz) mushrooms, sliced
225g (8oz) green beans, blanched and sliced
2 tomatoes, quartered
4 spring onions, chopped
★1tbsp fresh coriander leaves, chopped
salt and pepper to taste
2tbsp vinaigrette dressing

Peel, quarter and finely slice the chayotes, then blanch in boiling water for 1 minute, refresh in cold water and drain. Add the remaining vegetables and coriander leaves, season to taste and toss in vinaigrette dressing.

CURLY ENDIVE AND BACON SALAD
USA

A marvellous contrast of textures, flavours and temperatures are all gathered in this American-style appetiser.

SERVES 4
★1 curly-leaved endive, washed and torn into manageable pieces
170g (6oz) smoked bacon, diced
4 slices of bread, cubed and fried in garlic-flavoured olive oil
½ cup garlicky French dressing

Divide the endive into individual bowls. Just before serving, scatter on the fried bacon and croûtons. Serve dressing separately.

CYPRUS ARTICHOKES
Cyprus

These may be served as a first course or to accompany grilled lamb or chicken.

SERVES 4–6
3tbsp olive oil
★455g (1lb) artichoke hearts, quartered
6tbsp red wine
salt and pepper
2tbsp coriander seeds, crushed

Heat the oil and gently fry the artichokes until golden. Lower the heat and add the wine and salt and pepper to taste. Cover and simmer gently until tender—about 15 minutes. Add the coriander seeds and simmer for a further 3 minutes.

FATTOUSH
Syria

This bread salad, literally 'moistened bread', is popular in the Middle East. The inclusion of purslane is desirable but not essential.

SERVES 6
1 pitta bread, toasted and torn into small pieces
★1 small bunch of purslane leaves
1 cucumber, previously diced, salted and drained
1 small lettuce or lettuce heart, shredded
4 tomatoes, diced
★1 green capsicum, diced
3tbsp parsley, finely chopped
2tbsp mint, chopped
1 onion, finely chopped

Dressing:
★2 cloves garlic, crushed
3½tbsp lemon juice
3½tbsp olive oil
salt and pepper to taste

Place the bread in a large bowl together with the vegetables and herbs. Mix the garlic, lemon juice, oil and seasoning thoroughly and add to the salad. Toss well and chill for 30 minutes before serving.

FENNEL WITH PARMESAN CHEESE

Italy

It really is worth buying fresh parmesan cheese for this traditional recipe.

SERVES 4
★4 fennel heads, trimmed and halved
55g (2oz) butter
55g (2oz) parmesan cheese, grated

Cook the fennel in boiling, salted water until tender, about 10 minutes. Butter an ovenproof dish, arrange the fennel halves and dot with more butter. Sprinkle with the cheese and bake in the oven at 190°C (375°F), gas mark 5 for 10–15 minutes until golden brown.

FUFU

Ghana

This Ghanaian recipe is much quicker and easier to make if you have a food processor. Serve like dumplings with peppery soups and stews.

SERVES 4
★455g (1lb) cassava, prepared and cut into large chunks

Cook the cassava in boiling water until done, about 45–50 minutes. Drain, allow to cool a little and process or pound to a thick dough-like consistency. You may have to do this in batches depending on the size of your processor or mortar. Now wet your hands and shape the cassava into egg-sized balls.

GADO GADO

Indonesia

A cooked salad which is served warm with a hot and spicy peanut sauce. Take great care not to overcook the vegetables.

SERVES 4–6

Sauce:
1 onion, grated
★2 cloves garlic, crushed
★4 fresh red chillies, finely chopped
2tsp brown sugar
1tbsp oil
170g (6oz) peanut butter, coarse or smooth
1tbsp lemon juice
★1 cup coconut milk—85g (3oz) creamed coconut mixed with 1 cup hot water
salt to taste

Salad:
★225g (8oz) bean sprouts (see Sprouted Seeds), blanched
1/2 cabbage heart, shredded and blanched
2 carrots, sliced into large matchsticks and boiled until just tender
1 cucumber, thinly sliced
225g (8oz) French beans, cut into 2.5cm (1in) lengths and boiled until just tender
2 potatoes, cooked and sliced
2 eggs, hard boiled and sliced
1 onion, sliced into rings and fried
a few prawn crackers, crumbled (optional)

To make the sauce: with a pestle and mortar or food processor pound together the onion, garlic, chillies and sugar. Fry this mixture in oil for a minute, stirring. Gradually add the remaining ingredients, bring to the boil and simmer until a thick pouring consistency is reached. Salt to taste and refrigerate until needed. This sauce keeps for at least a week and should be gently reheated.

Arrange the salad vegetables in layers in a bowl with the potatoes at the bottom. Top with slices of egg, onion rings and a sprinkling of prawn crackers. Serve with the sauce.

JERUSALEM ARTICHOKE PURÉE

France

This is an unusual accompaniment to duck or game dishes.

SERVES 4–6
★1kg (2lb) Jerusalem artichokes
30g (1oz) butter
2tbsp cream
1–2tsp lemon juice
pinch nutmeg
salt and pepper to taste

Peel the artichokes and cook in salted acidulated water until tender. Drain and pass them through a sieve or purée them in a food processor. Beat in the butter, cream and lemon juice, together with the nutmeg, salt and pepper. Reheat very gently if necessary.

JERUSALEM ARTICHOKES WITH TOMATOES AND DILL

Mediterranean

Good with roast lamb or veal.

SERVES 4–6
★1kg (2lb) Jerusalem artichokes
3tbsp olive oil
1 onion, chopped
★1 clove garlic, crushed
395g (14oz) can tomato pieces
½tsp dill weed
salt and pepper
1tbsp parsley

Peel the artichokes and cut into 2.5cm (1in) pieces. Boil in salted, acidulated water for 15 minutes, drain and set aside. Heat the oil in a fairly deep pan and fry the onion and garlic until golden. Add the artichokes and tomatoes and bring to the boil. Now stir in the dill, season to taste and simmer for about 10 minutes until the artichokes are tender and the sauce is reduced to quite a thick consistency. Turn into a serving dish, sprinkle with parsley and serve.

JICAMA SALAD

Mexico

Crisp and crunchy—an ideal salad to accompany cold duck or turkey.

SERVES 2
★115g (4oz) jicama, peeled and diced
¼ cucumber, sliced
2 spring onions, finely sliced
1 small orange, peeled and sliced into thin rounds
3tbsp French dressing
½ crisp lettuce
1tbsp chopped parsley

Combine the jicama, cucumber, onions and orange and toss well with the dressing. Divide the lettuce and arrange on two plates. Top with the salad mixture and sprinkle with parsley before serving.

MATTAR PANEER

India

An arresting combination, spicy and unusual. A good side dish for an Asian meal.

SERVES 4
2tbsp oil
1 onion, finely chopped
★1 clove garlic
★½ green chilli, chopped
★1cm (½in) grated ginger
★1cm (½in) turmeric or ½tsp turmeric powder
½tsp coriander seed
½tsp chilli powder
55g (2oz) tomatoes, skinned and chopped
salt to taste
★225g (8oz) shelled pigeon peas (see Beans and Peas) or garden peas
115g (4oz) paneer or home-made cream cheese, cut into squares and fried
water
1tbsp parsley

Heat the oil and add the onion, garlic, chilli, ginger and turmeric (if using fresh turmeric) and fry until golden. Add the remaining spices, stir-fry for a minute then add the tomatoes and salt and cook for a further minute. Add the peas and cheese, just cover with water, put on a lid and cook until the peas are tender. Serve sprinkled with parsley.

METHI POTATOES
India

A spicy way of serving new potatoes, to go with an Indian meal or to accompany roast meat.

SERVES 4
3tbsp oil
1/2tsp whole cumin seeds
1tsp turmeric powder
1tsp chilli powder
455g (1lb) small new potatoes, scrubbed and halved
★1 bunch fenugreek leaves (methi), chopped, tough stalks removed
1/2tsp garam masala (optional—see page 213)
1tsp salt

Heat the oil in a saucepan, add the cumin seeds and fry until they pop. Immediately stir in the turmeric and chilli and cook for a few seconds. Now add the potatoes and fenugreek leaves with 2–3 tablespoons of water. Cover and cook very slowly until the potatoes are done. Add a little more water if necessary and sprinkle on the *garam masala* and salt just before the end of cooking time.

MONGRI BAJI
India

A spicy side dish with a crunchy texture to accompany an Indian meal.

SERVES 4
1tbsp oil
1/4tsp cumin seeds
1 onion, finely chopped
1tsp ground coriander
1/4tsp chilli powder
1/2tsp turmeric powder
1/4tsp salt
★225g (8oz) mongri, washed and trimmed
4tbsp water

Heat the oil, add the cumin seeds and fry until they pop. Immediately add the onion and fry until tender and golden. Stir in the remaining spices and salt and cook for half a minute. Add the mongri and water and cook for about 10 minutes until the water has evaporated.

MUSHROOM-FILLED ARTICHOKES
England

The delicately-flavoured filling makes a special start to any meal.

SERVES 4
★8 globe artichoke cups (fresh or canned)
1tbsp butter
1 onion, finely chopped
1 rasher streaky bacon, chopped
55g (2oz) mushrooms, chopped
4tbsp fresh breadcrumbs
1tbsp parsley, chopped
pinch thyme
pinch nutmeg, grated
salt and pepper to taste
2tbsp white wine
6tbsp white stock

Cook the artichoke cups (if using the fresh vegetable) in boiling, salted, acidulated water for 15 minutes. Drain and set aside. Melt the butter and fry the onions and bacon until soft and golden. Add the mushrooms and fry for a few more minutes. Remove from the heat and mix in the breadcrumbs, herbs and seasonings. Moisten with the wine and spoon the mixture into the artichokes. Butter an ovenproof dish small enough for the artichokes to nestle snugly side by side. Put in the artichokes, surround with the stock and bake in the oven at 190°C (375°F) gas mark 5 for 20 minutes.

OKRA WITH TOMATOES
Middle East

A simple dish, served hot to accompany grills, or on its own, hot or cold.

SERVES 4
2tbsp olive oil
1 onion, finely sliced
★1 clove garlic, slivered
★455g (1lb) okra, prepared whole
1 tin tomatoes with liquid, chopped
★1 dried chilli, crushed
salt and pepper to taste
3tbsp lemon juice

Heat the oil gently and fry the onion and garlic until soft and golden. Add the okra and fry for about 10 minutes, stirring frequently. Add the tomatoes, chilli, salt and pepper and bring to a simmer. Cover and cook for about 50 minutes until tender. Add the lemon juice and simmer a further 10 minutes.

PAK CHOI SALAD
Holland

A creamy side salad or light luncheon dish.

SERVES 4
115g (4oz) quark or low-fat cream cheese
1tbsp mayonnaise
1tsp Dijon mustard
salt and pepper to taste
2tbsp chopped parsley
★1 bunch pak choi (see Oriental Leaf Vegetables)

Mix all the ingredients together except for the leaves. Shred the leaves, place in a salad bowl and top with the dressing.

PAPAYA CHEESE SALAD
Europe

A slimmer's salad for a sunny summer's day.

SERVES 4
★1 ripe papaya
225g (8oz) cottage cheese
1 stick celery, finely chopped
6 spring onions, finely chopped
55g (2oz) pecan nuts, chopped
1tbsp parsley, finely chopped
salt and pepper to taste
2tsp papaya seeds
1 lettuce

Peel the papaya, slice into 2cm (¾in) rings, then remove the seeds (save 2tsp) and membrane. The cavity will be star-shaped. Into this spoon a mixture of the cottage cheese, celery, onions, nuts and parsley, after seasoning to taste. Garnish with the seeds and serve on a bed of lettuce.

RICE AND LENTIL ROLLS
Lebanon

A delicately-spiced filling in chard leaves.

SERVES 4
3tbsp olive oil
1 large onion, finely chopped
225g (8oz) cooked rice
225g (8oz) cooked green lentils
3tbsp parsley, chopped
3tbsp mint, chopped
1tsp mixed spice
salt and pepper to taste
★225g (8oz) chard leaves, stems removed
★2 cloves garlic, slivered
4tbsp lemon juice

Heat the oil in a medium-sized saucepan and fry the onion gently until soft.

Turn into a bowl and mix in the rice, lentils, herbs, mixed spice and seasoning. Set aside. Pour boiling water over the chard leaves to render them pliable. Drain. Lay each leaf flat, veined side uppermost and place on it about a tablespoon of filling—the exact amount will depend on the size of the leaf. Roll up like a cigar, taking care to tuck in the ends. Pack the rolls back into the pan quite tightly in two layers, then poke garlic slivers into the spaces. Sprinkle with lemon juice and just cover with hot water. Weight down with a plate, cover and simmer for 20 minutes.

SPICY BEANS AND POTATOES
India

This could be served as a side dish or on its own with Indian bread and salad.

SERVES 2–4
1tbsp ghee or oil
½tsp cumin seeds
½tsp mustard seeds
½tsp chilli powder
½tsp ground turmeric
★455g (1lb) beans (cowpeas or any other green beans), chopped into 4cm (1½in) lengths
340g (12oz) potatoes, peeled and cut into small chunks
4tbsp water
½tsp salt
½tsp garam masala (see page 213)

In a large frying pan melt the ghee and fry the cumin and mustard seeds over medium heat until they pop, then add the chilli and turmeric and stir for a few seconds. Add the vegetables and stir around until they are well coated with the spices. Add the water and salt, cover and simmer gently for 10–15 minutes until cooked, stirring occasionally. Sprinkle with *garam masala*, stir and serve.

STIR-FRIED ANGLED LOOFAH
China

Serve as a delicate accompaniment to a Chinese meal or with grilled chicken or pork.

SERVES 6–8
4tbsp oil
1tbsp spring onion, finely chopped
★1 clove garlic, minced
★2 medium angled loofahs (see Gourds), peeled and cut into wedges
1tsp salt
2tbsp chicken stock or water
1tsp cornflour mixed with a little water
½tsp sesame oil (optional)

Heat the oil in a wok or frying pan and stir-fry the onion and garlic for a few seconds. Add the loofahs, salt and stock and stir-fry for a minute or so. Add the cornflour and stir until smooth. Aromatise with sesame oil before serving if desired.

STUFFED CHAYOTES
Mexico

A light and spicy vegetarian supper dish.

SERVES 2–4
★2 medium chayotes, washed
1 onion, finely chopped
★1 clove garlic, crushed
1tbsp corn oil
2 tomatoes, skinned and chopped
★1 green chilli, finely chopped
3tbsp sweetcorn kernels (fresh, canned or frozen)
½tsp oregano
salt and pepper to taste
2tbsp breadcrumbs, fresh
2tbsp cheese, grated

Boil the chayotes for 30–40 minutes until tender. Halve, scoop out the flesh and mash, including seeds. Reserve the skins and pulp. Fry the onion and garlic in the oil until soft and golden; add the remaining ingredients except for the breadcrumbs and cheese. Combine with the chayote pulp and fill the shells with the mixture. Top with the breadcrumbs and cheese, brown under a hot grill and serve.

SURAN CURRY
India

Suran, or elephant foot yam, has a firm meaty consistency and makes a popular North Indian curry, accompanied with rice.

SERVES 2–4
3tbsp oil
★455g (1lb) elephant foot yam (see Eddoe, Dasheen, etc), peeled, cut into 2.5cm (1in) cubes
3 cloves
2 cardamom pods
5cm (2in) cinnamon stick
6 peppercorns
1 onion, finely chopped
★2.5cm (1in) ginger, grated
★1 clove garlic, crushed
★1 fresh green chilli, finely chopped
1tsp ground coriander
1tsp powdered turmeric
½tsp chilli powder
1 tomato, chopped
★1tbsp fresh coriander leaves, chopped

Heat the oil in a large frying pan and fry the yam until golden brown; remove and set aside. Add the whole spices to the oil and fry for about a minute. Add the onion, ginger, garlic and chilli and fry until the onion is golden. Now add the ground spices and fry for a further minute. Add the yam, tomato and sufficient water to cover. Simmer gently for about 45 minutes. Serve garnished with coriander leaves.

UNDIHU
India

A substantial mixed vegetable curry from the Gujarat district of India. Vary the proportions of the ingredients as you wish.

SERVES 6
3tbsp oil
★455g (1lb) yam or sweet potato, peeled and cut into 2.5cm (1in) chunks
★225g (8oz) aubergine, cut into 2.5cm (1in) slices or chunks
225g (8oz) onion, chopped
★2 fresh chillies, chopped
★2.5cm (1in) ginger, grated
½tsp asafoetida
2tsp ground coriander
1tsp turmeric powder
115g (4oz) pigeon peas, blanched 3 minutes or use frozen ones
★115g (4oz) chickpeas (see Beans and Peas), blanched 3 minutes
★115g (4oz) kantola (see Gourds), whole and blanched 3 minutes
★2 cooking bananas, peeled and sliced
455g (1lb) tomatoes, coarsely chopped
1tsp sugar
1tsp salt
★1tbsp grated coconut
★1tbsp chopped coriander leaves

Heat the oil in a large casserole and stir-fry the yam and aubergine for a few minutes until golden brown. Reserve. In the same oil stir in the onion, chillies, ginger and ground spices and cook for a minute. Return the yam and aubergine to the pan together with the peas, chickpeas, kantola, bananas, tomatoes, sugar and salt. Bring to the boil, cover and simmer gently for about 20 minutes until tender, adding a little water if necessary. Serve sprinkled with coconut and coriander leaves.

PUDDINGS AND DESSERTS

ALMOND CREAM
Indonesia

Embellish a fruit salad with these almondy diamonds of jelly.

1/2 cup water
1/2tsp powdered agar-agar or 2tsp gelatine
1/2 cup milk
1tbsp sugar
1/2tsp almond essence

Bring the water to the boil in a saucepan, sprinkle on the *agar-agar* and stir until dissolved. Take the pan off the heat and add the remaining ingredients. Pour into a small shallow tin or mould and leave to set. Cut into diamond shapes and add to the fruit salad.

BLUEBERRIES NEUCHÂTEL
Switzerland

Tart, fresh blueberries with rum.

SERVES 6
★*340g (12oz) blueberries*
6tbsp rum
2tbsp vanilla sugar
1/2 cup whipping cream
1/2tsp cinnamon

Put the blueberries in a bowl with the rum and sugar. Stir well and leave in the refrigerator for several hours to macerate. Spoon into individual glasses, top with whipped cream and a sprinkling of cinnamon.

CHAYOTE RELLENOS
Mexico

SERVES 4
★*2 chayotes or small squashes*
2 eggs
85g (3oz) sugar
1/2tsp ground nutmeg
115g (4oz) sponge cake crumbs
85g (3oz) raisins
6tbsp sherry
55g (2oz) almonds, ground
55g (2oz) almonds, flaked

Boil the chayotes in their skins until tender, about 40 minutes. Halve, carefully scoop out the flesh, mash and allow to cool. Reserve the skins. Blend the eggs, sugar, nutmeg and chayote pulp together. Mix well with the cake crumbs then stir in the raisins and sherry. Add the ground almonds then spoon the mixture into the skins, sprinkle with the flaked almonds and bake in a moderate oven at 180°C (350°F), gas mark 4 for 30 minutes. Serve hot or cold with cream.

CRANBERRY AND BLACKBERRY KISSEL
Russia

SERVES 6
★*225g (8oz) cranberries*
225g (8oz) blackberries
2 cups water
85g (3oz) sugar
1/2 cup dry cider or white wine
3tbsp arrowroot powder

Wash the berries and put them in a saucepan with the water. Bring to the boil and simmer for 15 minutes. Strain the juice through a fine sieve, then return it to the pan. Add the sugar and bring slowly to the boil. Mix the cider and arrowroot and stir into the juice. Stir constantly until it thickens. Turn into a serving dish or individual bowls and chill until required.

FRUIT CREAM
World

A rich dessert that can be made with any fruit juice. Adjust the amount of sugar according to the acidity of the fruit and decorate with slices of fruit, chocolate or nuts.

SERVES 8
11g (½oz) gelatine (1 packet)
1 tbsp water
4 egg yolks
225g (8oz) sugar
1 cup dessert white wine
1 cup fruit juice
1tbsp lemon juice (optional)
1 cup double or whipping cream

Soak the gelatine in water for 10 minutes. In a bowl, beat the egg yolks and sugar until creamy. Add the wine and place the bowl in a saucepan of hot water. Cook, stirring constantly until the mixture coats the back of a spoon. Add the gelatine and stir until dissolved. Remove from the heat and stir in the fruit juice. Cool, then chill until just beginning to set. Lightly whip the cream and fold it into the mixture. Chill well before serving.

MANGO SNOW
Caribbean

Any fruit purée can be used for this light and fluffy pudding. Particularly suitable are custard apple, babaco and papaya.

SERVES 2–4
2 eggs separated
★½ cup mango purée
30–55g (1–2oz) sugar
wafer biscuits

Beat the egg yolks, mango purée and sugar together. Whisk the egg whites until stiff and fold into the mango mixture. Chill for several hours before serving with wafer biscuits.

MELON ALASKA
Bermuda

Simply a gorgeous dessert.

SERVES 4
3 egg whites
pinch of salt
85g (3oz) caster sugar
★2 small round melons, well chilled
1½ cups hard vanilla ice-cream
1tbsp flaked almonds

Whisk the egg whites and salt until firm peaks are formed. Gradually beat in the sugar until the meringue is stiff and satiny. Halve the melons, scoop out the seeds and fill the centres with ice-cream. Spread the meringue over the top and sprinkle with the flaked almonds. Cook in a very hot pre-heated oven at 230°C (450°F), gas mark 8 for 2 minutes. Serve immediately.

PASSION FRUIT MOUSSE
Kenya

SERVES 8
★12 passion fruits
1 cup water
1½tbsp sugar
juice of 2 oranges
1tbsp gelatine, soaked in a little water
2 eggs, separated

Halve the passion fruits and scrape out the pulp and seeds into a saucepan. Add the water and bring to a simmer for a few moments then firmly sieve the mixture into a bowl, discarding the seeds. Add the sugar, orange juice and gelatine. Return this to the saucepan and heat, stirring until the gelatine is completely dissolved. Leave until lukewarm then stir in the lightly-beaten egg yolks. When the mixture begins to set, fold in the stiffly-beaten egg whites. Refrigerate until completely set and serve with whipped cream and wafer biscuits.

SHARON GINGER CREAM
Australia

SERVES 6
★2 persimmons, peeled, 1 sliced, 1 chopped
115g (4oz) cream cheese
1–2tbsp caster sugar
30g (1oz) walnuts, finely chopped
30g (1oz) preserved ginger, finely chopped
½ cup double cream
55g (2oz) butter
115g (4oz) digestive biscuits, crushed
1tbsp brown sugar

Arrange the slices of persimmon in the bottom of a small loaf tin. Beat the cream cheese with the sugar until light and smooth, then fold in the chopped fruit, nuts and ginger. Whip the cream, fold into the mixture and carefully pour into the tin and refrigerate until firm. Melt the butter and mix thoroughly together with the biscuit and brown sugar. Spread this onto the cheese mixture, patting it well down. Refrigerate until required. To serve, turn out onto a dish and cut into slices.

SOURSOP SORBET
West Indies

SERVES 8
115g (4oz) sugar
½ cup water
★1 cup soursop pulp (see Custard Apple), sieved
★1tsp lime juice
1 egg white, beaten

Make a syrup by dissolving the sugar in the water over very low heat. Bring to the boil, simmer for 5 minutes and let cool. Mix the syrup with the soursop purée, add the lime juice and fold in the beaten egg white. Turn the mixture into a plastic container and freeze until the sorbet is still just able to be stirred. Beat the mixture with a hand whisk or in a food processor until light and fluffy. Return to the container and freeze until required. Take it out of the freezer 30 minutes before serving.

SOUTHERN PUDDING
USA

SERVES 4
★340g (12oz) sweet potatoes, peeled and boiled
3tbsp sugar
115g (4oz) butter, melted
4 eggs, separated
1tsp lemon rind, grated
½ cup orange juice
½tsp cinnamon

Sieve or purée the potatoes. Add 2 tablespoons of the sugar, and the butter, and mix thoroughly. Beat the egg yolks and add to the potatoes together with the lemon rind and orange juice. Beat the egg whites until stiff and fold into the mixture. Pour into a soufflé dish, sprinkle with the remaining sugar and the cinnamon and bake in the oven at 180°C (350°F), gas mark 4 for 25 mins.

STICKY RICE
Thailand

SERVES 4
115g (4oz) glutinous rice, soaked overnight in water and drained
★10cm (4in) length of pandanus leaf
1 cup water
★½ cup coconut milk, reduced to two-thirds by boiling
3tbsp sugar
★2 medium-sized mangoes, sliced and chilled

Put the rice, pandanus leaf and water in a saucepan, bring to the boil, cover and simmer for about 10 minutes until tender. Put the coconut milk in a bowl with the sugar and stir in the rice. Leave it for 45 minutes and then chill thoroughly. Serve with the mango slices.

SAUCES

CRANBERRY AND ORANGE SAUCE
USA

A version of traditional cranberry sauce, good with poultry, game or ice-cream.

SERVES 8
*225g (8oz) cranberries
1/2 cup water
85g (3oz) sugar
1 orange, peeled, seeded, roughly chopped

Put all the ingredients in a pan, bring to the boil and simmer until cooked—about 25 minutes. If you like a smooth sauce, rub through a sieve, otherwise leave it just as it is. Refrigerate until required; it will keep for several days.

KIMISU DRESSING
Japan

This incredibly light, Japanese salad dressing is delicious with almost any vegetable, cooked or raw. The diet-conscious will note it contains no oil.

MAKES ABOUT 3/4 CUP
2 egg yolks
1/2 cup water
3tbsp rice vinegar or white wine vinegar
1tbsp sugar
2tsp cornflour
1tsp wasabi (Japanese horseradish), or mustard powder

Beat all the ingredients together or mix in a processor or blender. Pour into a small, thick-bottomed saucepan and cook over a very low heat, stirring constantly, until the mixture thickens enough to coat the back of a spoon. On no account allow the dressing to boil or it will curdle. Chill until required.

ROUILLE
France

A warm-flavoured red pepper sauce for fish soups and bouillabaisse, and (unconventionally) lovely with pasta.

MAKES 1/2–3/4 CUP
*1 red capsicum, skinned, seeded and chopped
*1 fresh red chilli, or 1 dried and soaked
*2 cloves garlic
1 slice bread, about 30g (1oz), soaked in water and squeezed out
3tbsp fish stock, hot
2tbsp olive oil

Blend the capsicum, chilli, garlic and bread with 2 tablespoons of the stock in a liquidiser. Gradually add the oil until you reach the consistency of thin mayonnaise. Thin out with the remaining stock if necessary.

SKORTHALIA
Greece

If you like garlic you will love this Greek sauce which has a robust and pungent taste and is perfect for adding flavour to a cooked vegetable dish, fried fish or as a general savoury dip.

SERVES 8–10
*6 cloves garlic
1/2tsp salt
1 cup olive oil
4tbsp lemon juice
2 cups mashed potato

Combine the garlic, salt, oil and lemon juice in a blender or processor until smooth. Add the potato and blend until creamy. Thin down with a little water if necessary.

SNACKS

INDIAN ASPARAGUS
England/India

Drumsticks are known as Indian asparagus because when they are cooked they have a similar flavour. They are long and narrow and can be eaten like asparagus—a little more fiddly but well worth it.

SERVES 4
★455g (1lb) drumsticks
115g (4oz) butter, melted
lemon wedges
black pepper

Cut the drumsticks into 8cm (3in) lengths and cook in boiling water for 15 minutes. To eat: cut the drumsticks in half lengthways, dip into the melted butter, add a squeeze of lemon and a dash of pepper and scrape the flesh off between the teeth.

AUBERGINE WITH TAHINI
Middle East

A flavoursome light dip with the warm savour of sesame.

SERVES 8
★1 aubergine 340–455g (12oz–1lb)
★2 cloves garlic, crushed
4tbsp lemon juice
1tbsp oil
3tbsp tahini (sesame seed paste)
1tsp salt
½tsp cayenne
½tsp cumin (optional)
1tbsp parsley

Bake the aubergine in a medium-hot oven at 190°C (375°F), gas mark 5 for about an hour until soft. Liquidise or thoroughly mash the aubergine with the garlic and gradually blend in the lemon juice, oil and tahini. Season with salt and spices, turn out into a bowl and chill. Sprinkle with parsley.

CASSAVA CRISPS
Africa

Great served hot or cool with drinks.

★cassava root
oil
salt

Peel the cassava and slice very thinly—a food processor is ideal. Steep in cold water for 30 minutes. Drain, pat thoroughly dry and deep-fry in oil, several pieces at once, until golden brown. Sprinkle with salt and serve.

CHINESE CHIVE KNOTS
China

An intriguing snack, these chive knots are easy and fun to make.

SERVES 10–12
85g (3oz) plain flour
1tbsp cornflour
pinch of salt
1 egg
6tbsp water
★1 bunch chives or kuchai—approx 115g (4oz)—washed and dried
oil for frying
plum or hoisin sauce

Make a batter by sifting the flour, cornflour and salt into a bowl. Mix in the egg and gradually add the water until smooth. Set aside. Take 3 chives and fold them in 3 to make a bundle. Bind each bundle quite tightly with a single chive, weaving in the end to secure. Heat the oil, coat each bundle with batter and deep-fry a few at a time until golden brown. Cut each bundle diagonally into 4 or 5 pieces and serve with a dip of Chinese plum or *hoisin* sauce.

CHINESE 'SEAWEED' OR GREEN FLOSS

China

An expensive delicacy in a restaurant, 'seaweed' can be made from any greens for just a few pence.

SERVES 4
★225g (8oz) pak choi (see Oriental Leaf Vegetables) or other leaves, washed and dried with central stalk removed
oil for deep-frying
½tsp sugar
pinch of salt

Pack the leaves one on top of the other and roll them up tightly. With a sharp knife or cleaver shred them as finely as possible. Heat the oil and deep-fry for a minute or two. The timing depends on the thickness of the shreds—take care not to burn them. Drain well and leave for a little to crisp. Sprinkle with the sugar and salt and serve.

FENUGREEK AND ONION FRITTERS

India

MAKES AT LEAST 12
115g (4oz) besan (chickpea flour)
½–1tsp chilli powder
½tsp ground cumin
½tsp turmeric powder
½tsp black cumin seeds (optional)
½tsp salt
water
1 onion, finely sliced
★1 cup fenugreek leaves, chopped
oil for deep-frying

Mix the flour with the spices and salt and add sufficient water to make a fairly stiff batter. Stir in the onion and fenugreek leaves. Heat the oil, and drop tablespoons of the mixture, a few at a time, turning occasionally until crisp and golden.

HAM WITH PAPAYA

Europe

A variation on the more traditional melon and Parma ham. Serve this starter with crusty rolls and unsalted butter.

SERVES 4
★1 papaya
8 slices Parma ham
★1 lime, quartered
black pepper

Peel the papaya then cut it in half lengthways. Scoop out the seeds and membrane then cut each section in half once again. There are now four pieces, cut these crossways making eight pieces in all. Fold a slice of ham over each piece and serve with a wedge of lime and pepper.

MA HO

Thailand

Serve these 'Galloping Horses' as a colourful party snack.

ABOUT 36 PIECES
2tbsp oil
★4 cloves garlic, crushed
225g (8oz) minced pork
★3tbsp groundnuts (peanuts), coarsely ground
2tbsp dark brown sugar
2tsp oyster sauce
½tsp black pepper
½tsp salt
★6 kiwifruits (or equivalent tangerines, lychees or pineapple)
★1tbsp coriander leaves or parsley, chopped
★1–2 chillies, fresh, seeded and finely sliced

Heat the oil, fry the garlic for a minute, add the pork and stir until evenly brown. Now add the nuts, sugar, oyster sauce, pepper and salt and cook for about 10 minutes, stirring constantly. Set aside. Skin and cut the kiwifruits across into 6mm (¼in) slices. Put a little of the mixture on each slice and top with coriander and a slice of chilli. If using tangerines, halve the segments by slitting through from the fat side without severing them completely, open out and place skin side down; if using lychees, fill the centres; pineapple can be cut into pieces about the size of a kiwifruit cross-section.

PATARVEL
India

A very spicy snack.

6 LEAVES WILL YIELD 12 'DISKS'
85g (3oz) besan (chickpea flour)
½tsp ground turmeric
1tsp ground coriander seeds
½tsp garam masala (see page 213)
30g (1oz) grated jaggery or brown sugar
★*1 green chilli, finely chopped, or chilli powder to taste*
★*30g (1oz) tamarind, covered with boiling water, steeped until cool and passed through a sieve*
½tsp salt
water
★*6 arvi leaves, washed and with central stem removed*
★*lime or lemon juice*
oil
★*fresh coriander leaves, optional*

Mix the ingredients from besan to salt with sufficient water to form a smooth paste. Lay one arvi leaf smooth side down and spread on an even layer of paste. Lay another leaf on top and repeat until all the leaves are used. Roll up into a sausage shape, tucking in the ends, and secure at intervals with cotton thread, taking care not to bite into the leaves. Steam for 35 minutes and allow to cool. Remove the thread, cut into 1cm (½in) slices and deep-fry in oil until they turn to a dark bronze colour. Serve hot with a squeeze of lime or lemon juice and a sprinkling of chopped coriander if liked.

YAUTIA FRITTERS
South America

Serve these sweet fritters with meat, like sweetcorn. They also accompany Chicken Maryland or can be served simply as a snack.

SERVES 6
★*455g (1lb) tannia (yautia), grated raw (see Eddoe, Dasheen, etc)*
1 egg
½tsp salt
★*grated peel of one lime*
55g (2oz) cream or cottage cheese
1tbsp sugar
oil for deep-frying

Combine all the ingredients and mix well. Heat the oil and fry tablespoonfuls of the mixture, three or four at a time, until golden brown, turning once. Drain and keep warm.

CHUTNEYS, PICKLES AND SIDE DISHES

BEAN RAITA
India

Prepare this cooling addition to a curry meal just before serving.

SERVES 3–4
170g (6oz) green beans, barely cooked, cooled and cut into 1cm (½in) pieces
1 cup plain yoghurt
1tbsp oil
★2 dried red chillies or ½tsp chilli powder
★6 curry leaves
1tsp mustard seeds

Mix the beans with the yoghurt. Heat the oil in a pan, add the spices and fry until the mustard seeds pop. Pour over the yoghurt mixture and serve immediately.

CHILLI SAMBAL
Indonesia

A hot condiment to accompany *satays*, *kebabs* and sausages.

SERVES 6
1tbsp oil
1tsp blachan
1 onion, finely chopped
3 tomatoes, chopped
★2 chillies, finely chopped

Heat the oil and fry the *blachan* for a minute. Add the onion, tomatoes and chillies and cook until soft, stirring frequently, moistening with a little water if required. Serve warm or cold.

CORIANDER AND MINT RAITA
India

Serve this with Indian dishes—it goes especially well with *pakoras* and *samosas*.

SERVES 6
★½ cup fresh coriander leaves
½ cup fresh mint leaves
★1 small green chilli, seeded
6tbsp yoghurt
1tsp lemon juice
½tsp sugar
½tsp salt

Chop the leaves and chilli very finely, preferably in a food processor. Stir into the yoghurt, add the lemon juice, sugar and salt. Chill until required.

FALSA PICKLE
India

This is an authentic north Indian pickle using lots of spices. It is hot and has a tart flavour.
MAKES 455g (1lb)
1tbsp black mustard seeds
1tsp asafoetida powder
2tsp turmeric powder
1tsp whole fennel seeds
2tsp whole coriander seeds
2tsp fenugreek seeds
★10 dried red chillies
2tsp salt
★455g (1lb) falsa fruit
455ml (16fl oz) mustard oil

Grind the mustard seeds and mix with the asafoetida and turmeric. Gently dry roast the remaining spices for a minute before grinding them. Mix with the salt and fruit and put into sterilised jars with a spoonful of oil to moisten. Heat the remaining oil and allow to cool. The following day, fill the jars with the oil and seal. Leave for at least a month before using.

GUNDA PICKLE
India

Gunda fruit makes a sour and spicy pickle.

MAKES 1kg (2lb)
★455g (1lb) gundas
4 cups water
170g (6oz) salt
pickling ingredients as for Falsa Pickle (see page 206)

Remove the stalks and wash the gundas well. Make a slit in the side of each fruit and take out the stone. Put the water, salt and gundas in a bowl and leave for 24 hours. Follow recipe for Falsa Pickle.

INDIAN PAPAYA PICKLE
India

An unripe papaya may be used for this 'fresh' pickle. Serve with fish or vegetable curries. It will keep for a week or so in the refrigerator.

MAKES ABOUT 225g (8oz)
1tsp panch phora (see page 214)
2tbsp mustard oil
★1 papaya—about 340g (12oz)—seeded, peeled, diced, steamed and mashed
★1tbsp grated ginger
30g (1oz) sultanas
1–2tsp chilli powder
2tbsp grated jaggery or brown sugar
1tsp salt
★2tbsp tamarind water
1tsp ground turmeric

Grind the panch phora coarsely and fry for a few minutes in the mustard oil. Add the remaining ingredients and simmer gently until thick. Cool slightly and bottle until required.

LIME SAMBAL
Sri Lanka

This is a particularly zesty relish which can be enjoyed served with a curry, to add a hot, sour flavour.

SERVES 4
2 small salted limes (see page 208), finely sliced
4 spring onions, finely sliced
★½ green capsicum, finely chopped
★1 fresh chilli (red), seeded and chopped
★2tsp lime or lemon juice

Combine the limes and vegetables, sprinkle with lime juice and turn into a bowl.

PICKLED BEAN SPROUTS
Indonesia

Bean sprouts with a bit of zest—these will keep for at least a week and are served as a side salad.

SERVES 2
★170g (6oz) bean sprouts (see Sprouted Seeds)
3tsp salt
2tsp brown sugar
1tbsp rice vinegar (available from oriental food stores) or wine vinegar
water

Place the bean sprouts in a jar and sprinkle on the salt and sugar. Add the vinegar and sufficient water to cover. Leave for 3 days loosely covered, then cover tightly and refrigerate until required.

SALTED LIMES
India

A pickle of remarkable flavour. Salted limes are deliciously sour and salty—ideal for adding to other condiments, or eaten as such. They keep almost indefinitely. Use salt that is free of additives. Jar lids must be non-metallic.

MAKES 455g (1lb)
★455g (1lb) small Indian limes
170g (6oz) rock salt

Wash and dry the limes. Take a sharp knife and in each lime make two cross cuts, nearly all the way through, from top to bottom, as if to quarter, but without severing the pieces completely. Rub about a teaspoon of salt well into each lime and pack into one or two glass jars. Seal well, and leave for a week on a sunny windowsill if possible. Store for several months before using in chutneys, pickles and *sambals*.

SAMBAL BAJAK
Indonesia

Although this fiery condiment may be bought in jars, it can be made at home at a fraction of the cost, when red chillies are available. It will keep for at least a month.

MAKES 225g (8oz)
★115g (4oz) fresh red chillies, roughly chopped
1 medium onion, roughly chopped
★3 cloves garlic
½tsp laos powder
1tbsp brown sugar
1tsp salt
4 brazil nuts
1tsp trasi or blachan
★4tbsp tamarind water
4tbsp oil

Place all the ingredients except the oil into a blender or food processor and blend until a smooth paste is formed. Heat the oil in a wok or frying pan and stir-fry the paste quite gently until it is dark red and the liquid has evaporated. This will take about 30 minutes. Store in small jars and use sparingly.

SAMPHIRE PICKLE
England

Try this samphire pickle with your favourite cheeses and cold meats.

MAKES 2 JARS
4 cups white vinegar
4tbsp pickling spice
★1kg (2lb) samphire, roots discarded, sprigs cut into 2.5cm (1in) lengths

Bring the vinegar and spices slowly to the boil, remove from the heat and allow to cool, then strain. Pack the samphire into jars, cover with the spiced vinegar and seal. The pickle will be ready in a week but is best after 2 or 3 months.

SPICY CORIANDER RELISH
India

Bright green, hot and pungent, this condiment is ideal with mild curries for those who prefer a hotter dish, and can be added to other dishes for extra flavour or used as a base for a *pilau*.

ENOUGH FOR 8
★½ cup coriander leaves
★2.5cm (1in) fresh ginger root, roughly chopped
★2 cloves garlic, roughly chopped
★1 green chilli, deseeded and chopped
3tbsp water

Place all the ingredients in a blender or food processor and reduce to a pulp. Alternatively, grind with a pestle and mortar adding the water afterwards. We recommend the first method—a little extra water may be required with old-fashioned blenders.

SPICE MIXTURES

CHAT MASALA
India

This spice mixture will enhance both sweet and savoury snacks. *Kala namak* is available from Indian shops.

2tbsp amchur (dried mango powder)
2tsp black salt (kala namak)
1tsp chilli powder
2tsp ground coriander
2tsp ground cumin
1tsp ground fennel
1tsp ground fenugreek

Mix all the ingredients together and store in an airtight container. Sprinkle over a selection of mixed diced fruit such as banana, ber, falsa, pear and pineapple, with cucumber, cooked sweet potato, sprouted mung beans and a generous squeeze of lemon juice.

GREEN CURRY PASTE
Thailand

A curry paste from Thailand that can be kept for up to a month. This recipe makes enough for 4 chickens or 4kg (8lb) of meat.

★*2.5cm (1in) galangal, chopped*
★*1 finger Chinese keys (optional)*
★*2.5cm (1in) lemon grass, chopped*
★*½tsp lime peel, grated*
★*4–8 fresh green chillies, chopped*
★*1tbsp coriander root or stalk, chopped*
 1tbsp coriander seeds, ground
 ½tsp kapi
★*6 cloves garlic*
 1 onion, chopped
 2tsp salt
 3tbsp oil

Place all the ingredients in a food processor, blender or pestle and mortar and grind together until a smooth paste is obtained. Seal and refrigerate until required or divide into portions and freeze.

SUPARI
India

Complete your meal with originality—homemade pan. Proportions are for 1 pan leaf; all ingredients are available from Indian suppliers.

★*1 pan leaf*
 ½tsp lime paste
 2 pinches of sliced areca nuts
 1 pinch of sugar balls
 1 pinch of aniseed or fennel seeds
 1 pinch of cardamom seeds
★*1 pinch of grated coconut*
 1 pinch of cucumber or melon seeds
 1 whole clove

Lay the pan leaf veined side down on a flat surface and smear the lime paste over its centre. Add the pinches of spices in a heap in the centre, then fold the leaf over into a triangle. Finally fix the 'parcel' with the clove. Make it neat and small for a single mouthful.

TSIRE POWDER
Nigeria

A spicy, peanut-based coating for kebabs and barbecued meats and poultry. Ingredients are given in proportions only. Make quantities as required.

1 part chilli powder
1 part mixed spice
★*4 parts ground peanuts (groundnuts)*
salt

Mix all the ingredients together and store in an airtight container until required.

PRESERVES AND SWEETMEATS

FIG AND APPLE PRESERVE
Europe

This is an unusual jam combining figs and apples and it has a pleasant crunchy texture.

MAKES APPROX 3kg (6lb)
★1kg (2lb) figs, washed and chopped
2kg (4lb) cooking apples, peeled, cored and chopped
2.5kg (5lb) sugar
3 cups water

Place all the ingredients in a saucepan and simmer for about an hour. Cool before bottling.

FORBIDDEN CANDY
Barbados

An enticing candy to be eaten as a sweet, used for decorating cakes and puddings or delicious added to mince-meat. Save the flesh for a fruit salad.

★peel of 1 pomelo
455g (1lb) granulated sugar

Cover the pomelo peel with water and leave overnight. Drain, cover with fresh water, bring to the boil and drain again. Squeeze gently in a cloth to extract moisture and repeat this process three times. Put the sugar in a large thick-bottomed saucepan with a cup of water. Bring slowly to simmering point, stirring until the sugar has dissolved. Add the pomelo peel and simmer until the liquid is thick and the rind is translucent. Drain, cool and dust with a little sugar. When completely cold store in an airtight container.

JICAMA SWEETMEATS
Mexico

You will love these Mexican sweetmeats with a tropical taste.

MAKES 20 PIECES
★115g (4oz) grated jicama
★30g (1oz) grated or desiccated coconut
¼ cup orange juice
115g (4oz) white sugar

Place all the ingredients in a saucepan and stir continuously over a low heat until the sugar is dissolved and the mixture quite liquid. Now increase the heat a little and, still stirring, cook until the liquid is reduced and the mixture becomes sticky, making sure it does not burn. Take heaped teaspoonfuls of the mixture and turn into little mounds on a piece of oiled foil. Allow to cool and keep in an airtight container.

KUMQUAT PRESERVE
England

A decorative garnish for roast game and duck.

MAKES 1kg (2lb)
★455g (1lb) kumquats
2 cups water
455g (1lb) sugar
5cm (2in) cinnamon stick
6 cloves

Wash the kumquats, and put them in a saucepan, with water to cover. Bring to the boil, and then drain. Pierce each fruit in several places with a knitting needle. Bring the water and sugar to the boil, stirring until the sugar is dissolved, and boil for 10 minutes. Add the fruit and spices, and simmer until the fruit is shiny and transparent. Pack into sterilised jars and cover with the syrup.

QUINCE SWEETMEATS
Venezuela

Made from autumn quinces, these sweets make ideal Christmas presents. Sprinkle with sugar if you like.

1kg (2 lb) QUINCES MAKE 50 SWEETS
*quinces, washed, peeled, cored and sliced
lemon juice—1/2 lemon to 455g (1lb)
quinces
granulated sugar*

Put the quinces and lemon juice in a pan with sufficient water to cover. Bring to the boil and simmer gently until the fruit is tender. Strain and press through a sieve or blend to obtain a purée. To each cup of purée add an equal quantity of sugar and return to the pan. Stir over a low heat until the sugar is dissolved. Bring to simmering point and cook for 30–40 minutes, stirring occasionally to prevent burning. When the purée leaves the sides of the pan and is darker in colour, beat well and pour into a shallow baking tin. Leave to dry for about 3 days at room temperature. Slice into diamond shapes, wrap in waxed paper and store in an airtight container.

ROSELLA JELLY
Trinidad and Tobago

A lovely tangy-flavoured jelly with a brilliant red colour which can be served with meat or at teatime.

MAKES ABOUT 1½ CUPS
*225g (8oz) sorrel 'flowers'—you will need to buy 455g (1lb)
water
2tsp lemon juice
340g (12oz) sugar*

Roughly chop the 'flowers', cover with water and simmer until tender, about 20 minutes. Strain through a cloth overnight—it will yield about 1½ cups of juice. Put the juices and sugar in a saucepan, bring to the boil and cook rapidly for 5–10 minutes until setting point is reached. Pour into small jars and seal.

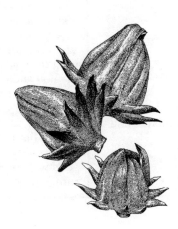

DRINKS

GINGER BEER
Caribbean

Notice the difference in this spicy and refreshing beer made with fresh green ginger instead of the powdered version.

MAKES 4.5 LITRES (1 GAL)
★85g (3oz) fresh ginger, finely grated
16 cups water
8 cloves
5tbsp lemon juice
1tbsp grated lemon rind
670g (1½lb) sugar
1 slice toast
1tsp dried yeast

Put the ginger into a large crock or bucket, pour on the boiling water and leave until tepid. Add the cloves, lemon juice, rind and sugar and stir until all the sugar is dissolved. Float the toast on top of the liquid and sprinkle over the yeast. Cover and leave for 24 hours in a warm place. Strain into bottles, cork or seal and leave for at least 48 hours at room temperature. Serve well chilled.

HAWAIIAN NECTAR
Tropics

Babaco is also ideal for this delicious tropical drink.

SERVES 6
★1 cup mango pulp
1 cup orange juice
½ cup lemon juice
1½ cups water
sugar to taste

Blend all the ingredients together and serve well chilled.

PASSION FRUIT JUICE
Tropics

A sweet and tangy concentrate for flavouring drinks and fruit salads.

MAKES 1½ CUPS
★12 passion fruits
1 cup water
juice of 2 oranges or 2 lemons according to taste
sugar as needed

Halve the fruits and scrape out the pulp and seeds into a saucepan. Add the water and bring to simmering point. Cool, add orange or lemon juice and sugar to taste. Refrigerate until required.

SORREL
West Indies

Sorrel or roselle is in season during Christmas time in the Caribbean and makes a festive, bright-red drink.

SERVES 6
★455g (1lb) seeded sorrel 'flowers'—you will need 1kg (2lb) whole sorrel
10cm (4in) cinnamon stick
8 cloves
6 cups water
170–225g (6–8oz) sugar
rum (optional)

Wash the sorrel and place in a large pan with the spices and the water. Bring to the boil and cook for 5 minutes then leave to cool for 24 hours. Strain into a large jug or crock. Add ½ cup water to the pulp, mash well and strain this second liquid into the first. Stir in the sugar and refrigerate well before serving with crushed ice and a tot of rum.

GLOSSARY
OF CULINARY TERMS

acidulated water To prevent discoloration; 1 teaspoon of lemon juice or vinegar to 1 cup of water.

agar-agar A gelatinous setting agent made from seaweed used in oriental cookery; available in dried sheets or powdered.

aka-miso Red soybean paste, see *miso*.

amchur Dried mango powder, an Indian souring agent.

anise-pepper A fragrant Chinese spice from the dried rust-coloured berries of *Zanthoxylum piperitum*.

asafoetida A strong-smelling resin extracted from giant fennel and used in small quantities in Indian cookery.

beans, salted, yellow or black Chinese flavouring of salted and fermented soybeans. Salty and tangy.

besan Chickpea flour used in Indian cookery.

blachan See *dried shrimp paste*.

chapati Indian unleavened bread, round and flat, usually served with curries etc.

dashi Japanese stock made from dried tuna fish and seaweed.

dried shrimp paste (blachan, kapi, trasi) Southeast Asian flavouring made from dried shrimps or prawns, essential to most regional savoury dishes. Acts as a catalyst for other flavours and loses its own very fishy aroma and flavour in cooking.

fish sauce (nam pla) Southeast Asian flavouring sauce made from dried fermented fish, added to almost every local dish.

five spice powder Chinese spice powder mixture of anise-pepper, cinnamon, cloves, fennel and star anise.

foo foo See recipe for Fufu page 193.

garam masala A fragrant spice mixture of cardamom, cinnamon, cloves, cumin, peppercorn and nutmeg, roasted and then ground. Often sprinkled over curries before serving.

ghee Clarified butter or vegetable oil, essential in Indian cooking.

glutinous rice Type of rice that becomes sticky on cooking, used in Indonesian and Thai cookery.

glykos Greek 'spoon sweet' or preserve made from fruits or citrus peel. Traditionally offered to guests on arrival.

gur See *jaggery*.

halva Middle Eastern and Indian sweet made with honey.

hoisin sauce Traditional Chinese barbecue sauce containing chilli, flour, garlic, ginger, red rice, salt, sesame, soybeans, sugar and vinegar.

jaggery (gur) Indian sugar, brown and rich.

kala namak Indian black salt (actually grey) essential for authentic Indian dishes.

kapi See *dried shrimp paste*.

kewra Sweet-perfumed essence from a pandanus flower, used in Indian sweets and puddings.

kofta Indian meatball of spiced ground meat. Served as a snack or with sauce and rice as a main dish.

laos powder Spice powder made from dried greater galangal. Used in many Indonesian dishes.

mezze Greek and Middle Eastern hors-d'oeuvres.

mirin Rice wine, used in Chinese and Japanese cookery; sherry (dry) can be substituted.

miso Japanese fermented soybean paste, white, red (*aka*) or brown and very salty.

msg, monosodium glutamate Flavour enhancer made from glutamic acid, much used in Chinese and Japanese cookery and processed foods in the West. Gives food a salty and meaty flavour.

naan Puffy Punjabi bread baked in the tandoor oven, spiced with nigella seeds and sometimes stuffed with minced meat.

nam pla See *fish sauce*.

pakora   Indian spiced vegetable fritter.

panch phora   Literally 'five seeds', a Bengali mixture of whole spices: cumin, fennel, fengureek, black mustard and nigella.

paneer   Indian cream cheese.

paratha   Indian flaky wholemeal bread cooked with ghee, sometimes stuffed with spiced vegetables or meat.

pastrami   Spiced and smoked beef.

pitta bread   Middle Eastern unleavened bread.

poi   Polynesian dish made from baked, pounded and fermented eddoe or dasheen.

raita   Indian salad or dip of yoghurt with vegetables and spices.

rijsttafel   Dutch-Indonesian buffet-style meal consisting of rice with a myriad of meat, seafood, vegetable, fruit dishes and condiments.

sambal   Indonesian accompaniment, usually hot, midway between a sauce and a condiment.

samosa   Indian snack of triangular pastry stuffed with well-spiced meat or vegetable mixture and deep fried.

satay   Indonesian and Malay kebab.

sesame oil   Oil from toasted sesame seeds used to aromatise Chinese and Japanese food.

sherbet, sharbut   Indian and Middle Eastern fresh fruit drink.

shichimi-togarashi   Japanese condiment consisting of a mixture of chilli, poppy, rape, hemp seed, anise-pepper, sesame seeds (black and white), dried citrus peel. Seasons soups, noodles, *tempura* etc.

shoyu   Japanese soy sauce.

Sichuan pepper   See *anise-pepper*.

soybean paste   See *miso*.

star anise   Anise-flavoured spice from the orient, with seed pods in the shape of a star.

sukiyaki   Japanese beef fondue with bamboo shoots, spring onions, mushrooms, beancurd etc. cooked at table and dipped in raw egg.

sumac   Middle Eastern souring agent, a coarse-grained, purple-red powder from the dried berries of a Mediterranean bush of the cashew family.

swizzle   West Indian wooden stirrer for rapid mixing and blending.

tahini   Oily paste made from sesame seeds used in Greek and Middle Eastern cookery.

tofu   Japanese soybean curd.

trasi   See *dried shrimp paste*.

wasabi   Japanese horseradish, dried and ground as a flavouring like European mustard.

yudofu   Like *sukiyaki*, a Japanese-style fondue with beancurd (*tofu*) pieces, mushrooms and chrysanthemum leaves in a seaweed stock.

INDEXES

COMMON NAMES

This index gives all the names (bold type) used in the title entries and most of the common, also known as 'country' or 'trivial', names that we have come across for the fruit and vegetables in this book.

Abalone Mushroom – oyster mushroom, 124
Adam's Apple – common lime, 99
Adam's Fig – banana, 15
Aerial Radish – mongri, 112
African Cucumber – bitter melon, 75
Alkekengi – physalis, 136
Alligator Pear – avocado, 12
Amaranth, 117
Am Haldi, 165
Anise – fennel, 63
Annona – custard apples, 50
Apaeya – papaya, 128
Apple of Jerusalem – kantola, 76
Apple of Love – aubergine, 11
Apple of Paradise – banana, 15
Aromatic Ginger – greater galangal, 68
Arridari – prickly pear, 142
Arrowhead, 5
Artichoke, Globe, 6
Artichoke, Jerusalem, 8
Avri Leaves, 9
Asparagus Bean – yard long bean, 21
Assyrian Plum – gunda, 85
Australian Plum – gunda, 85
Atemoya, 51
Aubergine, 11
Avocado, 12

Babaco, 14
Bair – ber, Indian jujube, 23
Balsam Apple, Pear – bitter melon, 75; kantola, 76
Bamie, Bamya – okra, 115
Bana, Banner – hyacinth bean, 20
Banana, 15
Barbados Gooseberry – physalis, 136
Barbary Fig, Pear – prickly pear, 142
Basil, 17
Bastard Fig – prickly pear, 142
Batavia – broad-leaved endive, 60
Beans and Peas, 18
Chickpea, 19; Cowpea, 19; Hyacinth Bean, 20; Mangetout, 20; Pigeon Pea, 21; Yard Long Bean, 21
Bedara – ber, Indian jujube, 23

Bell Apple – passion fruit, 130
Bell Pepper – capsicum, 27
Bendee – okra, 115
Bengal Gram – chickpea, 19
Ben (Oil) Tree – drumstick, 54
Ber, 23
Berseem – alfalfa, 153
Betel Pepper – pan, 125
Big Sprouts – soybean sprouts, 153
Bilberry – blueberry, 24
Bird Pepper – chilli, 37
Bird's Foot – fenugreek, 65
Bitter Lettuce – wild chicory, 37
Blackeye Pea – cowpea (mature), 19
Black Ginger – greater galangal, 68
Black Gram – mung bean, 153
Black Oyster Plant – scorzonera, 147
Black Radish, Salsify – scorzonera, 147
Blimbing – carambola, 29
Blueberry, 24
Blue Succory – wild chicory, 37
Bonnet Pepper – chilli, 37
Bor – ber, Indian jujube, 23
Bottle Gourd – doodhi, 78
Bounceberry – cranberry, 46
Bracket Mushroom – oyster mushroom, 124
Brazilian Arrowroot – cassava, 30
Brazilian Guava – feijoa, 62
Breadfruit, 25
Bringall, Brinjal – aubergine, 11
Broccoli, Sprouting, 26
Brussels Chicory – chicory, chicon, 35
Buffalo Herb – alfalfa, 153
Bullnose Pepper – capsicum, 27
Bullock's Heart, 51
Butter Pear – avocado, 12

Cabbage Turnip – kohlrabi, 92
Cactus Berry, Pear – prickly pear, 142
Calabash Gourd – doodhi, 78
Calabrese, 26
Callaloo – arvi (leaf), 9
Camel's Hay – lemon grass, 97
Cam-quit – kumquat, 95
Canada Potato – Jerusalem artichoke, 8
Canadian Apple, Truffle – Jerusalem artichoke, 8
Canteloupe – melon, 110
Cantonese Onion – kuchai, 94
Cape Gooseberry – physalis, 136
Capsicum, 27
Carambola, 29
Carille Fruit – bitter melon, 75

Cassava, 30
Catarrh Root, East Indian – lesser galangal, 68
Cauli-broc – calabrese, 26
Celeriac, 31
Celery Cabbage – petsai (Chinese leaves), 120
Celery Rave, Root – celeriac, 31
Chaci, Chaco, Chaka – chayote, 34
Chard, 33
Chataigne – breadnut, 25
Chaulai – amaranth, 117
Chayote, 34
Chefoo Cabbage – petsai (Chinese leaves), 120
Cherimalla, -ola – cherimoya, 50
Cherimoya, 50
Cherry Tomato – physalis, 136
Chicken Claws – marsh samphire, 19
Chickpea, 19
Chico, Chicu – sapodilla, 150
Chicory, 35
Chicory (US) – endive, 60
Chihli Cabbage – petsai (Chinese leaves), 120
Chilli, 37
China Root – lesser galangal, 68
Chinese Apple – ber, Indian jujube, 23
Chinese Artichoke – crosnes, 47
Chinese Boxthorn (Gau Gei), 121
Chinese Broccoli – gai lan (Chinese kale), 118
Chinese Cabbage – pak choi, 118; petsai, 120
Chinese Cherry – lychee, 105
Chinese Chives – kuchai, 94
Chinese Flowering Cabbage (Choi Sum), 119
Chinese Ginger – lesser galangal, 68
Chinese Gooseberry – carambola, 29; kiwifruit, 90
Chinese Kale (Gai Lan), 118
Chinese Keys, 39
Chinese Leaves (Petsai), 120
Chinese Leeks – kuchai, 94
Chinese Okra – angled loofah, 77
Chinese Onion – kuchai, 94
Chinese Parsley – coriander, 43
Chinese Potato – dasheen, eddoe, 57
Chinese Radish – mooli, daikon, 113
Chinese Spinach – amaranth, 117
Chinese Water Chestnut, 169
Chinese Water Lily – lotus root, 103

CHINESE NAMES

No attempt has been made to rationalise the multiplicity of spellings of this selected list of Chinese names. Apostrophes and hyphens have been omitted.